Flop Idol

THE HILARIOUS DIARY OF A POP IDOL WANNABE

TV broadcaster Jonathan Maitland reported for Radio 4's *Today* programme for six years before moving to BBC 1's *Watchdog*. He currently works for ITV as a reporter on the *Tonight* programme with Trevor McDonald. He has also presented two consumer watchdog series, *House of Horrors*, which exposes cowboy builders, and *The Man in the Van*.

Jonathan Maitland's previous book was *How to Make Your Million from the Internet (and what to do if you don't)*:

'His efforts are chronicled in laugh-out-loud diary entries that owe much to Adrian Mole ... Many of the insights are so spot-on ... Zips along at a blistering pace' *The Sunday Times*

'A mixture of bullishness, naivety and hubris combined into a funny and riveting read' *Esquire*

'Maitland takes you with him every step of the way: prepare to laugh, learn ... and bite your nails. Excellent stuff' Adam Faith

Flop Idol

THE HILARIOUS DIARY OF A POP IDOL WANNABE

JONATHAN MAITLAND

POCKET
BOOKS

LONDON • SYDNEY • NEW YORK • TOKYO • SINGAPORE • TORONTO

First published in Great Britain by Simon & Schuster UK Ltd,
under the title *How to have a No. 1 Hit Single*, 2002
This edition first published by Pocket Books, 2003
An imprint of Simon & Schuster UK
A Viacom company

1 3 5 7 9 10 8 6 4 2

Simon & Schuster UK Ltd
Africa House
64–78 Kingsway
London WC2B 6AH

www.simonsays.co.uk

Simon & Schuster Australia
Sydney

A CIP catalogue record for this book is
available from the British Library

ISBN 0-7434-3025-5

Typeset by M Rules
Printed and bound in Denmark by
Nørhaven Paperback A/S, Viborg

ACKNOWLEDGEMENTS

Thank you to everyone who's given me their time, effort, ears and talent in connection with this thing. I'd especially like to thank John and Jackie (and not just for the pipe of peace), Kate Lyall Grant (for editing this book) and Emily (for everything).

I'd also like to thank Prince, The Rolling Stones, The Beatles, Al Green, The Electric Light Orchestra (scoff if you like but they were really good, actually), Sheryl Crow, Thin Lizzy, Doctor Feelgood, John Cougar Mellencamp, Burt Bacharach and Hal David, Crowded House (I think you know where I'm coming from by now, don't you?), Marc Bolan, Holland/Dozier/Holland, Rod Stewart before he met Britt Ekland, The Faces, Elvis, Del Amitri, the Black Crowes, The Monkees, The Hollies, The Sundays and, above all, Squeeze for giving me so much enjoyment and inspiration. Finally, thank you for buying this book. I hope you like it.

JM

CONTENTS

PART ONE

★★★★★

I'M DOWN

TUESDAY, 1 MAY

I haven't been having a very good time lately. I have just had to endure the double whammy of turning forty and the break-up of a relationship which, although it didn't actually crash on takeoff, saw its engines fall off into a field about five miles outside Gatwick.

So here I am, surveying the twin wreckages of my youth and my love life, wondering what to do with myself. There's my career, of course. I have a good job, reporting on current affairs for *Tonight with Trevor McDonald* and helping to ensnare dodgy builders on *House of Horrors*, both on ITV. And there's my cricket: I have played with my mates in a team called the Riverbank Ramblers for the last fourteen years and not missed a single game in all that time. But I need more passion and excitement in my life. I need a new challenge.

So, I have decided to do something about it. I am going to exploit my love for, and knowledge of, pop music. I am not a musician, though: I would love to be a brilliant instrumentalist, or even a good one. But I'm not. Having spent the last five years in hand-to-hand combat with my bass, I have reached only the barest level of competence. Like a one-fingered typist, I'm slow, I make mistakes and there are no frills.

This has not stopped me performing in public, mind you. I am in a band called Surf 'n' Turf. We are not bad. If it wasn't for me, we'd actually be quite good. But the other three members (Jackie, Matt and Pete) can't get rid of me, partly because they're good friends but mainly because I get all the gigs.

Our last two engagements, for example, were a mate of mine's fortieth, followed by another friend's fiftieth. Our next – yet to be confirmed – is for a work colleague's father's sixtieth. I'm not making this up, by the way. At this rate we should be playing our first funeral by the end of the year. So even though I have the same effect on the band as two large bags of sugar tied to the waist of a long jumper, I am indispensable.

But what of our music? As you may have gathered, cutting edge we are not. Our motto, emblazoned on our bottom-of-the-range business cards, tells prospective punters all they need to know: 'Proper Music, Played by Professionals.' In essence, this means that anything by Burt Bacharach – indeed, anything with a decent tune – is in. Provided I can play it, that is. The rest – noisy, unappealing drug music – is very much out. Come to think of it, our motto is a bit dishonest, as our music may be 'proper' but it is not played by 'professionals' – at least, not professional musicians. The only one of us who can lay claim to that is Pete, our good-looking Scottish drummer whose girl-friend's hair changes colour every time I see her. He is in a band called Rialto, who are actually quite good (think David Bowie meets John Barry) and have had four hits. At the moment, though, he is, as they say, 'between gigs', i.e. working on a building site.

As for the rest of us, Jackie, our vocalist, used to be a session singer – she did backing vocals on Pink Floyd's *The Wall* album – but is now a full-time wife and mother of two living in Stoke Newington, and our guitarist Matt, like me, is a grade C celebrity TV presenter (i.e. we occasionally get recognized in public by people who don't know who we are or what we do but think they might have met us at a party in East London recently).

Anyway, the point is this: I have plans for Surf 'n' Turf. Big plans. I want us to get to number one.

I don't see why we can't do it: it's not as if you need to be talented to have hits. (See Halliwell, Geri.) What you do require, however, is an almost psychotic desire to be the centre of attention at all times, raging determination, a lack of shame and an ability to bullshit. These, thankfully, are qualities I possess. That is why I have just rung up a bloke called Graham Sharpe, of William Hill the bookmakers, and told him that I want to place a bet on Surf 'n' Turf to have a number-one hit single by the end of 2002.

He is going to work out the odds and will ring me back tomorrow.

WEDNESDAY, 2 MAY

09.03: Why am I doing this? Well, I like a challenge – as readers of my last book, *How to Make Your Million from the Internet (And what to do if you don't)*, will know. That told the story of my attempts to make a million quid from the Great Internet Phenomenon of the year 2000: I mortgaged my house for fifty grand and gambled the lot on the stock market.

Unfortunately, I missed out on the million. By approximately a million. This was due to my rather poor timing. Just after I crashed through the front door of the Hotel Internet, all the smart people quietly let themselves out the back. There was one consolation, though: the book sold well. (In fact, if the Inland Revenue are reading this, my name is Belinda Matthews.)

My Internet trauma hasn't put me off, however. In fact, I reckon I stand a far better chance of making a million from music than I ever did from the Internet: I knew nothing about cyberspace and the stock market before I started my last project, and cared even less – but I love music.

Or rather, pop music. I am one of those boring trivia buffs who can tell you everything you need to know about the 1960s, '70s, '80s and early '90s (i.e. until those dreadful druggy records that sound like someone using an industrial drill in a metal factory started polluting the charts).

I know which member of the Hollies wore a lady's wig (Bobby Elliot, the drummer), who got to number one with 'Sugar Baby

Love' (the Rubettes, stupid), and which member of Fleetwood Mac
went off to join a cult called the Children of God (Jeremy Spencer).

That is why I have accepted rather ungenerous odds of 50–1
from Graham Sharpe of William Hill, and just sent him a cheque
for a hundred quid. If Surf 'n' Turf get to number one by the end of
this book, I will win £5000.

Here we go!

14.04: Everyone needs a strategy: I am putting plan A into operation. I am going to get the help of a small, dark, furry musical
genius. Hence the following e-mail:

From: jmaitland@ukgateway.net
To: www.npgmusicclub.com
Sent: 2 May 2001
Subject: You scratch my back and I'll scratch yours

Dear Artist Formerly Known As Prince

I was wondering if you could help me.

I am in a band called Surf 'n' Turf. We perform passable versions of other people's
hits (including your own) at fortieth birthday parties, small Italian bistros in South-
West London, and weddings.

I am a fan of yours. At home, in my music room, I have a 'wall of fame' where I
have hung pictures of my main musical influences. You, you will be pleased to
hear, were inducted in a special ceremony which took place last November. You are
placed to the right of Wilko Johnson, to the left of Glen Tillbrook, and just under
Sheryl Crow (not a bad place to be).

Anyway, the point is this: I have placed a sizeable bet on Surf 'n' Turf having a
number one in the next twelve months. Trouble is, I don't write songs. You do, of
course. Lots. I was wondering if you could knock one off the top for me, so to
speak, given that you've done the same thing for people like Sinead, the Bangles
and Cyndi.

What's in it for you? Royalties, a nice warm feeling and a free meal at my local
curry house, the Akash.

Doubtless you will have a few questions you might want to ask me first, so feel free to get in touch on any of the phone numbers below.

Love and peace

Jonathan

PART TWO

★★★★★

WISHIN' AND HOPIN'

THURSDAY, 3 MAY

The Artist Formerly Known As Prince hasn't got back to me yet.

I thought this might happen. Which is why I have plan B.

Matt has a Very Useful Person Indeed living in the flat above him: Iain, the guitarist from Del Amitri. Del Amitri are fab: I have all their albums. They are a bit like Crowded House, only Scottish, a bit rockier and more depressed. They are very successful and have had several hits. (One, 'Kiss This Thing Goodbye', has the best mouth organ intro this side of 'Love Me Do'.)

Matt is trying to set up a charity gig, Turf Aid, featuring three bands: Surf 'n' Turf, the Gents (an R 'n' B outfit fronted by Matt's financial adviser, Bob, who lives in Watford) and – yes – Del Amitri.

If they say yes – and, Matt tells me, the omens are good – then I will use the occasion to bond, musician to musician, with the boys from the band and try to persuade them to help us out: I'm sure they fancy a bit of fun.

FRIDAY, 4 MAY

09.34: Oh, yes. It is happening. Turf Aid takes place at the Irish Centre, Hammersmith, on Sunday week. Del Amitri have confirmed.

Del Amitri! Maybe they will let me join them on stage! Mind you, they are rock stars and as such may change their minds. I will not believe it until it happens.

FRIDAY, 4 MAY (CONTINUED)

16.17: Everything is now on hold, for the moment. The day job has got in the way. But intriguingly so. There is a General Election coming up and I have just been chosen to interview the Prime Minister, no less. Oh yes. And Charles Kennedy. And William Hague. This means I have got a very busy few days ahead. Who knows? I might be able to get a gig for Surf 'n' Turf at Number 10.

SATURDAY, 5 MAY

10.13: Arse. A rumour has surfaced that I may not be doing those big political interviews after all. Ulrika Jonsson suddenly appears to be in the frame. It's like being told you're in the team, you're playing, get your kit on, sonny, and then being told to hold on, the manager is having second thoughts.

And before you start saying, 'Why on earth are they thinking of getting Ulrika to interview the PM?', wait a minute. It's not as daft as it might sound. When she interviewed Gordon Brown a few years ago for the BBC, about European monetary union, he came over all shy and slightly flirty and we saw a side of him we previously hadn't glimpsed, so it made more-than-averagely-interesting-tv-given-the-subject-matter.

The way I see it, these interviews can be conducted in two ways:

1) The combative, willie-waving method, favoured by the likes of Paxman, Dimbleby jnr and John Humphrys, where the interviewers say 'I put it to you' and 'In your last manifesto you said you would put up state earnings-related pensions by 2.3p but in real terms they have gone up by just 1.6p' a lot.

    The trouble with these interviews is that very few people really appreciate the detail of what's being said: they're all about point-scoring. They tell you very little about the character of the person being interviewed. But that doesn't mean that Paxo, Dim-Doms and Humph aren't great interviewers: there are plenty of viewers who will tell you they are. But I work for ITV, which is a commercial channel.

To survive, and indeed prosper, as a business it has to appeal to as many people as possible. The moment we start losing sight of that fact (i.e. asking loads of questions about state earnings-related pensions on prime-time telly), we are in trouble. Some polenta-chompers reckon this is evidence of dumbing down: it ain't. It's called Brightening Up. Yes, of course we need to discuss pensions; they are important. But prime-time TV ain't the best place to do it.

So that leads us nicely on to interview style number

2) i.e. the Try And Get To Know What They're Really Like By Asking Them The Kind Of Questions The Man In The Street Would Ask Method.

This is much favoured by moi, as I don't know enough about politics to be able to do a Paxo-style interview and I'm much more interested in personalities anyway. Fortunately, personality, rather than politics, seems to be the overriding issue this time round, and so that's why the big cheeses at ITV are opting for method 2, i.e. Tap Them Lightly On Both Sides Of The Cheek With A Velvet Glove rather than method 1, i.e. Smash Them In The Face With An Iron Fist.

And that's why I am now competing with Ulrika for the attentions of the PM.

SUNDAY, 6 MAY

Eureka. I am doing the interviews after all. Woof!

MONDAY, 7 MAY

Did interview with Charles Kennedy today. He was thinner than I thought he'd be, and quite nervous to begin with. I think this is because he was required to be 'normal' and 'relaxed' and 'at home' on camera (we did the interview in his London flat), which, of course, he never has to be when he's on *News at Ten*.

In an effort to achieve the required effect, he wore – oh yes – A Casual Green Army-Style Jumper. So when he said, halfway through the interview, 'Most people watching this won't be listening to what we're saying, but judging how we come across', I was able to ask 'What will they make of that jumper then?' Being a politician, he had a ready answer, of course. 'They will say that it was chosen for me by my girlfriend, just before you came, because it's the kind of thing I like to wear.' (Aha! The 'I'm not just a politician, I'm an ordinary bloke' answer.)

There was a good bit, I think (you can never really tell until you see it played back), when I asked him if he thought he really had what it took to be the leader of the country. He said yes (of course) and then asked what I thought. Well, you can only be honest, can't you? I said he seemed like a nice bloke, but I wasn't sure he had the necessary steel. I can't be sure, but I think he looked a bit crestfallen. He shrugged, did the 'We shall see' bit and then we moved on. Mind you, the whole thing is a bit of a charade anyway. Everyone knows his chances of being PM are, as Elvis Costello once sang on one of the best albums ever made, less than zero. I'd put good money on Surf 'n' Turf getting to number one long before Charles Kennedy gets to Number 10.

In fact, come to think of it, I already have.

For someone who looks so square, Kennedy is a surprisingly well-informed pop fan. He had several David Bowie CDs laid out on his kitchen table. I asked whether this was a calculated attempt to appear hip 'n' trendy in front of the cameras, but he said it wasn't, and so I asked him to name his favourite David Bowie album. 'Er, I think it would have to be *Station to Station*.'

Apart from being a genuine Bowie fan, then, Chazza likes a party. And I'm not talking about the Lib Dem kind. On his kitchen sideboard there was a packet of Silk Cut Ultra, and judging by his breath he had clearly had a drink or two at lunchtime.

Anyway. I am interviewing the Prime Minister tomorrow. Eek!

TUESDAY, 8 MAY

I have just spent the day with Tony Blair. What was he like? Well, Winston Churchill once described Russia as 'a riddle wrapped inside a mystery wrapped inside an enigma' but he could have been talking about TB.

You can't get a real sense of him in such a short space of time: in fact, he's so tightly wound, so in control, and such a good performer that someone in my position is never going to get a real handle on the real him. He was dead earnest, though. I can see why comedians compare him with a preacher.

We met at 10.06 this morning at a school just down the road from the Blair family home in Sedgefield, near Durham. I knew it was 10.06 because there was a dark-suited security type whose walkie-talkie kept crackling into life: '09.57, PM nine minutes away . . . 09.59, PM seven minutes away.' We'd engineered it so that when we met for the first time, it would be captured on camera. That way, we hoped to make the whole thing spontaneous, real and relaxed. His PR woman (Alastair Campbell was nowhere to be seen) had obviously told him we were hoping for a relaxed and spontaneous performance because when I went up to him for the first time and said, 'Hello, how are you?', he replied, 'Fine, I'm feeling very relaxed'.

Anyway. The PM, as you may know, likes a bit of rock. (Recently, there have been shots of him on the news walking into Number 10 carrying a guitar case – good for the image or what?) During a filming break, and in an attempt to ingratiate myself, I asked him about one of his favourite bands, Free. He came over all wistful. 'Yeah, saw them in the 1970s. It was the last gig they did. Paul Kossof [the guitarist] was just out of his mind on drugs. Very sad.'

Obviously, he hasn't got the time to play CDs all night, but he keeps his hand in by listening to what his kids play: I can now reveal that the Prime Minister's current favourite bands are the Foo Fighters and U2. And the first song he ever bought was 'I Wanna

Hold Your Hand' by the Beatles. Also favoured were David Bowie (the politician's favourite!), the Doobie Brothers, Led Zeppelin and the Stones. He apparently does a very useful Mick Jagger impersonation which, for some reason, he was reluctant to do for me. I asked him if he used to move around a bit when he sang on stage. 'I used to, yeah, believe it or not.' Blimey. What an image.

That got me thinking: wouldn't it be an amazing TV programme if we could get the ultimate supergroup together, i.e. one that featured current, or former, world leaders? It was a thought I couldn't get out of my mind.

Later on, we found ourselves sitting in his garden with a few minutes to kill before the main interview started. I had to say something to keep the atmosphere congenial, so I asked him which world leaders he would ask to join the band.

'Well, Bill, of course. He's into soul and jazz. I mean, he's actually a good musician.' So: Bill Clinton on sax, Tony Blair on guitar. What about vocals?

'The Chinese President.'

'Really?'

'Yeah. He sings.' The PM smiled at the – clearly slightly painful – memory of the Chinese President's vocal ability.

'You could do a great set list,' I said. 'Start with "If I Ruled the World" and do "It's My Party" for an encore.' He smiled again – more out of politeness this time, I thought – and then I got the sign that the cameras were running, so we were off.

We talked about how his dad's death had affected him (badly), how he met Cherie and whether it was love at first sight (at a gathering of barristers and mind your own business), why people thought he was out of touch (he's not; he speaks to ordinary people a lot, honest) and whether, if William Hague was six feet tall and, like Tony, had a full head of hair, he'd get more votes ('I don't know, Jonny. You'd better ask him.' 'All right then, I will.').

One thing I did notice about him was that he was a bit of a Zelig. As in the role played by Woody Allen in the film of the same name. Zelig was a human chameleon who adopted the mannerisms and characteristics of whoever he was talking to. When I'm a bit nervous – as I was today – I say 'you know' and 'I mean' a lot. A few minutes into the interview, the PM started saying 'you know' and 'I mean' a lot too. Curious.

Afterwards, there wasn't much time for pleasantries, so I thought I'd seize the moment. 'Erm, if you ever need a band for one of those Number 10 cocktail parties . . .' I handed him a Surf 'n' Turf card from my wallet. He looked at it, holding it at arm's length like a smelly piece of fish. Unlike his wife, who earlier on had said, 'Ooh, great', and put it in her handbag, even though we both knew it was heading for the Prime Ministerial dustbin.

'You want to give it back to me, don't you?' I laughed. 'Well, you can't.' I put my hands in my pockets and the PM, realizing what he was up against, placed the card on the table.

After a quick photo for the mantelpiece featuring the crew, me, the PM and Cherie, that was it.

WEDNESDAY, 9 MAY

Did William Hague today. He arrived at the interview (at his old school, in North Yorkshire) in a helicopter, with Sebastian Coe. The sixth-former in me wanted to greet him with a *Carry On*-style 'Nice chopper, mate' gag as an icebreaker but something inside me said, 'No, don't do it', so I didn't. I quite liked him. Like Kennedy, he's a bit square, but then what do you expect from someone whose idea of a good time when he was a teenager was speaking at the Tory Party Conference? That footage (greasy hair, high-pitched voice) has come back to haunt him, of course. It's getting shown all the time on TV at the moment. Which is why he kept playing the 'I was a normal teenager too, you know' card during our interview. It felt a bit forced, though. For example, when I asked him what he got up to as a kid, apart from politics, he said: 'Well, I used to go out to the cinema a lot with GIRLS, and just go for walks in the country with, er, GIRLS, and just hang around a bit, as you do, with, you know, GIRLS.'

All right, William! We get the picture!

SUNDAY, 13 MAY
5.30 p.m.: I am excited. Turf Aid is tonight! What's more, two record company execs, husbands of friends of ours, are going to be there, metaphorical chequebooks at the ready. This is going to be a crucial opportunity to impress.

MONDAY, 14 MAY
Very early in the morning: Oh, dear. My head feels like the brain has been taken out and replaced with a rusty spanner. I don't normally drink very much, but they had extra-strong lager on sale at 60p a pint and I had a lot of time to kill before we went on stage.

Maybe I was still feeling nervous from having to do our sound check, on stage, in front of the chaps from Del Amitri: I couldn't have felt more inadequate if I'd been practising my backhand in front of Pete Sampras.

Things seemed to go reasonably well last night. I think.

Actually, now I come to think of it, there was a problem with the stand-up comedian who we got to do the warm-up.

He did exactly the opposite. Because the crowd wasn't laughing enough (OK, at all) he went into insult-the-audience mode. This made things even worse, and he got the equivalent of a middle-class lynching when someone threw a ciabatta roll at him. I couldn't have cared less, though, as by this time I had successfully cornered Del Amitri's guitarist, Iain, by the bar, to tell him about my project. Unfortunately, meaningful communication proved difficult, as a) I had drunk a fair bit of 60p-per-pint lager by then, and b) his Scottish accent, which even under normal circumstances would take some deciphering, was completely drowned out anyway thanks to the thunderous sound of the Gents, the R 'n' B band fronted by Rocking Bob, Matt's financial adviser who lives in Watford.

So thunderous, in fact, that just after the Gents' seventh Doctor Feelgood cover version, someone noticed smoke coming from the side of the stage: one of the amps had exploded. Unfortunately, the amp in question was the one powering all the microphones, so Jackie, our singer and trump card (she can sound like Minnie Ripperton or Chrissie Hynde: take your pick), couldn't be heard.

Even so, I feel we acquitted ourselves rather well: I felt unusually relaxed and didn't spend the whole time, as I normally do when I'm playing, staring vigorously at the fret-board on my bass to make sure that I'm playing the right notes.

After we left the stage there was a long gap while Matt and the chaps from Del Amitri poked around the offending amp, occasionally prodding it with screwdrivers. At one stage it looked as if they weren't going to play – which would have been the end of the world – but thankfully, in the end, the amp was brought partially back to life. That meant we got to hear some vocals, but not much. A bit like my conversation with Iain the guitarist, in fact. Del Amitri only did four songs but, my God, they sounded fantastic. I have a hazy memory of Matt standing by the stage while they were playing, fanning the smoking amp with a large piece of cardboard in an effort to stop it overheating again.

Rock and roll!

By the end of the gig I was barely able to walk, so I left and fell into a taxi. I feel like shit and am going back to sleep.

09.23: Oh, dear. Jackie has just phoned. Things don't seem to have gone quite as well as I thought. She sounded pissed off. She said that I'd ruined things by being a) out of tune for fifty per cent of our performance and b) out of time during the other fifty per cent. She told me I was unprofessional, selfish and that I'd spoiled it for everyone else. 'You might think you sound great when you're pissed, Jonny,' she said, 'but you're the only who does. Alcohol completely buggers up your faculties.' Jackie told me she'd got worried when she saw me, seconds before we were due to start playing, looking a bit dazed and trying to plug my guitar in. 'In the end Matt had to do it for you.'

Apparently, I stood on stage beaming like a goon for the whole gig (so much for looking cool) and at the end of the evening, when we were packing up the gear, I dropped my guitar, said, 'Fuck it', and stumbled into the night, leaving behind my wallet, my coat, all my equipment and, very nearly, my fledgling musical career. This is not big and it's not clever. I have promised Jackie it will never happen again.

13.12: The people who run the Irish Centre in Hammersmith (the venue for Turf Aid) are now threatening to sue Matt for blowing up their public-address system. This doesn't seem very fair. We raised three grand for charity, for goodness' sake. Whatever happened to karma?

And as for the big cheese record company execs . . . there has been a very loud (albeit diplomatic) silence. I have single-handedly blown it. I am in disgrace. On the bright side, however, I have received a complimentary e-mail from Rocking Bob, Matt's financial adviser who lives in Watford, who says my behaviour on Saturday night (i.e. leaving my bass guitar where it fell) was 'the most rock 'n' roll thing I've ever seen'.

Mind you, there's Rocking Bob's idea of what constitutes rock 'n' roll behaviour, and then there's the real thing, as contained in a book called *The Dirt*, the autobiography of probably the most depraved rock group ever, Motley Crue. I'm only up to page 168, but it's clear I have some way to go before I can compete with those boys. In fact, I have the book here with me now. Let's have a look.

Here we go. Page 142: 'As I shot more and more cocaine, paranoia set in and soon I hardly let anyone in the house . . . I would sit around naked, day and night. My veins were collapsing and I would scour my body to find fresh ones: on my legs, my feet, my hands, my neck, and when the veins everywhere else had dried out, my d**k.'

Then there's the sex. These boys had so much, with so many people, that they used to employ a novel trick to make sure their partners didn't suspect them: just before they went home, they would place their guilty members in kebabs to disguise the smell. Eeeeuuuurrrgh.

And as for the incident on page 114, involving a naked groupie, a hotel room and a strategically placed telephone at the other end of which was the groupie's mum ... ahem, I think we'd better leave it there.

Me? Rock 'n' roll? I don't think so.

WEDNESDAY, 16 MAY

23.55: Just got back from seeing the Eagles at Earls Court on the last date of their Paying The School Fees Tour, as the *Spectator*'s music critic calls it. It was a good deal more professional than Turf Aid, I must say.

The Eagles may not be cutting edge – it's rock, with all the nasty bits taken out – but, my God, they're huge. They've become one of the most successful bands in the world ever without anyone noticing: their *Greatest Hits* CD is one of the top ten biggest selling albums of all time. But I can't quite work out why. It certainly has nothing to do with stage presence: two of them look like golf pros on the pull at the local wine bar. Then, during 'Hotel California' it came to me – as I watched a middle-aged bloke in front of me holding his mobile aloft so his mate at the other end could hear the guitar solo, in fact. The Eagles are safe. Comfortable. Unthreatening.

Their music has been expertly refined and homogenized, like processed food. That's why it slips down so easily. And, of course, it makes people like me nostalgic for the time when they could fit into thirty-four-inch-waist jeans. In the mid-1970s, as any public schoolboy will tell you, owning a copy of 'Hotel California' was compulsory. (Circa 1976, on the clothes list that boarders used to receive before term started – Rugby shirts: 4. Plain grey ankle socks: 6. Black shoes: 2. – they might as well have added: 'Hotel California': 1.)

But to be fair all the blokes in the band can sing. And play. Big time. And they made a lot of people happy tonight (even if the Don Henley/Glen Frey solo tracks sounded horribly *Miami Vice*). And some of the lyrics are quite intriguing, i.e. the title track of *Hotel California*, which mentions a beast of uncertain origin being stabbed with steely knives and people checking out but never leaving, etc. In fact, when the listeners of the Terry Wogan show on Radio 2 were asked to name their all-time favourite song, it was 'Hotel California' that came out on top. Why?

1) It's got atmosphere. (Think of that guitar intro.)
2) Enigmatic lyrics. (See above.)
3) It goes in the folder marked 'Story in a Song'. (Along with 'Stairway to Heaven' and that one about the girl who jumped off the Tallahassee Bridge.)

However: leafing through my *Guinness Book of British Hit Singles*, I notice that the band have never had a number-one hit single in this country.

I wonder if Surf 'n' Turf can succeed where the Eagles have failed?

WEDNESDAY, 23 MAY

Nearly one month into the project and I've got nowhere. The roads marked 'Del Amitri' and 'Prince' have both turned out to be culs-de-sac. I keep having bright ideas for novelty singles but that's about it. Going down the bad taste route, I've thought of trying to get 'Conversations with Dead Rock Stars' by Surf 'n' Turf featuring Doris Stokes off the ground. I was quite enthusiastic about that one for a bit. Especially as it would surely be in with a good chance of getting banned. And as everyone knows, especially Serge Gainsbourg and Jane Birkin and Frankie Goes to Hollywood, a ban dramatically increases your chances of having a hit. I've also thought of getting the Poet Laureate, Andrew Motion, to write us some lyrics that we would then put to music. Trouble is, it would make a good story, and get us plenty of publicity ('Poet Laureate Goes Pop!'), but would the record sell? I doubt it.

Very few proper poems ever reach the charts, unless you count the rather frightful 'Desiderata' by Les Crane, which – OK, I admit it – I bought in 1972. It featured the aforementioned Les, droning

'Go placidly, amongst the noise and haste . . .' over a Muzak-style backing track. The chorus was good: loads of heavenly-sounding females chanting 'De–si–de–ra . . . De–si–de–ra–ta'.

Clearly, I need help. And I know who to ask. Fourteen years ago, I interviewed a bloke called Bill Drummond, when I used to work on Radio 4's *Today* programme. He had just written a book called *The Manual (How to Have a Number One the Easy Way)*. Unlike me, he had actually made a record first, seen it get to number one, and then written a book about it. The song was called 'Doctorin' the Tardis' by the Timelords. I am meeting him and his co-author Jimmy Cauty in a couple of weeks' time.

But in the meantime I have another interesting interview to conduct for *Tonight*, with the most famous singer in the world, no less, give or take the odd Michael Jackson: Luciano Pavarotti.

FRIDAY, 25 MAY
This is all very jolly. Tonight we are having dinner in Modena with Pav's PR lady, Teri, and tomorrow we are to drive up into the mountains of Tuscany to meet 'Maestro' himself, as I have been told to call him. H'm. 'Surf 'n' Turf featuring Pavarotti'. That would be a coup. On the other hand, he is said to have a bit of an ego so it might turn out to be 'Pavarotti with Surf 'n' Turf', but I could go with that. It's not as unlikely as it might sound: Pav has sung with plenty of popsters in the past, including Bono, Elton John and even the Spice Girls. Having said that, the reason I am here is not to talk him into making a single with an unknown covers band but to interview him for *Tonight*. And as I know next to nothing about the most famous opera singer in the world, I had better get cracking and read all about him.

SATURDAY, 26 MAY
Have just interviewed Pav. It took place at his holiday villa. I was expecting a bit of a palace but it was actually quite modest. It had a small swimming pool and, I couldn't help noticing, a table football game.

We (i.e. Teri, his PR girl, George the cameraman, Keith the sound man, Liz the producer and the veteran *Daily Mirror* hack Sue Carroll, who was here to interview him too) hung around for forty-five minutes while he got himself ready. During that time I took the opportunity to sniff around his front room. It wasn't huge – there was space for an antique dinner table with six chairs and not much else – and there were loads of books about his favourite footie team, Juventus, lying around. There was also a small bar in the corner, with one of those plastic singing fish on it: Billy the Bass, I think it's called.

The first thing that struck me about Pav when he finally appeared was that he had smeared thick make-up on his eyebrows to make them look darker. It was really obvious, like he had a dead sardine over each eye. He wasn't nearly as fat as I'd expected him to be. Although he looked like he had a small volleyball under his shirt, his legs (he was wearing shorts) were surprisingly skinny. He is clearly a ladies' man: when he met us, he made a point of introducing himself to the girls first.

''Ello, bee-you-teeful,' he said to Teri, his PR girl, kissing her on both cheeks.

''Ello, bee-you-teeful,' he said to Liz, the producer, doing likewise.

''Ello, bee-you-teeful,' he said to Sue Carroll from the *Mirror*, who had chosen to wear a black chiffon evening dress and full make-up for the occasion, even though it wasn't yet midday.

Then it was my turn.

'Ello . . .,' he said, shaking my hand, while at the same time pulling a comedy face to show that I was clearly not quite as 'bee–you–teeful' as my three predecessors. He then lapped up the laughter for what was obviously a well-worn routine. Sue Carroll did him first, by the pool. Even from where we were, in the lounge, we could tell there was a bit of flirting going on, as every so often we could hear deep, rumbling laughter, punctuated by her coquettish tinkles. When it was time for photos at the end of her chat, he kept putting his arm around her and snuggling up close, on one occasion with a rose clenched between his teeth. Watching all this, I couldn't help feeling that I was going to be a great disappointment to him.

The time had finally come. Well, almost. Maestro insisted that before we could get going, there was the small matter of 'getting the shot right' to be addressed. George the cameraman spent the best part of twenty minutes adjusting the shot before Maestro finally declared things to be 'bee-you-teeful'. ('OK, ten centeemee-tres to the left . . . nononononono, too much. OK, dark, much more darker . . .'.)

Once we had started, he was very engaging: he spoke about his pre-singing career ('I sell insurance. I very, very good. I always special pick the lady of the house.'), his weight ('Ees very deefeecult. When I stop football, I carry on with the pasta.') and his new girl-friend, who is young enough to be his daughter ('She make-a me feel like-a young agayn.').

Then it was time for lunch. His, not ours. When he is staying at the villa, he has it every day, with his three beloved daughters, by the pool. Trouble is, we had no pictures of him that we could use to 'set up' the interview, i.e. pictures other than those of us talking, over which we could run some commentary.

I suggested a quick game of table football.

'No.'

'Oh, go on . . . just a few seconds . . . you're not worried about getting beaten by England, are you?'

'Ha ha ha. No.'

In the end we went for the rather clichéd 'meet and greet' shot, i.e. him saying hello to me as if we had just met.

Mind you, there was one difference. Clearly still a little self-conscious about his weight, Pav hid his entire body behind his front door (no mean feat) so that the camera could see only his head popping out sideways, rather like Eric Morecambe's trick with the stage curtain, when he used to pretend to throttle himself.

And that really was it. As we left, I caught my last – strangely memorable – sight of him. There he was, the world's greatest opera singer, in his kitchen, straining the boiled potatoes for his lunch. It was then I realized that I had forgotten to ask him about Surf 'n' Turf. It was too late, though: I couldn't come between Maestro, his boiled potatoes and his daughters.

FRIDAY, 8 JUNE
As expected, Tony Blair has won the election by a country mile and William Hague has resigned. He has shown heroic dignity and poise in defeat. I hope he goes off and makes millions and has loads of kids and is happy ever after. He deserves to be, after all the shit he's had to take.

SATURDAY, 9 JUNE
H'm. William Hague is at a loose end. I wonder if he can sing?

SUNDAY, 10 JUNE
Forget it. It didn't even seem like a good idea at the time.

MONDAY, 11 JUNE
This morning I met Bill Drummond and Jimmy Cauty, authors of *The Manual (How to Have a Number One the Easy Way)* at Café Nero, near Oxford Circus. They had a bloke called Angus with them, who was wearing North London-style heavy-rimmed glasses. He, it turned out, was writing a book too. It was about Bill and Jimmy, and it was called *How to Be an Artist*. This was his first day on the job.

So let's get this straight: he was there to write a book on them, which means he will be writing about this book which is an attempt to emulate their book. Very media. Although Jimmy (good teeth, wild grey hair, attractive, witty, torn jeans, slightly on a different planet) and Bill (bad teeth, thinning black hair, tall, charismatic, witty, Scottish, sharp) made their names as pop stars, they are now full-time artists. Their big artistic statement, a few years ago, was to burn a million quid in cash and film it. I never quite got that one. To me it seemed a bit of a waste of money. (If indeed it really happened. Bill and Jimmy assured me it did.) I'm not great on art appreciation, I said, so you'll have to forgive me, but how can you call the act of burning a million quid 'art'? Am I missing something?

'Look,' said Bill, sounding impatient. 'Are you glad you're writing this book?'

'Yes.'

'Are you glad you wrote your last book?'

'Yes.'

'Well, we're glad we burned the million pounds.'

'Right, I see . . . right, OK, I get it now,' I said, not getting it at all but not wanting to get into an argument about what constitutes art. Clearly, Bill's and Jimmy's circle and mine don't have a great deal of Venn diagram-style overlap. Apart from our mutual interest in pop music, of course.

Talking of which, their book gives several interesting bits of advice to would-be chart-toppers, such as:

1) Make the song short, i.e. less than three and a half minutes.
2) Don't try to be original; it's all been done before.
3) Make sure you have a killer intro to the song.
4) Don't do a cover version as you'll lose loads of writing royalties.

Bill's and Jimmy's thesis is that number-one hit singles have far more in common than you might think. Take two number ones from opposite ends of the musical spectrum, for example, like the punk classic 'God Save the Queen' by the Sex Pistols and 'Raindrops Keep Falling on My Head' by Sacha Distel. These two songs, reckon Bill and Jimmy, have more in common with each other than they do with other songs from their respective genres, i.e. the categories marked 'punk' and 'poppy ballad'. The two tracks got to the top, say Bill and Jimmy, because they followed 'the golden rules'. Some of those rules are listed above, but the most important one of all is that the record should have a compelling quality, a soul: one that shines through the music. This will come from the person(s) who made that record. Their personality will be stamped on the sound, and it will demand the listeners' attention. Curiously, the pair's own number one, 'Doctorin' the Tardis', did not observe all of these rules. It brazenly broke rule number 4), i.e. the one that says don't do a cover version. Actually, it was six cover versions in one. They simply edited together bits from half a dozen of their favourite songs, including the intro from 'Blockbuster' by the Sweet and the chorus from 'Rock 'n' Roll (Part One)' by Gary Glitter, shouted 'Doctor Who' a lot over the resulting melee, and – hey presto – got to number one. They were professional magpies, in other words. Shameless, tongue-in-cheek magpies.

But that was then. This is now. Has anything changed in the intervening fourteen years, I asked. Is it now harder, or easier, to have a number one?

Bill reckoned the latter. The charts are more volatile now, he said. Far more songs get to number one in the course of a year nowadays than they used to. A glance at the *Guinness Book of British Hit Singles* proves his point. In 1988, for example, there were only nineteen number ones. But in 2000 there were more than forty. So in this day and age you've got roughly twice as much chance of hitting the top. (You just won't stay there quite so long.) Also, you don't need to sell as many records to get there. In the 1960s you could sometimes shift 100,000 singles in a week and not get to number one. But nowadays, 40,000 (in a very quiet week, i.e. early January) could do it for you. Having said that, Bill told me, there are still huge hurdles to overcome. You have to persuade the retailers to stock your record. Woolworths are the most important of all, he said. If they don't sell your single, your record is going to be as much use to the chart compilers as an ashtray on a motorbike.

Who would have thought it? In the mad, crazy, excessive world of rock 'n' roll, the kingmakers aren't the drug lords, the fat-cat record company execs, or even the fans themselves, but ...

Woolies. Good old pick 'n' mix selling, plastic garden furniture stocking Woolies.

Before I said goodbye to Bill and Jimmy (who hadn't said much but had retained a benign/bemused smile throughout), I mused out loud about how we had all arrived at the same notional destination ('backstage at *Top of the Pops*', as Bill put it) but from totally opposite directions. They – i.e. Bill and Jimmy – had come via the route marked 'art' and 'experimentation'. I had travelled the road marked 'journalism' and 'proper music played by professionals'. It was like ending up on the same square of the A–Z of London, I said, but having got there via completely different pages.

They agreed. We shook hands, wished each other luck and off we went. In different directions, naturally.

MONDAY, 18 JUNE

I have been a bit busy recently filming *House of Horrors* for ITV. This is the show where I and my pretend TV wife set up home somewhere, invite dodgy builders in and get ripped off by them. As usual, the builders haven't failed to disappoint. In the last few weeks they have been filmed by our secret cameras a) pissing in our sink, b) nicking money from us and c) charging us £700 for a job that should have cost only £20.

I now have a bit of time to spare before I start work on another ITV show, *The Man in the Van*, so I have decided it's time to get proactive again. (*The Man in the Van* involves me going around the country, in a white van, saying 'Hello, I'm the man in the van' a lot, solving people's problems.)

This time I am going to hawk Surf 'n' Turf's wares direct to some of the biggest cheeses in the record biz, in a bid to get them to give us a deal. The wares in question are two songs: a nifty cover version of the old Rolling Stones track 'Tumbling Dice', which is one of the best noises I've ever heard (their version, not ours), and our interpretation of the lovely Bacharach/David song 'Walk On By'.

I have asked my cousin Stephen Budd, who works in the music biz, who the three biggest cheeses in the industry are when it comes to this sort of thing and he has come up with the following list:

1) Colin Barlow at Polydor.
2) Tony Wadsworth at EMI.
3) Muff Winwood at Sony. (I've heard of him already. His full name is actually 'Legendary A & R Man Muff Winwood', which is how he always gets referred to in music mags like *Q* and *Mojo*.)

All, apparently, have the power to sign acts up on the spot and offer them multi-album deals with several noughts on the end. So I have rung up their secretaries and asked for appointments. No one has said yes – yet – but I've been asked to send an e-mail saying what I want. If I were honest, I'd fire one off saying: 'A record deal, please. Yours sincerely, Jonathan Maitland.' But I suspect I wouldn't get very far, so I have covered my true intentions with a journalistic fig leaf by telling each of them I want to interview them for this book.

Which is true. Conveniently.

FRIDAY, 22 JUNE
Looking good. I am booked in to see Colin Barlow at Polydor on Monday, and this morning I got a letter from Legendary A & R Man Muff Winwood.

Sony Music Entertainment (UK) Limited
10 Great Marlborough Street
London W1F 7LP

Dear Jonathan
I don't mind answering a few of your questions for your new book but I'm not sure what you're trying to do with Surf 'n' Turf. Is this part of the plot?

If you call my assistant Dawn she will make an appointment.

Yours sincerely

Muff Winwood

(Senior Vice-President, A & R)

This is rather exciting. I will go and see Colin Barlow on Monday and play the charming, enthusiastic and persuasive card from the bottom of the pack. And then who knows? We could be on the way. First off, though, it's down to the South Coast for a joint fortieth birthday party. Five friends whom I was at school with (we've all been mates since we were thirteen) are celebrating their fortieths this summer at a cottage in Bognor.

SUNDAY, 24 JUNE

The fortieth party was fun, if a little depressing. I never used to worry about being forty as it always seemed like such a long way off. I would say to myself, 'I won't be forty until 2001. That's years away', but then all of sudden it *was* 2001 and not only was I turning forty but all my friends were too.

The sick feeling in my stomach that I felt in the run-up to being forty has now been replaced by a low-level depression. All my life I've been young. Now I'm not. I keep repeating the figure to myself. Forty. Forty. Forty. It sounds so old! Forty! I am now closer to fifty than I am to thirty. God, I feel sick.

Anyway, back to the party. Events were brightened up considerably by the unveiling, at the start of the evening, of a life-size ice sculpture in the shape of a human being. Not any old human being, mind you: this one had a large pair of breasts and a huge penis.

The idea was to select one of two frozen orifices – nipple or cock – through which you wished to receive your chosen drink, and clamp your mouth around it. Someone then poured a coloured vodka cocktail down one of two entry holes in the sculpture's head, and a few seconds later the liquid spurted, suitably chilled, out of the nipple or cock and into your gob.

As the evening progressed, everyone became a lot more relaxed (i.e. the blokes migrated from the tit to the cock) and by the end one or two exhibitionist/drunks were attempting tit/cock/tit/cock quadruples, which was quite entertaining, if a little messy. Not one for the vicar's tea party.

MONDAY, 25 JUNE

Saw Colin Barlow, head of A & R at Polydor, at his office in Hammersmith today. I made sure to be nice to his secretary, Sorcha. (Rule number one when seeing bigwigs: always take time to charm their secretary. It can pay off in spades.) He was a lot younger than I thought he'd be. I expected him to be forty-plus but, annoyingly, he looked about twenty-three. He was pretty, blond, tanned and a dead ringer for athlete-turned-TV-presenter Roger Black. We got on well. We talked about music, non-stop, for more than an hour. (When I left, I apologized for taking so much of his time and he said: 'No problem, mate. I could talk about music all day.') We also talked about his record company's logo. It was part of my youth, that red Polydor label, with its white letters and the small black half-circle thing. I can see it now, whirring around the metal maypole of my record player. Polydor. Home of the Jam, Slade, the Who and, most important of all, as far as I was concerned, the Hollies. 'It's funny you should say that,' he said. 'The bosses wanted to get rid of the logo a few years back but I said no fucking way.'

Colin reckons the record bizzo is becoming too obsessed with the short term: i.e. signing up acts of a Hear'Say nature (a Polydor band, in fact) who may last two years if they're lucky, when they should, like pigs sniffing for truffles, be pointing their snouts in the direction of U2-type bands, who may not crash into the charts at number one with their first single but will prove to be better bets – commercially and artistically – in the long term.

'Aha,' I said. 'Good headline. "Hear'Say Trashed by Their Own Boss Shocker!"'

'Not at all. I approve of Hear'Say, coz they pay for us to develop the U2s of this world.'

The modus operandi of the music business, he said, pretty much involves bunging loads of mud against the wall and hoping some sticks. A lot of acts 'happen' by chance, by default, he said. That took me neatly on to my first question. 'What do you think of my odds of 50–1, on Surf 'n' Turf getting a number one?'

'Given the business you're in, and the access you have, I reckon you have as good a chance as any. Fifty to one's not bad, actually.' I nervously fingered my cassette tape.

He, like Bill Drummond, reckons it's easier to have a number one nowadays than it used to be. There are a lot more outlets around, he said, where you can get your track heard. Like Capital Radio and all the commercial stations.

In the old days, if you didn't get played on Radio 1, you were a dead duck. Now, it's hugely helpful but not essential. Atomic Kitten, for example, got there with no help from Radio 1 at all. A few TV appearances and a bit of press cracked it for them.

Who is the biggest star he – Colin – had signed, and what made him sign them?

'Ronan Keating.'

What, even with those trousers that look like they've been made out of a middle-aged woman's crocodile-skin handbag?

'Yeah, I've had a word with him about that.'

Ronan, according to Colin, has two essential qualities:

1) He listens to advice. This means he will not let his judgement get so clouded by his initial success that he insists on releasing an album full of Gregorian chants set to a hardcore Finnish ambient trance backing, thereby alienating his core audience, i.e. conservative fifteen- to forty-five-year-olds like me who thought his debut single, 'Life Is a Rollercoaster', was a thing of great joy.

2) He puts in the hard work. Or, as Colin puts it, he is not only prepared to go to Norway at the weekend and shake hands with punters in an Oslo record shop and thank them for buying his record, but he will actually enjoy doing so.

Ronan, says Colin, is the Kevin Keegan of pop. In many people's eyes he might not be the most naturally talented bloke around, but he more than makes up for that by trying twice as hard as anyone else. He has, apparently, more drive than anyone else Colin has worked with and works a room brilliantly. (This is encouraging. I may not be able to sing but I've got more drive than Buckingham Palace and I'm not too bad at room-working.)

But that alone doesn't explain Ronan's success. He also needed the Right Song to break him as a solo act. And with 'Life Is a Rollercoaster' he found it. What a corker that track is: I love it. In fact, it's one of those songs that everybody likes, a bit like 'When You're Gone', by Bryan Adams and Mel C.

But here's the 64-zillion-dollar question. Why? What is it about that piece of music (or any other song) that makes it widely accepted as 'good'?

Colin had a stab. 'It's like Bob Marley said. When the music is that good, you feel no pain. You just hear the first few bars on the radio, you turn it up, you forget everything else, and you actually feel physically better.'

H'm. That explains what it does to you, but it still doesn't explain *why* it does it in the first place. Is there a technical explanation as to why we find some music 'good' and some music shite? Why do most of us turn up 'Hey, Jude' but switch off 'The Birdie Song'? Is it something to do with the notes, i.e. the order of them, which induces a chemical reaction in us? I once met a bloke at a party who looked a bit like Melvyn Bragg, but who turned out to be a conductor called Stephen Barlow. (He also happened to be married to Joanna Lumley.) We had a long chat about this. He reckoned there was a professor at Cambridge University doing research into this very question. I suspect he is trying to define the indefinable.

But back to 'Life Is a Rollercoaster'. Where did Colin find it? Turns out he'd flown over to LA to see Rick Nowels, a fab songwriter, who was responsible for that wonderful New Radicals song,

'You Get What You Give', to see if there was Any More Where That Came From.

When Rick played him a demo of 'Rollercoaster', over the corn-flakes, Colin realized there was. As soon as the chorus started sweeping over him, he turned off the machine, said 'I've heard enough' and bought it.

A few months later, said Colin, after Ronan had recorded his own version, he came to this very office where we were sitting now, with his wife, to hear the final mix. By the end, Ronan had tears in his eyes. All he said was, 'That's a number one, isn't it?' and then started jumping up and down. Colin and Mrs Ronan joined in and they all hugged each other. A few weeks later it was number one. 'That's why I love the bloke,' said Colin. 'Gary Barlow would never have done that.'

The only problem Ronan has now, reckons Colin, is the Niceness one, i.e. he must beware of becoming too nice. Pop stars always need a little bit of edge.

I'm not sure if Surf 'n' Turf have edge, I said, brandishing the tape, but what we do have is a good singer.

As the tape played, Colin sat there, legs crossed, with a serious look on his face. I detected a slight twitching of the right knee as he took in our (rather country-style) version of 'Tumbling Dice'. Then it was 'Walk On By'.

Alas, there was no jumping up and down and crying à la Ronan, and no brandishing of record contracts.

In fact, Colin didn't say much at all, apart from the fact that he was a big Rolling Stones fan and so, like me, thought 'Tumbling Dice' was completely fab. (Their version, not ours.) Oh, well. At least he knows we can play. After that, we did a bit more musical bonding (i.e. discussed whether 'Tempted' by Squeeze was one of the best records ever made) and then it was time to go.

TUESDAY, 26 JUNE
Sent Colin Barlow an e-mail today:

From: jmaitland@ukgateway.net
Sent: 26 June 2001
To: Sorcha Macdonald
Subject: Hello Sorcha can you pass this on to Colin ta v much! PS: is it too late to crack the 'phew what a . . .' gag?

Colin

That was a very pleasant hour spent with you yesterday. Thanks for your time. Now that you've heard me, and, more important, Surf 'n' Turf, what are our chances? I'm not asking for a lot: a one-album deal would do nicely, thank you very much. Failing that, what about a three-single deal? I can sense you're wavering a little, so here are five reasons why you should say yes:

1) Your right knee was twitching a bit as you listened to the Surf 'n' Turf rendition of 'Tumbling Dice'. Your instincts are strong. Listen to them.

2) You yourself said that someone in my position had as good a chance as anyone of getting to number one and that the odds of 50–1 I've been given on that happening weren't bad at all. That means I have a better chance of getting there than a lot of people you sign. So it makes good business sense to sign us if nothing else.

3) There is a trend out there: people are moving back to 'real' music, i.e. Eva Cassidy and the like. Surf 'n' Turf, with our motto 'Proper Music, Played by Professionals', are well placed to exploit this. OK, we can't claim to be so hip it hurts (although now I'm forty my hip hurts a bit) but then that woman from the BBC1 docusoap thing *The Cruise*, Jane Macdonald, wasn't exactly cutting edge either and she's done all right hasn't she?

4) It will be fun.

5) Er, that's it.

Kerrang!

All the best

Jonathan

FRIDAY, 29 JUNE

From: Sorcha Macdonald

To: jmaitland@ukgateway.net
Sent: 29 June 2001
Subject: Hey Jonathan. It's never too late to crack that one. Please see reply from
Colin below

Jonathan
Thank you for popping in to play me Surf 'n' Turf.
'Tumbling Dice' did indeed evoke a twitch in my right knee. However, it's an old
football injury that persists in returning.
As accomplished as the musicianship and interpretation were, I don't think either
song you played had the potential to evoke the 'real music' fans out to the record
stores in droves. Two well-interpreted covers are not enough for me to offer you a
deal, I'm afraid.
Kind regards
Colin Barlow

Oh, well. The Beatles got turned down by a bloke from Decca
before they hit paydirt, so I'm not too depressed. One big cheese
down, two to go.

FRIDAY, 6 JULY
I have had a bust-up with Mr Bedi, the local newsagent. This isn't
the first time. The last time it happened, last year, I boycotted him
for several months after he started abusing me in front of the other
customers. This was because I had fallen 2p short of the total
required to pay for my groceries. I asked him if I could let him have
the 2p next time and that was when the torrent started.

'You bloody always do this! Who you think you are? Bloody
come in here not have no money!'

It was deeply embarrassing and it meant that I was forced to use
the services of Mr Samad, his arch rival, for the next few months.
The only problem was that Mr Samad provided a heroically bad
service: most of his shelves were empty, most of the time. Mr
Samad, a large, genial, unkempt man, saw no problem with this.

Indeed, he and his equally large wife seemed to find it quite funny when I used to come in and say something like 'Don't tell me, you haven't got any sugar' and find that, yes, they didn't have any sugar. I stuck to my guns, though. Rather than lose face and go back to Mr Bedi's for sugar, I would walk the half-mile down the road to Somerfield. Now, however, Mr and Mrs Samad are no more. They sold out to a developer for half a million quid. And good luck to them.

I was hoping for a Tesco Metro mini-market to take their place – that would take care of Bedi once and for all – but, alas, the Samads have been replaced by, of all things, a tanning salon. Anyway, this unfortunate turn of events left me feeling that I should let bygones be bygones, and so I have started to sniff around Bedi's again. This morning, however, when I went in there talking on my mobile, he started having a go at me.

'Why you bloody come in here talking on bloody phone thing? Why can't you do this at home? This shop, not bloody hotel!'

This, from someone who charges me £2.50 to cash a cheque.

I said nothing, trying to control myself. There were customers there and I didn't want to embarrass them. So I gave him my best dirty look and walked out. But I am going to get my revenge on him. I have a plan. It will mean that I can never go back there again – but who cares? He has gone too far this time.

SATURDAY, 7 JULY

I have exacted my revenge on Bedi. It felt good. I went in there this morning and bought about twenty-five quid's worth of stuff. I could see his eyes bulge as I piled my basket higher and higher: his average customer spends only a couple of quid a time. When I got to the till he started being obsequious.

'How are you, Mr Jonathan?' and all that. After meticulously weighing and bagging up the lot, he stood there, announced the bill (£24.48p) and waited expectantly.

I looked at him and said, 'Actually, Bedi, I've changed my mind. You were unacceptably rude to me, again, the other day. I don't see why I should give you my custom, especially when you charge me £2.50 just to cash a cheque. Cheers, mate.' I could still hear the shouting thirty seconds later, as I opened my front door. Immature, petty and pathetic, I know. But deeply satisfying.

MONDAY, 16 JULY

Saw Legendary A & R Man Muff Winwood today. Or, to give him his full title, Senior Vice-President, Sony Records UK.

One of the perks of writing a book like this is that one day you can be struggling, like I have been, with the bass line to a song like 'Gimme Some Loving' by the Spencer Davis Group, and the next you are sitting opposite the bloke who not only played bass on the original but helped write it. Muff is that rare thing: someone who made a fair old fist of being a pop star in the 1960s (the Spencer Davis Group had two number ones, 'Keep On Running' and 'Somebody Help Me', and one number two, 'Gimme Some Loving') and then went on to have even more success behind the scenes. Acts produced/discovered/developed by him include Dire Straits, Sparks, Adam and the Ants, Shakin' Stevens, Bonnie Tyler, Paul Young, Wham!, Alison Moyet, Terence Trent D'Arby (God, he was good), Sade, the Stranglers, the Clash, Jamiroquai, Toploader and Reef. Unfortunately, the name Surf 'n' Turf will not be added to that list, but more of that later.

Muff is a tall bloke with slightly bouffant hair, a soft Brummie accent and glasses thick enough to make his eyes look slightly bigger than they are. He also cuts straight to the chase. He told me I didn't have a hope of getting to number one for a number of reasons, the first of which was that I was way too old. Most hits come from kids in their early twenties, he said. They're the ones who have the time and the energy to see what's happening in music and fashion. What's more, the target market – i.e. the people who buy singles – are that age too: how can someone my age know what someone half my age wants to hear?

How can I, a fat forty-year-old, connect with them, the record buyers? The odds are nigh on insurmountable, he said. Every week fifty or sixty tapes land on his desk from wannabes: he's never taken on one of them. The way acts get signed, he said, is simple. If they're any good at all, a buzz starts around them. Sooner or later, somebody will tell the bloke in the local record shop. He will then tell 'the local Svengali', as Muff calls it, or the visiting sales rep from EMI, Virgin, Sony or whatever. Then the whole thing is off and running.

'Right. But who, exactly,' I asked Muff, 'is the local Svengali?'

'You know . . . the bloke in the sheepskin coat, the local Mr Big, the guy that Michael Caine played in *Little Voice*, the bloke who bullshits a lot and says he knows all the right people in London.'

'OK, yeah, the local would-be Colonel Tom Parker.' (Colonel Tom was Elvis Presley's manager.)

'That's right. Colonel Tom, Brian Epstein. They were all local Svengalis to begin with.'

H'm. Can't quite see that happening with us. ('Hello. Might you be the local Svengali? I wondered if I might enlist your help.')

'And even then,' said Muff, 'even if we do sign 'em up, it's no guarantee of success.'

At the moment, Sony's hit rate is one in seven, which isn't bad. With some companies, it's one in ten. The economics of it all are scary. The cost of marketing a new act's single and debut album can be anything up to a million quid. And if that act is famous already, like an ex-Spice Girl, for instance, you can double or even triple that cost, because of all the things a star expects: hairdresser, make-up, limo, security, top producer, etc. If, after all that, the ex-Spice Girl doesn't sell at least a million records worldwide (a very tall order), then, says Muff, you're on the slippery slope. This, it would appear, is why Scary Spice is no longer required by her record company, despite having had a couple of chart hits. The worst (best?) example of this is Mariah Carey, who was given more than twenty million dollars upfront for a new record deal . . . just weeks before she had a breakdown. The chances of her record company recouping their twenty million are about the same as a one-legged man winning the World Arse-Kicking Championships.

Who on earth is going to invest that kind of money in us? Not Muff, that's for sure. Not on the evidence of his reaction to our tape, at any rate. Whereas Colin Barlow from Polydor sat through the whole lot, Muff was reaching for the OFF switch after ninety seconds. 'Can I turn it off now?' he pleaded. 'I can't really see the point even spending the time thinking of what to say to someone about that . . . it's so far off the mark. If you're going to make a tape, it should be new music, there should be something special about it, it should be the best recording you can make, it should be right in the pocket of what the kids are listening to today. And this tape is none of those. I don't think you realize how difficult it is to motivate people to actually buy records. I mean, I see trailers on the telly for films and I think, That's great, I'll see that. But I never actually get round to seeing it. So how difficult is it going to be for you lot to motivate a million people to say not only, "Cor that's good. I like that, I wanna buy it", but actually get them into the shops to physically buy it, the next day? That's what you're looking at.'

Oh, dear. I'll take that as a no then.

FRIDAY, 27 JULY

Three months down the line and I've got nowhere. Of the three big cheeses in the record bizzo that I have targeted, one hasn't even bothered getting back to me, and the other two have made it clear that it's not going to happen. I may be on the telly but that hasn't helped one bit.

In fact, it's a bit of a hindrance. In pop music, a bit of cred helps no end. Exposing dodgy plumbers may be entertaining, but it's not sexy or hip. The main problem, though, clearly, is going to be one of economics. Someone is going to have to invest, at the very least, tens of thousands of pounds in us, just to get a single out. Let's do the sums.

1) **Production**

Producing one song properly, in a studio, costs at least ten grand. Unless you get lucky and persuade a top record producer to do it for free, in the hope that it will be a hit, a bit like a barrister does when he takes a case on a no-win, no-fee basis.

2) **Manufacture**

Let's say you press 60,000 CDs: if they all get sold in the first week, that should, with luck, get you to number one, or at least within shouting distance of it, provided there aren't any other big releases out at the same time. Each CD costs 50p. So your manufacturing costs are £30,000. Total cost so far: £40,000.

3) **Shooting the video**

If you're George Michael or Michael Jackson, you'd be lucky to see change from a million quid but it's not impossible to do a decent-looking vid for less than five grand. Total so far: £45,000.

4) **Marketing/plugging, etc.**

I.e. advertising the song by plastering flyposters all over city centres and throwing big bashes, which influential members of the press are invited to. This is where it gets silly. You could spend – and some people have – hundreds of thousands. (See list of expensive marketing disasters coming up.) But to make the smallest of dents, a marketing budget of £20,000 would be needed. So that makes £65,000, all in all, just for us to get a single out there.

H'm. I now realize that having a hit – let alone a number one – is not as easy as I thought. Why should any record company want to release a single by Surf 'n' Turf when singles nearly always lose money? Singles, in effect, are merely promotional devices. They are loss leaders for albums. The hope is that punters who buy the single will then splash out on the album. And making an album costs an awful lot of money. Who is going to spend an awful lot of money taking an awfully big risk on an awfully obscure wedding band like us?

I can cut some corners, though: as a journo, I know how to cook up a story. With a bit of cute PR I could create loads of free publicity, thereby saving loads on the marketing budget. I did this quite successfully for my last project, creating, according to one expert, a quarter of a million pounds' worth of PR about my website. That, in turn, enabled me to charge companies lots of money to advertise on it. Trouble is, this is different: it's one thing to get someone to visit your website, but it's quite another to get them to buy your record. One costs nothing; the other costs £3.99.

But back to those marketing costs. This is where it gets really entertaining.

The landscape of pop is littered with the skeletons of bands who had trillions spent on hyping them. For instance:

1) **The Roaring Boys**
   This lot were supposed to be massive in the early 1980s. They were Oxbridge educated and had big hair, stupid clothes and wore make-up. Duran Duran with a degree, basically. They were signed for a huge advance and had the benefit of the most expensive stylists, video directors and producers around. Imagine how their record company, Epic, felt when their only single failed to make the top seventy-five.

2) **Sigue Sigue Sputnik**
   For a while, this lot got more press coverage than Princess Diana. Terrifyingly ugly (a badly disfigured Addams family in fright wigs), they were fronted by a bloke called Tony James, who got the press momentarily all excited by talking about how he was going to sell advertising on the spaces between the band's album tracks. EMI reputedly rewarded them with a £4 million deal. At least, this was the sum quoted in the press. Mind you, this figure will have included the predicted costs of making several SSS albums over several years: only a tiny fraction of it, if any, will have made its way through to

Tony's pockets. And his trousers were so tight he couldn't have fitted much in them anyway.

Unfortunately for Tony, the press hated SSS.

When that happens, the biggest marketing/PR/hype budget in the world won't change things. In fact, in SSS's case it probably made the situation worse, as the press like to think they've 'discovered' bands, and once word gets out – hype or no hype – that a band has had four mill spent on them, the press just loves to shoot them down. EMI's alleged four million, then, turned out to be Not A Good Investment. Although SSS's first single, 'Love Missile F1-11', got to number three, their next four bombed quicker than your average dotcom, leaving EMI with a lot of unsold albums and a very angry accountant.

3) **Girl Thing**

The giant record company BMG spent a mere one and a half million quid trying to turn this lot into the new Spice Girls. What did the money go on? Flying bucketloads of the press out to the Eiffel Tower and back, and wining and dining them for a start. Didn't work, though. The group got dropped at the end of 2000, poor things.

It is, though, possible to have a hit without shelling out loads of money. In fact, sometimes it can work in your favour. If you can record your track for 50p in your back bedroom – or pretend that you have – you will be guaranteed acres of press coverage should your song begin to catch on. As in 'Pop Music David Slays Record Business Goliaths'. Every year a song which has allegedly been recorded for 50p in someone's bedroom gets to number one. Songs like this don't need a fortune spent on marketing them; they just 'happen'. Usually, because someone influential, i.e. a DJ on Radios 1 or 2, starts playing them to death. But before I can even hope for that to happen to Surf 'n' Turf, I need to find the right song. And get it recorded properly. How am I going to do that?

Anyway. Tonight I am off to one of the highlights of the year: the

ITV summer party. This is when ITV spend shedloads of cash pouring champagne down the gob of every celebrity, from A+ to C−, who has ever appeared on the channel in the past year. Last year I passed out in the back of one of those big taxi van things while John Leslie attempted to snog every woman in sight. I must try to last the course this time.

SATURDAY, 28 JULY

Don't feel tooooooooo bad. I was, I am proud to report, one of the last men left standing. These parties are amazing, and very seductive. Free champagne and delicacies served on silver platters all night, in the grounds of one of the most famous buildings in the country, Kensington Palace, where Princess Diana used to live. There are loads of pictures of her on the walls near the bogs, in fact. And, of course, there are celebs. Ludicrous celebs, as far as the eye can see. Parties like these are one of the perks of the job, but trouble can start when you let yourself think that this is real life, and that the people here are your friends: it isn't, and they're not. OK, there are a few people who hang out exclusively with other famous people, like Dale Winton and Cilla (Babs! Cilla! Mwah! Mwah!), but that is not a world I want to be part of. I love observing it, though, and there was plenty to observe last night.

There is, it seems to me, a hierarchy of celebs. They all tend to know their own level instinctively, and cluster together accordingly. So, last night, there was Des Lynam, Trevor McDonald and Robson Greene talking with each other, over there in the corner were the kids from Hear'Say huddling with Ant and Dec and Cat Deeley, and there was I, punching slightly above my weight, talking to newsreaders Dermot Murnaghan, Katie Derham, Mary Nightingale and Action Man lookalike Mark Austin (ITN reporter and presenter of the much-hyped reality game show *Survivor*).

Dermot was a bit of a card: he told me he liked gambling (always a good sign) and that, remarkably, during the fuel crisis of September 2000 he had put a stonking £10,000 (big balls or what!)

on Labour to win the General Election. The odds were a remarkably generous 1–3. They had been 1–10, but the fuel crisis was making Labour wobble a bit. He surmised, correctly, of course, that free money was effectively on offer, and a few months later, that's what he got: a tax-free cheque for three grand's worth of profit made its way into his account. He'd got a thirty per cent return on his bet in the space of a few months. (He'd done much the same thing in the 1992 election, when, showing the exemplary even-handedness required of a good news presenter, he bet on the Tories to win.)

Mark Austin, ITN's senior reporter, took the piss out of me for being in showbiz – there is a certain snobbery among news and current affairs types about people like me who are supposed to be doing serious stuff on progs like *Tonight with Trevor McDonald* but let the side down by doing fluffier things like *House of Horrors* – but I was able to point out to him that he was on slightly dodgy ground himself, having spent the last few months poncing around an island presenting *Survivor*, saying things like: 'Fire represents your life on this island. Will you please extinguish your flame?' By the end of the evening I think he was regretting ever having brought it up as every time I wanted a light for a fag I asked him for one, on the basis that wherever there was fire, he wouldn't be too far away.

Other incidents included:

1) Martin Bashir agonizing over whether to ask Myleene from Hear'Say for her autograph for his daughter. (At least, he said it was for her.) He was too embarrassed, but I'd had a few by then so I volunteered to ask her myself. She looked a bit dazed – dunno why – and stared at me like I was from another planet.

2) Bruce Forsyth turning up with his glamorous ex-beauty queen wife in a white Rolls-Royce even though he'd appeared in the paper a few days earlier, slagging off ITV for not putting on his show at a more viewer-friendly time.

3) Me trying unsuccessfully to break the rule that celebs on one

rung shouldn't try to mix with those on a higher one by attempting to get into a conversation with Des Lynam and being completely blanked by him, although it may have had something to do with the fact that he was talking to a very glamorous woman at the time.

4) Having a very pleasant conversation with Simon Shepherd, the absurdly handsome geezer from *Peak Practice*, about the interview I'd done with William Hague.

5) Watching John Leslie trying to get off with half a dozen women.

6) Talking – briefly – to Richard, of Richard and Judy fame, and marvelling how completely like Alistair McGowan's impression of him he is.

FRIDAY, 3 AUGUST

I wonder if I should give up? I have sent e-mails and letters to lots of famous pop people in the last few weeks, asking them to help me, and none of them has even replied. Thanks, Sir Tim Rice. Thank you, Malcolm MacLaren. Thank you, Guy Chambers, the bloke behind Robbie Williams's hits. The trouble is, as the press agent of Cathy Dennis told me, when she turned me down for an interview with her client: 'If Cathy knew exactly how to have a hit single, why on earth would she be telling you all about it? She'd want to put it in her own book.' (Cathy, a former pop star, now writes mega-hits for other artists, like Kylie Minogue.)

I could, I suppose, tell Simon & Schuster, the publishers of this book, that it's not working out, and offer to return their advance. Then again, why give up now? If Manchester United can win the European Champions Cup after being 1–0 down in the second minute of injury time, then surely I have a chance – just a chance – of getting to number one in the next seventeen months?

SATURDAY, 5 AUGUST

I need a hit maker on my side. Someone who understands the busi-

ness inside out. Someone who has written and produced a hatful of
number ones. Someone who has invented hit acts out of nothing.
Someone, in fact, just like Jonathan King. Trouble is, he's currently
facing charges of assault on young boys. Mind you, innocent until
proven guilty and all that.

I sent him an e-mail yesterday, telling him what I was doing,
and asking if he remembered me from when I interviewed him for
the BBC's *Weekend Watchdog* programme a while back. Could he
help? This morning, the following e-mail popped up on my
screen:

From: tipsheetxx@aol.com
To: jmaitland@ukgateway.net
Sent: 5 August 2001
Subject: re your letter

Of course I remember you, you silly old queen. I consumed your book about
making money on the Internet and thought it was GREAT FUN and very well done.
I'd love to help with your new project – only problem is, I'm currently doing a
project of my own (called Defending Myself Against Spurious Charges) and it
rather depends how the trial goes. Anyway, for 3–4 weeks, I'm unavailable.
Hopefully, if the verdict goes the right way, I should be back in action and ready for
anything. So fingers crossed, watch the news, pray for me and in a couple of
months I'll give you a number one!
JK

Blimey. I never expected to hear from him at all, let alone so
soon. But even if he does get off, what would be the PR implica-
tions of having Jonathan King behind me, so to speak? Better wait
and see.

SATURDAY, 19 AUGUST
All this waiting and seeing is all very well, but it's not doing me or
my chances of success much good. I am worried. This project is

suffering from a serious case of drift. The way things are going, nothing is going to happen.

Apart, that is, from me occasionally getting rejected by important people in the record biz. At this rate I will have to give up. That means I won't be able to provide Simon & Schuster with the 80,000-odd words which they need for this book. That means I'll have to give them their money back, which will make me feel like I've failed, which will make me feel even more shit than I did at the start of this book. I am currently on cricket tour, in Devon. Let's face it, if I were a greyhound, I would still be in the traps, on my own, with the mechanical hare well out of sight. Right now I'm more likely to get a call from the England selectors asking me to open the batting against Australia than I am to be at number one in the charts by the end of 2002. I am consoling myself with the thought that it's impossible to get anything like this off the ground in the summer anyway, as everyone's on holiday. This self-delusion seems to be working, a bit.

SATURDAY, 1 SEPTEMBER

A small crisis. Surf 'n' Turf are playing a friend of mine's wedding, at the very posh National Liberal Club in London, in two weeks. Trouble is, Matt can't do it: the BBC1 *Holiday* programme have asked him to go grape-picking in France. We have never done a gig without him. He also plays guitar on every single track and sings on a few as well. This is like being told, just before you're due to put on *Hamlet*, that the leading man has gone AWOL and there's no understudy. I have tried to talk him out of doing it on the basis that doing the *Holiday* programme isn't good for your cred as a journo. Anyone who appears on it has to leave their critical faculties behind at the airport.

It's full of presenters who adopt fake looks of approval and go 'Mmm, delicious!' as they sip glasses of wine or try out the local delicacy. But as the father of an eight-week-old child, Matt has pointed out that he needs the money, so fair enough. This means, as Tony Blair would say, that I am 'Thinking the Unthinkable'. In

Blair's case that meant reforming the social security system and scrapping certain unemployment benefits: in my case it means contemplating getting my brother, Pete, to do the gig.

Pete is eight years older than me and has been a musician all his life. Mind you, he now bills himself (on the photocopied sheets of A4 paper he sticks in the windows of the pubs he plays) as an 'all-round entertainer'.

Like many an older brother, he shaped my musical taste. How can you fail to be affected by the sound of 'Revolver' being played, sixteen hours a day, seven days a week, for more than a year? I particularly remember him playing an Elton John track called 'Harmony', from the *Yellow Brick Road* album, non-stop, for much of 1973. At the time I thought it was the most amazing thing I'd ever heard. But then again, I was only twelve so there wasn't much to compete with. (I hadn't actually heard the track for twenty-five years until the other night when I caught Elt doing it on a TV docco. It still sounded lovely.)

My brother's defining characteristic is that when he meets people for the first time he will ask them dozens of questions, very quickly, without waiting for any of the answers. Often, questions one, three, eleven and fourteen will be exactly the same. I think it's his way of coping with nerves. Some people find this quaint and endearing, others bemusing.

He is also small, pushy and domineering. This may explain why, over the years, he has gone from playing in a four-piece band to a trio and then, via a duo, to his current solo act. There is something both heroic and tragic about his career. The tragic bit is that, like so many musicians and actors, he feels he has never fulfilled his talent. Although he plays bass well and can write good pop songs, with strong tunes and catchy hooks, he has never written a hit, or even played on one. He did get a faint whiff of the big time once. It was in the early 1970s. A famous team of songwriters – Bill Martin and Phil Coulter, who wrote 'Congratulations' for Cliff Richard – were thinking about getting Pete and his mates to do some of their songs. In the end, however, Martin and Coulter went for a band called Slik (featuring one Midge Ure) instead. A few weeks later, Slik were number one, and my brother was still playing the King's Head in Worcester Park, Surrey. Which is pretty much where he's still at today.

There was another brief sniff-ette of mini-stardom when he played with a band called the Nashville Teens, who had a big top-ten hit with a song called 'Tobacco Road'. Trouble is, Pete joined them in 1975: the hit was eleven years earlier. The heroic bit is that he still – just – has hope, and doesn't let the profoundly depressing experience of playing to half-empty North London working men's clubs, littered with uninterested kids, pissheads and thickos, get him down . . . not too much anyway.

You develop a thick skin playing in places like he does. You have to. The unintentional brutality of venues like those can be awesome, and hilarious. Jackie, our singer, was telling me the other day that her mum, Julie, played working men's clubs in the North for years. One night, just before closing time, she was giving Dusty Springfield's 'You Don't Have to Say You Love Me' the full treatment on stage, when halfway through the song the club manager walked on stage with a broom and started sweeping up around her.

On another occasion, when she was once again singing for Britain, a phone went off, very loudly, in the corner of the stage. The club manager answered it and, placing himself in between Jackie's mum and the microphone – while she was still singing, mind you – shouted out: 'Brian, it's for you.'

The risks of using my brother as a stand-in for the wedding gig, then, are these:

1) He will try to take over, like he always does (hence the down-sizing of his act over the years).
2) He refuses to rehearse, ever.
3) It will be impossible to stop him doing his cabaret act, i.e. Irish/mother-in-law gags. These invariably go down well at his

pub/club gigs, but could easily leave a posh wedding crowd at the National Liberal Club bemused/mystified/appalled.

Actually, come to think of it, it's too much of a risk.

SUNDAY, 2 SEPTEMBER

The trouble is, my brother knows loads of musicians who might be able to fill in, but I don't. So I've had to ring him and ask for their numbers. I could tell he was itching for me to ask him to do it, but I didn't. Anyway, he has given me the name of a bloke called Alan Lovell, who is in the Swinging Blue Jeans. They got to number two, thirty-eight years ago, with a song called 'Hippy Hippy Shake'. I have left a message for him.

MONDAY, 3 SEPTEMBER

Alan Lovell says he can do it. Woof! I have sent him our tape so he can learn the songs.

WEDNESDAY, 5 SEPTEMBER

Arse. Alan Lovell says the Swinging Blue Jeans have just been given a gig in Germany so he can't do the wedding. Either that or he doesn't fancy what he's heard on our tape. Have rung my brother again, and he has come up with a bloke called 'Scouse Billy', who, he assures me, will be just the ticket.

THURSDAY, 6 SEPTEMBER

Rock on! Scouse Billy says he can do it. I have just put our tape through the letterbox of his tiny Brixton council flat.

FRIDAY, 7 SEPTEMBER

Shite. Scouse Billy says there are too many songs to learn and it's not his bag. He has recommended someone called Bob, a plumber, from Streatham. He is coming over tomorrow.

SATURDAY, 8 SEPTEMBER

Oh, dear. Bob the plumber has just come over. He was covered in tattoos and looked, and sounded – how can I say this – a bit rough. Call me a snob, but I know the kind of crowd we're going to be playing to and he just won't fit in. Trouble is, he thinks he's doing the gig and getting £100 for it. I need to come up with a story, fast. Ironic, really. I've spent the last three years pissing off plumbers on *House of Horrors* and here I am, about to do it again. Oh, well. I need to find a replacement. Quickly. The wedding is in less than a week and I have told the groom, who is a worrier, that everything is Just Fine. But it clearly isn't. I am in danger of ruining a good friend's Big Day.

MONDAY, 10 SEPTEMBER

The deed is done. Told Bob the plumber a minor porkie – i.e. that Matt can now do the gig, after all – and apologized profusely. He took it very well, thank God. After crisis talks with Jackie, we are pinning our hopes on a bloke called Derek, whom she met at a parents' evening at her kids' school. She says she has a feeling he'll be fine. He had better be. An added worry is that the groom has insisted that we play his favourite song, 'Make Me Smile (Come Up and See Me)' by Cockney Rebel. The trouble is, the band will be meeting each other for the very first time just half an hour before the gig starts, so we won't have time to learn each other's names, let alone that particular song. Instead, I have sent tapes of it to everyone and am hoping for the best. I haven't told the groom this, though. He thinks we have been rehearsing and honing our act every night. He is so anal that if he knew we were winging it, the stress and uncertainty would destroy him.

TUESDAY, 11 SEPTEMBER

Have been watching TV all afternoon. Puts it all in perspective, really.

THURSDAY, 13 SEPTEMBER

So many people have been saying the world is now a very different place that it's become a cliché. But it's also true. Every single one of us has been affected in some way. At first I thought my mate might call off his wedding, but he's decided to go ahead. Trouble is, everyone is paranoid about setting foot outside their house at the moment, let alone venturing into Central London, where his wedding is due to take place, lest they get blown up by terrorists. Hopefully, we will all be feeling a bit less fragile come Saturday.

SATURDAY, 15 SEPTEMBER

14.04: Am about to set up all the gear for the gig here at the National Liberal Club, having driven through an unnervingly quiet London. Parking is a problem, as you'd expect: Downing Street is just 800 yards away.

SUNDAY, 16 SEPTEMBER

A number of people might have been worried about the imminent outbreak of the Third World War last night, but you wouldn't have guessed it. It was one of those evenings when the alcohol, the atmosphere and the music combined to push the partymeter up to a maximum of ten. In fact, I can remember the exact moment when the needle hit the max: it was just before midnight, and we were playing to every single guest at the wedding, all of whom were on the dance floor. We had just announced we would be playing 'Make Me Smile (Come Up and See Me)' completely unrehearsed, and that the groom, who by now had alcohol coming out of his ears and was therefore no longer anal, would be on drums.

This was a high-risk strategy. Rocking Bob, Matt's financial adviser who lives in Watford, who had been drafted on rhythm guitar to provide extra ballast to the Surf 'n' Turf sound, looked concerned, as if the mortgage rate had just gone up by two per cent. If we could get the intro right – as in 'Do do do do do doot-todootoodo. Dootodooto. Dodo' – we should be all right, I thought.

Derek, Jackie's mate, who had henceforth performed like a Trojan, shuffled the lyric sheet on the music stand in front of him so he could get a better view of the words. And the groom (a dead ringer for Elvis Presley in the hamburger years) sat there on the drum stool, confused and bleary in one of those large, brightly coloured wedding waistcoat things. He, at least, was not worried.

And off we went. It was like jumping off a cliff, not knowing if the parachute would open: it could have ended in death, or nice, floating euphoria. Thankfully, it was the latter. Every time the song stopped for a couple of seconds (which it does, after every verse) everyone went bonkers.

It was One Of Those Moments.

One Of Those Moments that only someone playing in a band can experience. And the wonderful thing is, that band can just as easily be Surf 'n' Turf as U2. I think it has something to do with social and musical alchemy. Our band isn't the best in the world, obviously, but last night its total was much greater than the sum of its parts. I know that sounds over the top, but we gave everyone a good time and that's priceless. Then again, maybe it was just a simple equation: COMPLETELY PISSED WEDDING PARTY + GROUP PLAYING WELL-KNOWN SONGS = GOOD TIME HAD BY ALL.

I can't believe a rock star performing in front of 80,000 scream-ing fans at Wembley Stadium could have got more out of it than I did last night. Oh, yes. Only music can do this!

TUESDAY, 18 SEPTEMBER

The wedding gig may have been a triumph the likes of which hadn't been seen since Live Aid in 1985 but it doesn't hide the fact that I am still nowhere near getting a hit single together. So I have decided to play the Use Your Famous Friend Card. Yes, I have a mate who is famous. Alistair McGowan, the impressionist.

It's not a Babs/Cilla/Dale thing, mind you. I've known him for ten years. In those early days he was just another stand-up comedian, fretting that the big break would never come. I liked him because, unlike a number of other comics I've met, he was more interested in finding out about other people than he was in talking about himself. And he didn't have that other irritating habit comics have, of com-peting with anyone who says anything funny by trying to say something even funnier. He is gentle, quite shy and a bit like an old woman in that he likes his routine and keeps cats. He also likes playing tennis (which he has regularly thrashed me at) and Scrabble (vice versa).

And, praise be, he is interested in doing something together. This is tremendous. It means going down the novelty single route, of course, but who cares about street cred? This is all about doing whatever it takes to get a number one. And I seem to remember an impressionist – Roger Kitter I think his name was – having a big hit years ago which consisted of a takeoff of John McEnroe swearing at all and sundry at Wimbledon.

I mentioned what I was doing to Alistair the other day and he said: 'Yeah, that sounds great. I'd love to help you.'

This is fab: the best-known impressions on Alistair's show are of Posh and Becks. What price a Posh and Becks rap getting to number one just before the World Cup, in June next year?

Ha! I think I may have cracked it.

WEDNESDAY, 19 SEPTEMBER

Alistair wants me to e-mail his agent with the details of what I'm planning. I am trying not to get too excited about it, but this has got to be in with a realistic chance of getting to number one. It's quite a prospect: the best-known impressionists in the country, Alistair and his comedy partner Ronni, doing a takeoff of the best-known couple in the country, just before the best-known sporting event in the world gets under way.

All we need now is a suitable song. I quite fancy a lyrically bas-tardized version of 'I Got You, Babe', the old Sonny and Cher song. I can just see Alistair and Ronni performing it on *Top of the Pops*, with Surf 'n' Turf providing the backing.

THURSDAY, 20 SEPTEMBER

Have spent all day in Liverpool, interviewing schoolkids about their feelings on the imminent war we're supposed to be having. The actual sight of what happened on 11 September has been haunting me ever since, so Lord knows what it must be doing to the minds of impressionable eight-year-olds. One chubby, bespectacled, Scouse-accented kid told me he'd been having a recurring nightmare. 'I dreamed that, em, Osama Bin Laden, like, followed me and me mam and me dad to Colwyn Bay, and he, like, shot me mam and me dad and then he killed me and then he dropped a bomb on Colwyn Bay and everybody died.'

FRIDAY, 21 SEPTEMBER
I am a bit ambivalent about cover versions. If Alistair and Ronni do an updated version of 'I Got You, Babe' by Sonny and Cher, with us, there will be one big thing in its favour, which is that everyone knows the song. All hits need immediacy, and what could be more immediate that a song that you already know? On the other hand, as we've already discussed, you aren't helping yourself financially by doing a cover version.

And artistically speaking, there isn't much point in covering a well-known song unless you can add something to the original. Eva Cassidy, for instance, brought a remarkable new quality to the old Judy Garland classic 'Over the Rainbow', and Joe Cocker actually managed that rarest of things with 'With a Little Help from My Friends', i.e. he redefined and improved a Beatles original.

Then again, I'm not speaking artistically: I don't give a shit about art, I just want a hit. And, anyway, it's not a crime to fail to improve on the original. I mean, few would argue that Boyzone added anything to Cat Stevens' 'Father and Son' when they covered it in 1995, but who cares? What's more, they will have turned on hundreds of thousands of kids to Cat's stuff, which has got to be a good thing. The point is, once those classic songs are released, they belong to everyone, and not just the person who wrote and/or performed them originally. The bloke who busks (quite appallingly) every day outside my local Woolwich Building Society in Clapham Junction has just as much right to play (or rather massacre) 'Yesterday' in public as Paul McCartney does.

So there. I've talked myself into it. I have nothing at all against cover versions. I like them. They are, after all, a very good way to make the title of this book come true. I also like cover bands, or rather tribute bands. In fact, there is a very good case to be made for saying that some tribute bands give better value for money than the real thing. Take the Counterfeit Stones, imitators of the Rolling Stones. (I've seen both bands live in concert so am qualified to judge.) At a Counterfeit gig, you can park, the tickets are less than a tenner and they play stonking note-for-note versions of all the hits. There's also humour. Like when the Mick Jagger impersonator introduces a song with the words: 'This one is for Bill Wyman. It's in his favourite key. A minor.'

As for the real thing, parking is a nightmare, and fifty quid will get you a partial sighting of four very wizened old men on the horizon. You can also bet your mortgage on them not playing all your favourite Stones' tracks.

SATURDAY, 22 SEPTEMBER

Oh, dear. Another day, yet another slammed door. I e-mailed Alistair's agent, Vivien, yesterday about the project and she doesn't think it's such a good idea. And neither, apparently, does Alistair now he's thought about it a bit more. She said Alistair felt bad about letting me down, which he hasn't, of course. However, I'm not too pissed off, as another light bulb has been switched on over my head. And the caption to this image consists of just one word: 'Eurovision.'

SUNDAY, 23 SEPTEMBER

A.M.: Blimey. I need to move fast. I have just found out that the closing date for the BBC's *Song for Europe* competition is in two weeks. Apparently, they are expecting around 600 entries, from which they will pick just one to represent the UK in the *Eurovision Song Contest 2002*, which is in Estonia next year. Trouble is, I don't write songs. But I know a man who does.

P.M.: Have just rung my brother, who says he will come up with three songs by the end of the weekend. The odds seem overwhelmingly against us, but as Mr Bedi, my local news-agent/grocer/arch enemy, used to say to me, when I was dithering about investing in some share or other: 'You got to be bloody innit to winnit, Jonathan.'

TUESDAY, 25 SEPTEMBER

Pete, true to his word, has come up with the goods. One is a post-11 September ode to world peace called 'World Come Together' that is so exquisitely excruciating that it has the potential to achieve what the Allied war effort has so far failed to, i.e. get Osama Bin Laden to surrender. It sounds like a cross between Bob Geldof's Live Aid single and 'Hark the Herald Angels Sing' performed by a pub singer. Actually, come to think of it, it doesn't sound *like* that – it *is* that. If the song – which he has just played me down the phone on his guitar – was to be broadcast loudly and continually over the mountains of Afghanistan, I could see it ending with OBL himself emerging from his hideaway, hands over his ears, white flag in tow. It's catchy, though (mind you, so is mumps).

He played me two more: 'I Give In' (wet, singalong ditty) and 'Tearing at My Heart' (quite good, actually: a poppy Motown thing. Pete said he was 'inspired' – ahem – to write it after listening to 'I Can't Help Myself' by the Four Tops and 'Build Me Up, Buttercup' by the Foundations).

This professional magpie approach to songwriting isn't new, of course. Everyone nicks off everyone else, sometimes wittingly, sometimes unwittingly. John Lennon, for instance, was completely open about the fact that the opening harmonica riff to 'Love Me Do', the Beatles first hit, was a straight nick from a song called 'Hey! Baby' by the American singer Bruce Channel.

I've always been fascinated by the case of Neil Sedaka, who went even further than that and took a completely academic approach to writing a hit. In the late 1950s he spent months poring over every single record that got into the American charts, and analysed each and every one of them, line by line, note by note. He worked out from this, apparently, that to have a hit you had to have lots of chord changes and mention a girl's name quite a few times. And from that, hey presto, he came up with 'Oh Carol', the world's first painted-by-numbers hit. (The 'Carol' in the song, incidentally, was Carole King, who went on to make one of the greatest albums of all time, *Tapestry*, which was compulsory listening for all bedsit dwellers in the early 1970s.)

The thing is, Pete's songs don't sound nearly as good as they might at the moment, because he is singing them, and he ain't no Elvis. But once we get Jackie, who has a voice as sweet as honey, on the case, they should come to life a bit more. To that end, I have booked a studio belonging to a mate of Pete's called Neil the Hippie, and we are recording there a week on Monday. It's not going to be a big-budget affair, mind you. The whole session should come in at comfortably less than the thirty million dollars that Michael Jackson's new album is rumoured to have cost (Neil the Hippie reckons we should see plenty of change from £100).

I have worked out a deal, just in case any of the songs gets anywhere. Unsurprisingly, Pete has accepted, as it means he won't have to part with any money. (The last time he opened his wallet, a bat flew out.) I am paying the costs of the recording myself – and the £80 entry fee for each of the three songs – in return for a writing credit on each of them.

I have also secured Jackie's services on the same basis. So our three *Eurovision* entries, although actually written solely by my brother, are now to be officially entered into the competition as 'Maitland/Collins/Maitland' compositions. H'm. 'Maitland/Collins/Maitland.' It has a rhythm to it, an internal balance, a meter, a symmetry, not unlike 'Holland/Dozier/Holland', the wonderful songwriting team responsible for countless superb Motown hits. Here we go!

I don't feel *too* bad about getting a writing credit for something I haven't written, and nor should I: there are plenty of precedents for this kind of thing.

From the very dawn of time, local Svengalis, some of whom

couldn't tell one end of a guitar from the other, have managed to get themselves a slice of the writing royalty pie in this way. This, as I am finding out, is how it actually happens in the music business.

So. One rung completed: only ninety-nine to go.

WEDNESDAY, 26 SEPTEMBER
23.55: Just got back from Brighton, and a 1980s revival gig, featuring Paul Young (lost his voice somewhere on the way: shockingly out of tune), Kim Wilde (only slightly out of tune: made up for it anyway by being so sweet-natured), Carol Decker of T'Pau (good voice, shame about the outfit, i.e. floral-print blouse and white trousers), Nick Heyward of Haircut 100 (funny, sounded great, and my God those were good songs, weren't they?), Go West (took themselves a bit too seriously: hence the tight black T-shirts), Heaven 17 (alarmingly portly, and slightly missed the point of the evening by doing groovy modern versions of their hits) and Ben Volepierre-Pierrot, former lead singer of Curiosity Killed the Cat and well-known lover of – ahem – 'the rock 'n' roll lifestyle'.

I took a particular interest in Ben's surprisingly good performance (he's a nifty dancer: loose-limbed and gangly, a bit like a blissed-out monkey) as I had bumped into him on the train on the way down. He was wearing a Peruvian woolly hat/tea cosy thing that covered his ears. I recognized him instantly: 'Down to Earth', his first single, still gets heavy rotation on my record player. He was friendly, in a spaced-out kind of way, and offered me a small strip of transparent material the size of a postage stamp, which I immediately, without thinking, whacked on to my tongue. He told me it was a mint-flavoured thing, but for a moment I panicked. What if he'd just given me some acid? I did actually feel strange for a few minutes after that, but I think it was a psychosomatic thing. Mind you, I suspect he subsequently went on to ingest something stronger than mints, as when he appeared on stage he started spouting the most bizarre, mumbled non sequiturs. He had a great voice, though: deep and sexy. But Lord knows what was going on inside his head.

Anyway, the point of all this is that when I told him about this book, he gave me his phone number. Who knows? It might come in useful in the next few months.

THURSDAY, 27 SEPTEMBER

I do love Planet Celebrity. A spat has broken out in the papers between Anne Robinson and Esther Rantzen. This reminds me of the fun we used to have when I worked at the BBC, playing a game called 'Who Would You Least Want to Be Stuck in a Lift With? Annie Or Esther?' (Self-explanatory, really.) Funnily enough, it was always Esther who won (or rather lost), on the basis that Annie could at least laugh at herself.

I am fascinated by the way the atmosphere on Planet Celebrity plays havoc with its occupants' perceptions of the world. Take EastEnders actor Michael Greco and his recent acceptance speech at the National TV Awards. The result of the award for Best Soap was announced by the heroes of New York, the fire officers who risked their lives on 11 September. They got a three-minute standing ovation. But poor old Michael failed to notice the prevailing wind of sentiment, and once the clapping had finished he didn't even mention the presence of the fire officers, but instead crowed about his show's ratings. Oh, dear.

Then there's the veteran showbiz figure – famous for his apparent ability to relate to the ordinary people who compete in his game shows – who's well known in the business for having it written into his contract that he must never, when being chauffered from airport to studio, 'drive through any run-down council estates or working-class areas'.

Or the camp TV host who hailed a taxi driver just a hundred yards from the entrance to a glitzy awards ceremony. When the cabbie pointed out that because of the area's one-way system it would be far quicker – and cheaper – to walk, the celeb said: 'Oh, no. I can't be seen to walk.'

Welcome to Planet Celebrity!

How is this relevant to having a hit single? Well, you could argue that to have a hit, you need to be ruthless and to possess that all-important 'star mentality', which, in effect, means behaving like the above.

In which case I'm in trouble as I am, I think, relatively normal.

FRIDAY, 28 SEPTEMBER

I am off to Portugal for the weekend. A friend of mine called Martin Bicknell, who is a professional cricketer (he plays for Surrey and he's dead good), is coming to the end of his career and has come up with a rather exciting business idea which he hopes to develop once the last ball has been bowled.

This is extremely sensible of him, as an awful lot of professional cricketers have found themselves in an awful lot of difficulty, post-retirement. They spend their twenties and early thirties having the time of their lives, like a cross between a student and a rock star, and then, overnight, suddenly find it's all over and they haven't got a clue what to do with their lives. This is why cricket boasts a most unenviable statistic: it has, proportionally, more suicides among its players than any other sport.

Since the turn of the century something like half a dozen pro cricketers have topped themselves, including David Bairstow, the well-known wicketkeeper, who played for Yorkshire and England. Martin, sensible bloke that he is, is already making plans for his next career. He has set up a company called Martin Bicknell Golf, which organizes golf tours for companies to Portugal, where he a) shows them a good time and b) gets them to play golf against his celebrity sporting chums. His inaugural event is this weekend, and he has invited me along as a reserve celeb in case one of the proper sporting celebs pulls out. I will get back to the UK on Monday at around 9 p.m.: which isn't very good timing, as Pete and Jackie are due to start recording our *Eurovision* efforts at Neil the Hippie's studio in Streatham that evening, starting at 7 p.m. Mind you, they don't really need me there, anyway. I'm just the cash cow.

MONDAY, 1 OCTOBER

16.00: Am on the plane back from Portugal. Drinking vast quantities of alcohol all night doesn't really agree with me, but I found myself doing it all weekend: it's not often that you find yourself in pretty Portuguese bars with sporting legends at one o'clock in the morning, so when you do you should make the most of it and not go to bed early. Martin had assembled quite a team of sportsmen: the non-cricketers included Frank McLintock, the captain of Arsenal's double-winning team of 1971 (annoyingly, he looks even fitter now than he did when he was playing), Dave Jessup, the ex-world speedway champion (not very tall but don't mention it to his face) and Dave Jacks, the ex-judo champion and bloke who was famous for doing a million press-ups or something on *Superstars*. (He spent the whole time doing card tricks for people.)

As for the cricketers, we had quite a team. I spent a lot of time wondering what sort of a performance Martin's mates would put on if the Australian cricket team (who whupped us in the Ashes series this summer) suddenly turned up for a game. We would have done OK in the bowling, that's for sure. Martin, a bowler himself, had, either consciously or subconsciously, packed the party with fellow practitioners of his art, like John Emburey (legendary England spinner, swears a lot), Gladstone Small (famed for lack of neck, smiles a lot), Pat Pocock (if you're sat next to him at dinner, don't expect to be awake when the dessert comes round) and Phil De Freitas (emotional, entertaining all-rounder with lots of stories to tell who has now decided he wants me to help him write his autobiography).

The batting fraternity was represented by Alistair Brown (who once scored about 200 runs in half an hour at Lord's) and the most interesting tourist of the lot, Mark Butcher, who, if you're a cricket fan, will need no introduction. If you're not, all you need to know is that one day this summer he achieved every sportsman's dream when he single-handedly took us to victory (our only one of the season) against the hated Australians. I very much wanted to ask him about that, but I sensed he was tired of talking about it and so we chuntered on about music instead.

Mark is a superb singer (I know because whenever we talked about songs he liked he started singing them) and guitarist: so much so that when England's county cricketers hold their annual bash at the Royal Albert Hall, he provides the live band. Not any old band, mind you: he packs the line-up with the best players in the biz. He has a lot of music in him. He told me how he used to listen to his dad's Deep Purple records when he was a kid, as well as the obligatory Tamla Motown stuff. It's a bit upsetting, really. I would have done anything to have been able to play the guitar properly, sing nicely and be brilliant at cricket.

In fact, I would have sold my soul for just one of the above, but it didn't happen. He, on the other hand, is insufferably good at all three. That is not fair. Why couldn't God have shared it out a bit more, i.e. let me have the musical talent, and Mark the cricketing ability? Or vice versa?

He also has stamina. One night he apparently forgot to go to bed, even though he was due to start his golf match at 7 a.m. In the end he simply left the bar he found himself in at 6.45 a.m. and, pausing only to pick up his clubs from his room, went straight to the tee. He won the game. He is having a turbulent time off the pitch, mind you. Yesterday he got a call from home saying that due to some shenanigans in his personal life there was a story about him plastered all over the *Sunday Mirror*. Such is the life of a National Sporting Hero.

Hello, we are touching down any moment now and then it's off to Streatham and Neil the Hippie's studio.

TUESDAY, 2 OCTOBER
Some recording studios are hi-tech palaces, fitted out with millions of pounds' worth of state-of-the-art equipment. Often they're to be found in glamorous locations like the South of France, Barbados or Hollywood. Teams of highly skilled technicians, engineers, produc-ers and musicians attend the artist's every whim. The best food,

drink and, of course, stimulants are laid on as well. Recording can take months, sometimes years, and cost millions of pounds.

Neil the Hippie's place is not like that.

I had to find the studio first: it's so difficult to locate that I had to ring Neil up from a local landmark (Sainsbury's in Streatham) and wait next to a red phone box for him to come and fetch me. To get to the studio, we had to go through a dark, cold, wet alleyway and down some steps into a basement. The sight – and smell – that greeted me inside was something I hadn't experienced since my student days. There were clothes, overflowing ashtrays and half-eaten takeaways all over the floor. In one corner there was a makeshift kitchen, which I didn't see at first, as it was obscured by a home-made bar, on top of which was a cat, eating its dinner out of a bowl. Half the light bulbs didn't work, and the ones that did were naked. The walls had cracks in them, and some of the wallpaper was torn, hanging off and suspended in midair. Jackie said it reminded her of the place in *The Silence of the Lambs* where Dr Hannibal Lecter used to keep his victims. To me it was more like how I imagine John McCarthy and Brian Keenan's cell must have looked after they had been sharing it for several years.

As for the aroma, poor old Jackie was so overcome with the pong that she came close to throwing up. (She had to eat her dinner – a sandwich from Sainsbury's – outside, just in case.) Mind you, if you want state-of-the-art recording, you have to pay state-of-the-art prices, so I'm not complaining.

The bill came to just £70 for three songs, which works out at £23.33p per track. (£23.33p would buy you about three and a half seconds in a 'proper' studio.)

Anyway, I've just listened to the songs and, well, they're not bad. OK, they're not cutting-edge hip-hop garage Ibiza-type songs, but don't forget this is Planet *Eurovision*, where a song with a title like 'Diggi–Loo, Diggi–Ley' is regarded as the pinnacle of artistic achievement. ('Diggi–Loo, Diggi–Ley' actually won the contest in 1984 by a mile. It was performed by three camp-looking young blokes from Sweden in tight white trousers and gold boots.) But the backing track on each of our three efforts is a little – how shall I put it? – rudimentary: i.e. Pete on acoustic guitar and backing vocals and – er – that's it. One song, though, 'Tearing at My Heart', Pete's Motown rip-off, is really very catchy. It has come alive thanks to our trump card, Jackie. She has a great voice. Right up there with Eva Cassidy: no nasty additives, no artificial E numbers, just pure, natural and gorgeous.

Anyway, it is now out of my hands. I have sent all three songs, each on a different cassette tape, in a large brown envelope to the HQ of the British Academy of Composers and Songwriters in Central London. Who knows? This could be the start of something big. Or maybe medium.

Then again, I must be realistic. We haven't got a hope of winning. Six hundred songs are being entered. I will know what has become of our efforts in December, when a jury of experts from the music biz will select just twenty to go through to the semi-finals. Then, some time in January 2002, those twenty will be whittled down to just eight by another panel of judges. That's when Radio 2 listeners get involved: they will then vote for four of those eight songs to go forward to the *Song for Europe* final, which will be shown live on BBC1 in March. It will then be down to the Great British viewing public to choose which one of those remaining four songs represents the UK in the *Eurovision Song Contest* in Estonia in May.

I'm not holding my breath.

WEDNESDAY, 3 OCTOBER

Was one of those memorably crap days that you sometimes get working in TV. I had to fly all the way up to an incredibly remote part of the Scottish Highlands at the crack of dawn this morning to do a piece for *Tonight with Trevor McDonald*, about 'Anthrax Island'. This is because everyone is getting scared about Islamic terrorists launching anthrax attacks on us. 'Anthrax Island' earned its name when the government deliberately infected it with bucketloads of the stuff back in the 1940s as part of an experiment to see just how deadly it was.

That's why I had to wear a ludicrous canary-yellow chemical warfare jumpsuit to go on the island: just in case it was still infected. In fact, I looked not unlike your typical *Eurovision Song Contest* entrant.

Trouble is, as I was attempting to haul myself out of the boat we were in, and on to the shore, I fell into the sea. Not only that, but as I fell I could feel my ridiculously flimsy canary-yellow jumpsuit ripping, from bow to stern. By the time I made it on to dry land, the whole thing was in shreds. I looked like the Incredible Hulk after he'd gone through his transformation from man to beast while wearing something bright yellow. What a great day. Soaked, freezing and, quite possibly, infected with one of the most deadly chemical warfare agents known to man.

THURSDAY, 4 OCTOBER

Clearly, I need a backup plan if (or rather when) the *Eurovision* option doesn't work. And even if it does work, and we do get selected to represent the UK in Estonia next year, that is absolutely no guarantee whatsoever that we will get a number one. Look at Katrina and the Waves: even though they won the contest in Dublin in 1997 with 'Love Shine a Light', they only got to number three in the charts. So I need a friendly record company. And I think I may have found one. The other day I was interviewing a bloke called Mark Borkowski, who is big in public relations, for *Tonight*. Mark, who has a round, friendly face, floppy blond hair, and looks a bit like the Pilsbury Dough Boy thirty years on, has an office in Camden populated, as is *de rigueur* in PR, by lots of attractive young women. And he wants to help. He is a useful bloke to know. In 1998 he was part of an ingenious scam that achieved what many might have thought was impossible. He made Cliff Richard cool. What happened was this: Cliff, who hadn't had a decent hit in years, suddenly woke up and realized what his big problem was. He wasn't getting played on Radio 1. It didn't matter how good his songs were, if they had his name on them, they weren't getting played. This was because Radio 1 was trying to reinvent itself as being hip, trendy and in touch, all three of which Cliff wasn't, and isn't. At least, he wasn't perceived to be. (Can I just say at this point that I still treasure the moment I saw him sing 'Devil Woman' on *Top of the Pops* in 1976, when he had a British Home Stores black leather jacket slung over his left shoulder, in the style of someone who's just appeared in the squash club bar, post-game, all freshly showered and sporty casual looking. This image has stayed with me for more than a quarter of a century. I don't quite know why.) Anyway, the scam Borkowski was involved in meant that Cliff's new record, 'Can't Keep This Feeling In', was released under a pseudonym, Black Knight. It was a funky dance track and had a single clue as to the identity of the singer: halfway through, a rapper shouted out 'CR! Tell it like it is!' Had it been released under Cliff's name, of course, radio stations would have treated it like a steak at a vegetarian barbecue. Instead, thinking it was some mysterious dude, black stations started playing it . . . as, indeed, eventually, did Radio 1. It was then that Borkowski let the press know that Radio 1 was, unwittingly, defying its own 'ban' on Cliff records. Result: lots of publicity, lots of airplay, and Cliff's first top-ten hit in more than five years.

Anyway, the point of this story is a) to show how useful PR can be in making hit records, but you probably know that, and b) the bloke who was Cliff's boss at EMI at the time and dreamed the whole stunt up was someone called Clive Black. Clive is a mate of Borkowksi's. In fact, they have offices in the same building in Camden. When I told Borkowski about my plan to get to number one, he thought it was a splendid wheeze, as Bertie Wooster might have said, and wanted to help in some way; so he told Clive about it. Clive got similarly aroused and told Borkowski that I should get in touch. So I am. Clive is my last chance, really: no other record companies seem remotely interested.

THURSDAY, 11 OCTOBER

Bit of a diversion. Got a call from a big cheese at ITV today. It seems there is some interest in me presenting the new series of *Survivor* on ITV. This is really quite exciting. The show, which is basically *Big Brother* meets *The Generation Game* on a desert island, wasn't a huge hit first time round. But it's being given another chance, and the presenter, Mark Austin, the man who's always useful if you need your ciggie lit at a party, has decided he doesn't want to do it again. What excites me greatly is a) the money (there were press reports at the time that Mark got 150,000 smackers for just over two months' work) and b) the career enhancement prospects. Some people might think it's dumb taking on a programme that has a reputation as being a bit of a turkey, but I disagree. When you're taking over a show which is perceived to have failed, the only way is up. If it tanks again, you can blame the programme and say: 'Well, we all knew it was going to flop, anyway, didn't we?' But if it succeeds, you can modestly claim the credit by subtly pointing out that the only difference between this series and the last one is you, and therefore you should get all the glory and even more money. On the other hand, if you take over a hit show from a well-known presenter, like *Watchdog* after Anne Robinson, or *Who Wants to Be a Millionaire?* after Chris Tarrant, then unless you're super-talented and/or extremely lucky, the only way is down. Anyway, I have two important meetings next week: one with Clive Black, record company boss, the other with Claudia Rosencrantz, ITV's Head of Entertainment.

MONDAY, 15 OCTOBER
Saw Clive Black today. His label is called Edel Records. They've had a couple of big hits, one of which is that one that goes 'Who Let the Dogs Out, Woof Woof!' by, I think, the Baha Men. Clive comes from good musical stock. His dad is Don Black, one of the most successful lyricists ever, who wrote the words to songs like 'Diamonds Are Forever', 'Born Free', 'To Sir with Love' and 'Ben', the sweet little ballad sung quite beautifully by a pre-pubescent Michael Jackson. In fact, when Clive's dad lived in Los Angeles, little Clive got to hang out with the equally little but slightly older Michael Jackson a fair bit. Clive claims his only memories of Jacko are that he was a bit of a pain in the arse and that he used to regularly smash

him at pool. Clive comes over as just a little bit wide, but with a twinkle in his eye, and he talks very quickly indeed. He is also clearly a bit of a lad. Just before he signed on the dotted line to become the youngest ever director at the mighty EMI record label, he asked for a clause in the contract to be removed. It was the one that said 'Please declare whether or not you have a drug problem, suffer from mental illness, or have a criminal record'. Clive's argument was that those were precisely the qualities you need to make it in the music business. This may be why he was once described in a magazine article as 'having a personality more colourful than any rock star'.

Anyway, I liked him. He struck me (not surprisingly) as someone who would be good fun at a party. And, praise the Lord, Clive appears to like me too: he Wants To Do Something. He says he will finance the recording of a single, provided I take a smaller royalty than normal. No problem, I said. At this stage I would be prepared to bend over and let you shove a cucumber up my arse if it meant I'd get a single out of it. By the time we'd finished talking (not very long: Clive fits three times more words into the time available than your average person) we reckoned we had three options: 1) To record a really great original, new song that will get to number one because it's just so damned good. 2) To do a souped-up modern dance-style cover version of an old song that everyone knows. Or 3) to do a crap novelty song.

The trouble with 1), though, is that it's a lot easier said than done. 2) is quite a good idea, and there are quite a few old songs that I'm dying to have a go at, like 'Groove Is in the Heart' by Dee-Lite, or 'Feel the Need in Me' by the Detroit Emeralds. But 3) is probably our best bet. As Clive pointed out, the majority of buyers of singles are young kids, so maybe we should do a novelty song that shamelessly and cynically appeals to young kids. Why don't we do a 'Stars on 45'-style single, I said, and splice together all the best-known children's hits like 'The Birdie Song', 'The Wombles', 'The Teletubbies Song', etc., etc., and then slap a disco backing on it? It would be a musical crime against humanity, but it would surely be in with a shout. Clive agreed. Let's mull it over, he said, and talk again soon.

TUESDAY, 16 OCTOBER

Met Claudia Big Cheese at ITV about *Survivor* today. She was accompanied by a thin-lipped woman called Mary who looked like a very senior woman in the police force but who turned out to be an accountant and the head of Planet 24, the independent TV company that ITV pays to make *Survivor*.

I felt like I got on well with Claudia, but there wasn't an awful lot of wattage flowing between Mary and me. For some reason I actually volunteered the fact that she reminded me of a police-woman. I dunno why; it just came out. This may – just may – have done my chances of landing the job no good at all.

However, they are seeing only one other person, so there's not a huge amount of competition. I want this job.

THURSDAY, 18 OCTOBER

I can't help myself, but I am getting very excited about the possi-bility of presenting *Survivor*. Or rather the probability. A couple of my insider TV chums have told me that it's looking very good for me. I keep picturing myself on the desert island, getting a suntan and earning life-changing amounts of money, while everyone else back home freezes their nuts off.

FRIDAY, 19 OCTOBER

From: jmaitland@ukgateway.net

To: Clive Black

Sent: 19 October 2001

Subject: How To Make Your Million From Pop Music. Mind You, At This Stage A Tenner Would Be A Result

Clivey Baby!

It was great to meet you the other day. I particularly liked the black and white pictures of you and various boxers/TV celebs on the walls of your office. It made me feel like I was in a cosy, family-run Italian restaurant, i.e. the type where the owner has plastered the place with signed photos of Henry Cooper, Paulo Rossi et al.

Anyway, I have given a lot of thought to the 120mph conversation that we had the other day and I really think the children's novelty song is the way to go.

As we both know, we have one key problem: getting young kids to buy our wares. If we splice together every well-known kiddy hit ever made, then we have surely gone a long way to cracking it.

Whaddya think?

Rock on

Jonathan

MONDAY, 22 OCTOBER

From: Clive Black

To: jmaitland@ukgateway.net

Sent: 22 October 2001

Subject: Think Big, My Son. Let's Go For Ten Million

Jonathan: what would be the chances of you getting some telly coverage if we went ahead with the Tots on 45 idea?

Cheers

Clive

PS Glad you like my office. Maybe I should get a dessert trolley thing (with a large bowl of tiramisù on the top, of course) to complete the effect.

From: jmaitland@ukgateway.net

To: Clive Black

Sent: 22 October 2001

Subject: I'm Getting Quite Excited

Clivey Baby!

I spoke to the head of children's programmes at both ITV and BBC today and told them what I was planning. Both were dead interested. At least, they seemed to be: you have to bear in mind that I work in an industry where 'Yes' actually means 'Maybe' and 'Maybe' means 'No'. In fact, sometimes 'Yes' actually means 'No'. Having said that, I told them we could give them some groovy filmed material for free (I'll get one of my cameramen mates to do it on the cheap) of, say, the audition process for the single, i.e. the bit where we select the kiddies who will perform on the single. *Tot Idol*, if you like.

Then we can film the actual recording of the single, and, hey presto, we will have enough material for a long news package on something like *Newsround*, or even a half-hour documentary (steady!) on, say, ITV, which, let's face it, wouldn't do the single's chances any harm.

Rock on

Jonathan

MONDAY, 29 OCTOBER

From: jmaitland@ukgateway.net
To: Clive Black
Sent: 29 October 2001
Subject: I'm Not Stalking You, Honest

Clivey Baby!

As the crowd at Charlton are wont to chant when our team goes 2–0 up: 'It's all gone quiet over there' . . . You're not losing the faith, are you? I hope not . . . but if you are, you've got to let me know quickly, so I can try to get someone else involved.

Rock on

Jonathan

TUESDAY, 30 OCTOBER

From: Clive Black
To: jmaitland@ukgateway.net
Sent: 30 October 2001
Subject: Keeping The Faith

Jonathan: good to hear from you. I am at home with the flu.

I think I am up for it, as long as it is fun and I don't lose money on it.

Even if we do things on the cheap it's still going to cost me at least tens of thousands to put the thing out.
Let me have more of a think about it and I'll get back to you.
Clive

From: jmaitland@ukgateway.net
To: Clive Black
Sent: 30 October 2001
Subject: What About This?

Clivey Baby!
I hear what you're saying. I can guarantee it will be fun. As for not losing money: well, there's always a bit of a risk involved in these things, isn't there?
I'm fairly confident we won't be running up any Mariah Carey-style losses, though.
As for keeping the costs down, leave the making of the video for the single to me: and feel free to rip me off when it comes to apportioning any royalties.
At this stage I just want to get a single out . . . any single . . .
Rock on
Jonathan

MONDAY, 5 NOVEMBER

From: Clive Black
To: jmaitland@ukgateway.net
Sent: 5 November 2001
Subject: Brainwave

OK, what about this? Surf 'n' Turf featuring Jordan, doing a cover version of 'Boys, Boys, Boys', produced by the guys that did 'Barbie Girl'?
Sounds like a summer smash to me!
Over and out
Clive

From: jmaitland@ukgateway.net
To: Clive Black
Sent: 5 November 2001
Subject: Er . . . Interesting One

Clivey Baby!

Blimey . . . that's a bit of an about-turn. Having just walked down Northcote Road and had a fag, these are my thoughts:

1) It's not very classy, is it? But then we're not in this to make 'Bohemian Rhapsody'. We just want to get to number one.

2) I can see the novelty value.

3) It's your record label so I guess it's your call in the end.

4) Can she sing?

Rock on

Jonathan

MONDAY, 12 NOVEMBER

From: jmaitland@ukgateway.net
To: Clive Black
Sent: 12 November 2001
Subject: I Think We May Have Been Overtaken By Events

Clivey Baby!

Have you seen the papers? Jordan is pregnant.

Give her six months and she'll look like an aerial map of the Himalayas.

Still think it's a good idea?

Rock on

Jonathan

From: Clive Black
To: jmaitland@ukgateway.net
Sent: 12 November 2001
Subject: You've Got A Point

Jordan up the duff is not a good look. I have a fall-back position. Give my
secretary a call later to arrange a meeting tomorrow.

Mazel Tov

Clive

WEDNESDAY, 14 NOVEMBER

From: jmaitland@ukgateway.net

To: Clive Black

Sent: 14 November 2001

Subject: A Much Better Idea Than The Jordan One

Clivey Baby!

Good to see you again yesterday.

This makes a lot more sense.

'"I Just Don't Know What To Do With Myself" by Surf 'n' Turf featuring Dale Winton' or,
if he pulls rank, 'Dale Winton with Surf 'n' Turf' sounds like a much better fit. Hopefully
his manager will still think it's a good idea when she wakes up tomorrow morning.
And thanks for setting me up to meet Ian Levine: I can't think of anyone more
suited to produce this strange union. I just did an Internet search on him. He has
one hell of a track record: Take That, Petula Clark, the Elgins ('Heaven Must Have
Sent You' is one of my all-time faves), Bob Marley, Edwin Starr and the rest.

Rock on

Jonathan

THURSDAY, 15 NOVEMBER

From: jmaitland@ukgateway.net

To: Clive Black

Sent: 15 November 2001

Subject: Not Your Typical Bloke, Is He?

Clivey Baby!

Went round to Ian Levine's last night. I see what you mean. Bit of a character and
all that. Eric Hall meets Danny DeVito meets Hank from Larry Sanders.

I still can't get over the house, or rather houses. Knocking them all through like that. It reminds me of the house the Beatles lived in, in *Help*.

I was rather struck by the enormous Dalek nestling behind the beige leather sofas in his front room, the full suit of armour in the dining room, and the door that looked like it was going to lead into an ordinary bedroom but which opened out into a slightly musty-smelling wood-walled gym and sauna. The twelve-seater personal cinema was nice too. The overall effect was Graceland comes to Ealing Common.

The way he'd covered the entire hallway with pictures of his mother was interesting too: but I also had a Jewish mum, so I understand. Admittedly our conversation was more of a monologue than a dialogue (he talks even further and faster than you), but it was a very entertaining one.

He is certainly enthused about the whole thing — and he isn't going to let anything stand in his way, in the manner of a tank on its way into Warsaw circa 1944.

He wants to get going right now: and I mean, right now.

I'm game if you are and if Dale is . . .

Rock on

Jonathan

From: Clive Black

To: jmaitland@ukgateway.net

Sent: 15 November 2001

Subject: You Can Say That Again

Glad it went well. Ian is a great talent even if he is a little overpowering.

Jan, Dale's manager, still thinks it's a good idea but Dale has a lot on his plate at the moment (he's doing a Christmas special for the BBC) and she doesn't want to rush into anything, so we're all going to meet up in the New Year. All we have to do now is calm Ian down.

Cheers

Clive

From: jmaitland@ukgateway.net

To: Clive Black

Sent: 15 November 2001

Subject: Loose Ends

Clivey Baby!

That sounds fab.

Rock on

Jonathan

Well, we are at least heading in the right direction, and on two horses. One called Dale, the other *Eurovision*. We could get thrown off at any moment, though.

FRIDAY, 30 NOVEMBER

08.22: An envelope has just shuffled through the letterbox and landed on the mat. It has 'British Academy of Composers and Songwriters' on it. This is the *Eurovision* verdict. I'm depressed already. It smells like rejection. I mean, look at the odds: 600 songs were entered, only 20 go through to the next phase. Maybe I should just throw it straight in the bin and cut out the middleman. I don't even know why I'm bothering to open it but here goes anyway.

08.22.11: Ohmygodivejustseenthefirstfewwordsoftheletteritsays'I am delighted to tell you . . .'idontbelieveitidontbelieveitidontbelieve itweareinthesemifinalsofthesongforeuropecontest2002idontbelieveit idontbelieveitidontbelieveitimustringpeteimustringjackieimustring mattimustringeveryoneiknowohmygodohmygodiamuncontrollably excited.

08.34: Bits of me are still on the ceiling, but the rest of me has managed to get through to the key players, i.e. my bro ('Really? Huh. It's not gonna get any further, though, is it?'), Matt ('No! No!') and Jackie ('Jonny! Oh, Jonny!'). Having read the letter through a few (well, six) times, it seems we are now, officially, in the semi-finals of *Song for Europe 2002*. On Tuesday 8 January eight of the remaining twenty songs, of which ours, 'I Give In', is one, will be, quote, 'chosen to go forward to the public for voting'. The irony is that 'I Give In' was, as far as I was concerned, such a weak song that I didn't even want it to be put forward in the first place, but on the basis that if you throw enough mud, we entered it anyway.

The point is, there are four more massive hurdles to clear before we achieve the impossible. I know I've listed them before, but just to recap:

1) 8 January: a panel of experts pare twenty songs down to eight.
2) Some time near the end of January, the eight get played on Terry Wogan's Radio 2 show, and his listeners vote for four to go through to a televised final on BBC1.
3) Some time in March, the remaining four get played on live TV and then The Nation Decides.
4) The song that gets the nod from the public will represent the UK in the *Eurovision Song Contest*, which is being held in Estonia on 25 May.

I have paced around in circles so many times that I have done the equivalent of the 5000 metres in my front room. I must calm down.

10.25: Reality check. OK, we've done well to get this far, but it's not like we've won a Grammy or anything. I am bracing myself for failure when they announce the last eight. I mean, what chance have we got of making it?

After all, it wasn't exactly a big-budget number: I spent just £23.33p on recording it. Some of the other efforts will have had a lot more than that thrown at them. I remember, for example, hearing a belter of a song called 'Only the Women Know' by a band called Six Chix, which was entered for the 1999 *Song for Europe* contest, with the full backing of the mighty EMI. It had a perfect *Eurovision* pedigree in that it was written, and played on, by the guys from Katrina and the Waves. A hundred thousand pounds went on that particular project: the song made the final eight but didn't win, and no one ever heard of it, or Six Chix, again.

Having said that, the odds are actually a lot more favourable than they were at the start, when 600-odd tracks were in the ring. Then, we had a one in thirty chance of getting through to the last twenty. Now we're in the last twenty, we have, roughly, a one in two chance of getting through to the last eight. Eek.

MONDAY, 3 DECEMBER
I was so excited about the letter from the BBC that I never actually read it properly. Now that I have, I realize that a delicious little morsel of irony has made its way on to my plate. The judges who decided which 20 of the 600 songs should get this far were, according to the letter, 'music industry experts, members of the British Academy of Composers and Songwriters, and leading figures from the music business, including Muff Winwood from Sony . . .'

Muff Winwood! The same Muff Winwood who almost threw himself out of the window when I played him a short burst of Surf 'n' Turf performing live!

He didn't know it was us he was listening to, mind you: all the judges heard the songs blind, without knowing who the writers or performers (or indeed local Svengalis) were.

Anyway. Time to take stock. We're not in a bad position. In the semi-finals of the BBC's *Song for Europe* contest and lined up for a duet with Dale Winton. On the other hand, we still have a journey of Tipperary-style proportions to go. Nothing has been put down on vinyl (OK, plastic) yet. Lots can go wrong.

TUESDAY, 4 DECEMBER
In fact, something just has. Mary, the thin-lipped TV boss who looks like a senior policewoman, rang me today. I didn't get the *Survivor* job. They've given it to a bloke who presents cricket on

Channel 4 called Mark Nicholas who has thick wavy hair and looks like he's just walked out of the yacht club. I am really depressed. I really thought I had it in the bag. I am going to bed.

WEDNESDAY, 5 DECEMBER
Not nearly as arsed off as I was yesterday. I mean, it's only telly, innit?

WEDNESDAY, 12 DECEMBER
It can be done. It is possible to be middle-aged, terminally unhip and out of touch and still get to number one. Step forward Gordon Haskell. Gordon is fifty-five, has a beard and comes from the West Country. He has spent the last fifteen years playing to drunks in bars. And he is the bookies' favourite to be this year's Christmas number one. Unlike so many of the acts in the top ten these days, Gordon is not a prefabricated, manufactured, all-singing and all-dancing mannequin. Neither is he an unwitting pawn in a massive marketing exercise. He is, instead – praise be – a purveyor of Proper Music, Played by Professionals.

I remember saying a few months ago that someone would hit the top of the charts before the year was out with one of those cheap home-made-type records and now it's happened. Gordon – apparently – got two hundred quid off his manager to record four tracks in one day, in a studio in Oxfordshire. (They could have done it cheaper at Neil the Hippie's place, mind you.) One of the quartet of songs was called 'Harry's Bar', a smoky Frank Sinatra-type croonalong (which I have to admit bores the arse off me, but there we go) about how life looks from the bottom of a beer glass. Gordon's manager sent the track to Johnnie Walker at Radio 2, who played it. The listeners went bonkers. They rang up in their droves, asking what the song was, and who it was by. And now, with two weeks to go to Christmas, Gordon looks like he's cracked it big-style.

Gordon has done exactly what I need to do. He has struck a deep chord with members of the public who don't normally buy singles. How has he done that? Well, he has managed to fulfil the golden rule, as laid down by Bill Drummond, author of *The Manual (How to Have a Number One the Easy Way)*. He has got something of his unique self, his soul, down on vinyl. (OK, plastic then.) 'Harry's Bar', whether you like it or not, conveys what Gordon's life has been like these past fifteen years. It reeks of pubs, smoke, world-weariness and wisdom. Good for him. If he can do it, then maybe so can I. But what sort of a song is going to capture the essence of my, and Surf 'n' Turf's, soul? And even if we find one that does, will Johnnie Walker want to play it? And even if he does, will anyone want to buy it?

WEDNESDAY, 26 DECEMBER

Gordon didn't quite make it: he got to number two. Ironically, he was kept off the top by 'Something Stupid', a song even more uncool than his own, but which had the advantage of having been recorded by Robbie Williams and Nicole Kidman. Not to worry, though. Gordon has inspired me. Roll on 2002, and look out charts . . . here comes Surf 'n' Turf!

FRIDAY, 28 DECEMBER

I have been looking more closely into the process by which Gordon Haskell got to the top of the charts (nearly), and it is very instructive. Getting the song played by Radio 2 was the crucial break he needed, but by no means the only one. A big hit single is a bit like a stool: it needs three legs to get off the ground. Those legs are, in order of importance, airplay, distribution and publicity.

There was no point in Gordon getting all that invaluable airplay if the song wasn't available in the shops. Someone had to persuade all the top record shops to stock it, and then distribute it to them. But this can be very hard. Woolworths, the most influential retailer by far when it comes to the singles chart, won't sell your single unless it has a good chance of getting into the top ten. But it can only get into the top ten if Woolworths agree to sell it to begin with. How can you persuade Woolies your song has got a good chance of getting into the top ten if they're not predisposed to stocking it in the first place? They certainly weren't keen on stocking Gordon's at first, as he was a total unknown. As far as they were concerned, he had no chance at all of making the top ten. Verily, said the local Svengali, we have a catch-22 situation. And it was this situation that Gordon's lot found themselves in, early last month. They'd managed to persuade Woolies, and WH Smith et al., to take a few hundred copies of the single, but that is nothing like the numbers needed to get in the charts at this time of year: not even the top fifty. But then Radio 2 played it. And kept on playing it. Suddenly, Gordon's lot were able to say to Woolies and co.: 'Look, this song has a chance of getting in the top ten. Why don't you start selling it in serious numbers?' It worked. The big record shops started ordering thousands of copies. Gordon's lot then had a corker of a story on their hands, of the pop-music-David-slays-record-industry-Goliath variety. They were able to tell the press that a bearded nobody from the West Country was vying with the biggest pop star in the country, i.e. Robbie Williams, for the coveted Christmas number-one slot.

The ball was rolling. The *Sunday Times*, for instance, ran a story headlined 'Middle-Aged Pop Crooner Set To Top The Christmas Charts'. This got the record shops even more excited, of course. By the second week of December, Woolies and co. had ordered 200,000 copies of the song. Which is more than enough to get it to number one, even at Christmas, provided every single one of those 200,000 copies actually gets sold, that is. Orders of 200,000 copies by big record stores doesn't automatically mean you're going to get 200,000 members of the public actually buying it.

Gordon's lot then delayed the official release of the single until Monday 17 December, by which time it had generated such a nice head of steam, what with all that airplay and all that publicity, that it sold like crazy. Of the 200,000, 90,000 got snapped up that week, and it went straight into the Christmas chart at number two. Robbie Williams, incidentally, sold 120,000. The timing was very important. Had they put Gordon's song out a week earlier, i.e. Monday 10 December, the sales would have been diluted and spread out over the two weeks before Christmas. In which case he might not have made the top five.

So that's what it takes. You need a) Woolies, b) a famous DJ and c) the press behind you. And good timing. Oh, dear. This is not going to be easy at all. Those odds that William Hill gave me, i.e. 50–1 against us getting to number one, are beginning to look ludicrously ungenerous; 500–1 would have been fairer.

TUESDAY, 1 JANUARY 2002

P.M.: Just got back from watching Charlton play Ipswich. A funny thing happened on the way to the match. As I was walking to the stadium, I noticed my all-time pop hero, Glen Tillbrook, the singer and guitarist with Squeeze, a few yards away. He is a Charlton fan too. That bloke supplied the soundtrack to my youth. When I was at college in the early 1980s, I got so evangel-ical about the band that I used to write out the lyrics to their songs and act them out. God, I was sad. Mind you, I still am. As Julie Burchill once said: 'There is nothing sadder than a man over the age of thirty writing about pop music in an arena any more public than his diary.' Anyway, getting back to my Squeeze-worshipping college days. In their song 'Tempted', Glen Tillbrook sang about being unfaithful to his partner, and how, when he left the scene of the crime, his hotel room, he packed 'a toothbrush, toothpaste, a flannel for my face, pyjamas, a hairbrush, new shoes and a case . . .'. I – don't ask me why – assembled all those items and then packed them up, item by item, in front of my bemused/amused mate, Ian from Sevenoaks, as Glen sang the rel-evant words.

Squeeze really connected with me. They sang about bits of London that I knew, and characters – usually dodgy, drunken ones – and situations I could relate to. On top of that, they were mega-catchy and tuneful and, in the case of 'Tempted' – the best song ever written – classy and soulful. Once, in 1982, during a gig at the London School of Economics, Glen forgot the words to 'Up the Junction'. 'Anyone else wanna have a go?' he shouted, half in jest, I think. Before he had finished the sentence, I had barged my way to the front, Jonah Lomu-style, and grabbed the mike. It sounded appalling, but I didn't care. Afterwards, someone introduced me to Chris Difford, Squeeze's rhythm guitarist and lyricist (Chris is the Poet Laureate of pop). 'Thanks for singing, mate,' he said.

And here he was now. Glen. Should I say something? What can you say? It's so naff to come over all star-struck. But Glen Tillbrook! Then I heard a voice saying 'Jonathan'. It was someone I knew from the BBC. He was with Glen. Obviously a mate of his. We said hello. 'Bloody hell,' I whispered. 'You're only going to the match with my all-time hero. He is God.'

'I know. Hold on a minute.' A few seconds later he introduced me to Glen.

I babbled. I couldn't help it. 'Yeah, it's funny, actually. I've got pictures of you on my walls at home, obviously, and I'm writing this book and I've mentioned you and it's like, about having a number one, or trying to, and . . .' Oh, dear.

'Well, if you find out how to do it, let me know.' Glen laughed, and then got momentarily distracted by someone else. I walked self-consciously alongside him for a few yards while he chatted to his new-found friend, but then he put me out of my misery, politely, by shaking my hand just before he entered the turnstile and saying: 'Nice to meet you, mate.' Glen Tillbrook! God! I just met him! Is this fate?

MONDAY, 7 JANUARY

23.45: The BBC's panel of experts decides on the final eight songs tomorrow. I feel that a few positive vibes won't go amiss, so I've just rung psychic superstar Uri Geller and asked for his help. I interviewed Uri recently for a report on Michael Jackson: the two are big mates. As you'd expect with someone who is a pal of Jacko's, Uri isn't the most conventional bloke in the world. He is also very intense. He seemed to take to me, though, possibly because I played the 'I'm Jewish too' card, from the bottom of the pack. He bent a few spoons for my entertainment and kept saying how he was getting vibes off me which were telling him: 'Very strongly, verrrry strongly, Jonathan, that you should be a stand-up comedian. No really. It's true.'

Anyway, I have just rung him and played him our *Eurovision* song down the phone and asked him to send out a few strong thought signals to the jury tomorrow.

'OK, Jonathan, I will do this for you. I take this verry, verrry seriously. I will be concentrating verrry hard all day tomorrow. Let me know what happens.'

TUESDAY, 8 JANUARY

13.45: Am on the train up to Manchester to do a story on the Queen's Golden Jubilee, which she celebrates this year, for *Tonight*. Kate, the editor of this book, has just rung and reminded me that today is the day that the last twenty in the *Song for Europe* contest get whittled down to eight. I know, I said, but I don't expect to hear from them until the end of the week, and anyway I don't want to tempt fate by getting all excited about it. If you don't hear from me, you can safely assume we've been eliminated, I said. In the unlikely event that we do get through, believe me, you'll be the first to know.

14.42: My mobile is ringing.

'Hello?'

'Hi. Kevin Bishop from the BBC here. Can I speak to Jonathan Maitland, please?'

'Yeah, it's me.' (Thinks: it's someone on a daytime TV show who wants me to be their naff consumer expert. How can I say, 'Never in a million years', but still sound grateful and polite?)

'Congratulations. You have got through to the finals of the *Song for Europe* contest.'

'Kevin. I'm sorry. I am going to explode. I am on a train right now and I'm going to ring everyone I know and go bonkers. I'll call you back tomorrow when I've calmed down.'

'I quite understand. Well done. Bye.'

WEDNESDAY, 9 JANUARY

I'm not looking forward to seeing my mobile phone bill for this month. Uri was pretty chuffed, though. I must remember to phone him again the night before the next big hurdle.

THURSDAY, 10 JANUARY

Well, well, well. There were 600 songs. Then there were twenty. Now there are eight. We are one of those eight. At the end of this month the eight will be played on Radio 2 and on Friday 1 February the listeners will vote for the last four to go through to a live, televised final. The question now is this: do we stick with our very basic recording of the song, which cost twenty-five quid to make at Neil the Hippie's outside toilet-cum-studio, or do we get it redone properly?

Kevin Bishop, the bloke from the BBC who broke the good news to me on the train this week, strongly advises the latter course of action. (Kevin's full title, by the way, is in fact Editor, Mainstream Programmes, Entertainment, which is very comforting as the mainstream is very much Surf 'n' Turf territory.) Kevin has just told me a salutary tale about a song like ours which made the final eight last year. It was recorded by a farmer's wife, in her back bedroom, and cost nothing to make. But when it came to playing it on the radio, the less-is-more low-tech charm was lost on the general public and it didn't make it through. H'm. I need to find someone who will produce our song for us, cheaply. And fast. But someone who is good.

FRIDAY, 11 JANUARY

11.25: Just spoke to Ian Levine. As in the producer bloke who lives in that bizarre Graceland-style house in Ealing, with the Dalek in the sitting room. Played him the track down the phone. He said he'd record it for us for three grand. I wouldn't mind shelling out that kind of dosh if I thought we had a good chance of recouping the money eventually, but what if we don't get any further? It would be money down the drain. I could try Clive Black, but he's already committed to our possible Dale Winton project.

11.32: Have just rung a bloke called Steve Levine (no relation) whom I once did a story on for *Tonight*. We got on well at the time and agreed to keep in touch on the basis that one day we might be able to scratch each other's backs a little. Steve is a record producer. He produced all those fab Culture Club hits in the early 1980s. It was he who was responsible for that wonderful mouth organ intro to 'Church of the Poisoned Mind' and the amazing over-the-top epic sound on 'Victims'. More recently he has done stuff with a girl band called Honeyz. And, serendipitously, he produced the Russian Eurovision entry in the 2000 competition, a ditty by a girl called Alsou, which came second. According to Jonathan King, it was by far and away the best track ever to have not won Eurovision.

He has asked me to drop off a copy of the track at his place and let him think about it. He only lives across the river from me (Fulham), so I'm on my way. I have taken a bottle of champagne out of my fridge to accompany the tape which hopefully will oil the wheels a little.

19.34:

From: Steve Levine
To: jmaitland@ukgateway.net
Sent: 11 January 2002
Subject: Your Euro Hit

I have just listened to the tape. It is a hit. I will get my manager to ring you up and sort out a deal. If we can come to a sensible agreement I'd be happy to help.
Thanks for the champagne, by the way . . . you needn't have.
All the best
Steve

19.40: By happy coincidence, Steve Levine's manager just happens to be my cousin, Stephen Budd, who is a big cheese in the music biz. Stephen has just called me to suggest that we give him (i.e. Steve Levine) a twenty-five per cent share of any royalties that the song might accrue, in return for which Steve will work for nothing. Great, I said. Like a no-win, no-fee thing. 'Precisely,' said Stephen. 'But you may have to shell out a few hundred quid on getting the thing mastered [whatever that is] and you might have to pay for proper session musicians, should Steve want to go with them rather than your lot in Surf 'n' Turf.'

'Fine,' I said.

'Steve is now going to listen to the track non-stop for two days and work out where he wants to go with it, and what he wants to do with it, and he will call you soon.'

'No problem,' I said.

Woof!

21.34: Have just rung my brother. 'Huh! It's all being taken out of my hands!' he said. I managed to calm him down by pointing out that it was, to a certain extent, now being taken out of my hands too. If we tried to produce the thing ourselves, we'd just end up coming to blows . . . too many chiefs and all that. At least this way we are all putting ourselves in the hands of someone who clearly knows what he is doing. And, anyway, just because you're the writer of the song, it doesn't mean you get to call the shots: in Hollywood, the writer is lucky to be let on the set at all.

'If we get through to the TV final, what date is that?'

'Sunday, 3 March. But don't count your chickens.'

'I've got a gig that day.'

'All right, Pete. I tell you what. You do your crappy little gig for a hundred quid or whatever and we'll appear on live TV, in front of millions, performing your song, without you. And then if we get through to the final, in Estonia, we'll perform it in front of a billion people, worldwide, without you too. And pocket the £100,000 royalties too.'

He laughed. Phew. Noel and Liam Gallagher-style fallout narrowly avoided. For the time being at least.

WEDNESDAY, 16 JANUARY
Things are getting interesting. Steve Levine wanted to meet Jackie before deciding on the final direction the track should take, so we popped over to his house this afternoon.

Steve, who looks a bit like the footballer Mark Hughes, made us a coffee in his kitchen before ushering us into his back garden. 'This is my studio,' he said, pointing at a medium-sized garden shed. It was a bit like walking into Dr Who's Tardis. It might have looked small and simple from the outside, but inside was quite a different matter. Banks of gleaming black hi-tech recording equipment covered all four walls. I am not very techie minded and there were objects there which I had never seen before. I assume they were for recording purposes, but they wouldn't have looked out of place at NASA's command and control centre in Houston. There were also three computer screens and four large comfy leather chairs, plus, on the small bit of wall that wasn't covered with machines, about half a dozen highly expensive-looking guitars and, of course, the obligatory gold discs. 'Not as good as Neil the Hippie's studio, is it?' I said to Jackie.

Steve got straight down to business. 'We've got to look at what the opposition are probably going to do,' he said.

Blimey, I thought, is this a song contest or a football match?

Steve reckoned that the majority of the other seven songs lined up against us would be up-tempo, bright, bouncy S Club 7- and Britney Spears-type productions. 'We could go for that approach,' he said, 'but having met Jackie, that wouldn't be right.'

It made sense to me. Jackie is an attractive, hippie-ish, earth mother-type. Getting her to do a Britney would look and feel all wrong. And luckily, said Steve, the hippie-chick look is in this year. He felt we should go for a natural, organic sound: a bit like Fairground Attraction (they did 'Perfect'), or that rather sweet song by Emma Bunton, 'What Took You So Long?'.

That way, he said, we would be playing to our strengths and, crucially, we would sound different from most of the opposition. And what's more, it might well play better with the most important group of all, i.e. Radio 2 listeners – i.e. the ones who are going to vote on which songs make the final four. 'They,' said Steve, 'are probably more into Fleetwood Mac lite than S Club 7 or Britney.'

Then it was on to logistics. 'I've got two days to do what normally takes me seven,' he said, 'so I want the people who can do the best possible job in the shortest possible time.' He said he knew a bloke called Hank, who plays with the Eagles, and who is one of the best guitarists he knows. He wanted to use him. No problem, I said, mentally working out how I was going to break the news to Matt.

'Hank lives in Los Angeles,' he added.

I looked suitably surprised.

'Don't worry. I'll lay down the backing track this Saturday and send it to Hank in the evening by computer. He will then have all day to work on it over there – they are ten hours behind us, don't forget – while we sleep. When I get up in the morning, his guitar parts will be waiting here on my computer for me.'

'Fine,' I said. I could hardly argue. It made perfect sense, musically and logistically. As for bass – my instrument – I wasn't even going to contemplate putting myself forward. Pete, my brother, plays it far better than I do. That means that I won't have actually written the song, or played on it: but then who cares? In the same way that Sir Alex Ferguson doesn't actually kick the ball but Manchester United are very much his team, Surf 'n' Turf's Euro adventure is very much my baby. I feel a bit of a fraud calling myself a musician, though: maybe I am that local Svengali Muff Winwood was telling me about a few months ago.

'There is one other factor we need to be really careful about,' said Steve. He went on to explain that the organizers of the competition, the European Broadcasting Union (EBU), sometimes come up with annoying little diktats that can be impossible to observe. When Steve did the Russian entry by Alsou a couple of years ago, he said, the EBU suddenly decided a few weeks before the contest that all the musicians and singers performing on the big night had to be from the same country of origin. This was a problem for Steve as his track had a black Russian girl – Alsou – singing lead vocals, and three large, black, British gospel singers doing the backing vocals. So he then had to spend the next week frantically searching London and phoning Moscow in a bid to locate three black Russians (singers, not cocktails). If we get that far with this song, he said, don't be surprised if the Euro muso bureaucrats from the EBU come up with something similar.

I've just been doing some research on a *Eurovision* website myself, and I can see how important these rules are. Take the quite tragic example of the Croatian entry a couple of years ago. The rules stated that although it was perfectly permissible for all the music to be on tape, all vocals on the night of the contest had to be a hundred per cent live. Since there was a smidgen of prerecorded vocals on their musical backing track, the Croats had thirty-three per cent of their final points tally docked. Imagine how they felt: it's like winning a Grand Prix and then having it taken away from you the next day because you had the wrong type of seat covers.

THURSDAY, 17 JANUARY

Spent last night reading *The Complete Eurovision Song Contest Companion* by, among others, Tim Rice and Paul Gambaccini. There is some interesting stuff in there, like:

1) The most successful language in Eurovision is not, as you might imagine, English. There have been fifteen winning entries performed in French. H'm. I suppose we could translate the lyrics to 'I Give In' into French, but it wouldn't play well with the Radio 2 crowd.

2) Songs featuring puppets, circuses, fairs and clowns generally do well. (See 'Puppet on a String', etc.) H'm. Our song has no mention of these items whatsoever – as you can see from its lyrics, reprinted here by kind permission of the author(s):

I give in, I give in now, baby.
I give in to your tender charms.
This is it, I surrender, darling.
You know I'm helpless
In your arms.

I only needed someone to lean on,
Somebody I could rely on,
But then you walked into my dreams.
Love isn't always all that it seems.

I give in, I give in now, baby.
I give in to your tender charms.
This is it, I surrender, darling.
You know I'm helpless
In your arms.

Please remember you were the one
That played around and had all the fun.
I was the fool who just waited here.
You broke my heart and you didn't care.

I give in, I give in now, baby.
I give in to your tender charms.
This is it, I surrender, darling.
You know I'm helpless
In your arms.

I give in, I give in now, baby.
I give in to your tender charms.
This is it, I surrender, darling.
You know I'm helpless
In your arms.

Why should I worry if you play the fool?
I know you can't always count on the rules.

Love let me down. I missed again.
Now I can't even call you a friend.

I give in, I give in now, baby.
I give in to your tender charms.
This is it, I surrender, darling.
You know I'm helpless
In your arms.

I give in, I give in now, baby.
I give in to your tender charms.
This is it, I surrender, darling.
You know I'm helpless
In your arms.

I give in, I give in now, baby.
I give in to your tender charms.
This is it, I surrender, darling.
You know I'm helpless
In you arms.

I give in, I give in now, baby.

Before you scoff, remember that pop lyrics were meant to be sung, not read. Anyway, I've written them out only to illustrate the fact that we have a potentially fatal lack of puppets, clowns, carousels and the like. Mind you, I could shoehorn a few in. How about this?

I'm a clown, I'm a clown, now baby,
On a fairground carousel.
A puppet, a puppet now, darling.
I'm in a circus.
Can't you tell?

Might sound a bit gratuitous though.

3) The best song doesn't necessarily win on the night. OK, we all know that, but did you know that 'Volare', as in Dean Martin, as in 'Volare, wo ho-ho-ho, cantare, wo-ho', one of the most famous songs of all time, was actually a *Eurovision* entry? It was performed by a bloke called Domenico Modugno in the 1958 contest, which was held in Holland. It came third. H'm. This is interesting. Another song that did crap on the night but became a worldwide hit was Gina G's 'Ooh Aah ... Just a Little Bit'. It came eighth for Britain in 1996 but went on to sell over four million copies worldwide. So. If ... if, if, if we get selected (I really shouldn't be thinking like this but I can't help myself) to represent the UK, but we don't win, we could still have a nice little earner on our hands.

FRIDAY, 18 JANUARY

Didn't get much sleep last night: couldn't stop worrying about the musical traffic wardens from the European Broadcasting Union. And then when I did drop off I had a nightmare that we'd won the entire competition in Estonia only to have it taken away from us in front of one billion people because one of the strings on our guitars didn't meet EU thickness regulation requirements.

I'm still fretting now. Last week the BBC asked me to send them a list of musicians who were going to play on the track, which I did straightaway. (Another rule: no more than six musicians/artists can perform on any one song.) Now, of course, that list has been over- taken by events, what with Steve Levine wanting to use his mate Hank in Los Angeles and maybe even another mate, Rob, on key- boards. My worry is that if (if, if, if, if) we get through to the final stage, i.e. the big BBC1 TV show on 3 March, the BBC/EBU musi- cal traffic wardens will start stroking their chins and consulting their rule books when they realize that the line-up on stage in front of them, i.e. me, Matt, Rocking Bob (Matt's financial adviser who lives in Watford), et al., doesn't correlate with the list of those who actually played on the track, i.e. the various mates of Steve Levine. So I've just rung Kevin Bishop, Editor, Mainstream Programmes,

Entertainment (titles are very important in the BBC, you know), and asked him whether it matters. Fortunately, it doesn't.

I've also decided to unleash the dogs of war, i.e. the tabloid press. This was a tough decision. I was worried that alerting the press to this story ('ITV man gets through to BBC Euro final!') might piss the BBC off in some way. But then I thought about it: if we get knocked out at this stage, and there's been no publicity whatsoever, we will have missed a golden opportunity to get some valuable PR for the record, the band and, of course, this book. So I've taken the plunge and rung nice Emily Smith, the TV reporter on the *Sun*. Funnily enough, she said she had spotted my name on a press release that the BBC put out last week detailing the writers of the eight finalists and was planning to ring me anyway. She thinks it's a great story – especially the bit about me putting £100 on myself at 50–1 to have a number one – and she is going to try to run it in Monday's edition. My only fear is that the BBC will think that my getting publicity before the big vote is unfair on the other seven finalists and so disqualify me or something (or just quietly ensure that we don't get through the next voting stage), but according to Emily, who has just rung the *Song for Europe* press officer, the BBC are delighted that the competition is getting some publicity at such an early stage.

I've also had to get her to promise not to start a 'Sun Says Vote Jonny' campaign as that, I fear, would piss the BBC off. Or would it? I dunno. Part of me would be embarrassed to be the subject of something like that. Bit undignified, innit? But then again the music biz generally is a bit undignified. I mean, look at Mick Jagger. And I can't really do this thing by half: in for a penny and all that. Mind you, there's no way, if we get through to the TV stage, that I'm wearing a) tight trousers or b) a frilly shirt.

SATURDAY, 19 JANUARY. THE BIG DAY (HOPEFULLY THE FIRST OF MANY)

Today we started the task of rerecording our charming but unacceptably thin-sounding ditty, with the aim of turning it into something more suitable for the *Eurovision Song Contest*. At the helm: ace producer Steve Levine. The venue: the studio in his back garden, not that far from Wandsworth Bridge.

I was supposed to be at Steve's at 11 a.m. but got there fifteen minutes late. When I walked into his studio Tardis it immediately felt like something was wrong. There was a tightly wound thing in the air. And it was pretty obvious why. My brother Pete, dressed in black, tight-fitting tracksuit bottoms which went almost up to his chest, was sitting on a stool in the middle of the studio, strumming the song on guitar. Next to him was a big bloke called Terl, who was playing the drums. (Not the full set but a mini-electronic kit called 'V' drums.) Pete, displaying the qualities that had seen him downsize from a four-piece band member to solo act in record time, was trying to take over. 'Yeah, yeah, OK, OK. Stop, every-one . . .! All right . . .! Can you play a bit more on the bass drum, mate? Just push it through, you know, push it through like this, you know: dooff do do do do DOOF do do do do DOOFF . . .'

I didn't know what to do. I daren't look at Steve Levine. It felt like someone had just walked on to a Steven Spielberg set and started ordering the cameramen around. In the end I couldn't escape Jackie's frantic look. Her expression was of the 'oh, my God what *is* he doing?' variety. My stomach was stewing. What if Steve Levine decided he couldn't work with Pete? It could be all over before it's even begun!

Suddenly, I caught Steve's eye. He looked at me, smiled and said: 'Don't worry. I have a gun.' Phew.

After that it was OK. In fact, when I nipped outside for a puff with Rob, Steve's engineer, and apologized for Pete, he said there was nothing to apologize for. 'That's nothing, mate,' he said. 'Steve's had to deal with ten times worse than that. He's had two-bit pop stars who've had a couple of hits and think they know everything and he's put them in their place. That's why he's so good.'

To be fair, Pete was behaving like that only because he was nerv-ous and excited. He's waited thirty years for this, so you can't

really blame him. But what he is having difficulty in understanding – like lots of writers, be they novelists, screenplay writers, or
songsmiths – is that once you've written it, you have to let go. The
successful creative process involves different people doing what
they're good at, and one person is hardly ever good at everything,
unless they are called Brian Wilson.

What I am rapidly coming to realize is that to have even a
chance of a hit single, you need four crucial things:

1) Someone to write a good tune (in our case, Pete).
2) Someone who can perform it well (in our case, Jackie).
3) Someone who can produce it well (in our case, Steve Levine).
4) Someone who makes the whole thing happen (i.e. the local
   Svengali).

I think I know which category I'm best suited to.

Talking of the creative process, it's very slow. By mid-afternoon,
i.e. 3 p.m., we hadn't even finished recording Terl's drums. Five
hours in, and they were still polishing and editing and honing every
single beat. At one stage I did a bit of a Pete myself. I quite fancy
hearing handclaps on the finished track, so I asked Steve: 'Are you
morally opposed to handclaps on the song?' This time Steve actually got his gun (an imitation, I presume) out of a drawer and
started waving it about.

Around 5 p.m. I got really bored and so went home and left
them to it.

Around 9 p.m. I called Jackie to see how things were going and
she sounded shattered. I said I'd see her tomorrow.

SUNDAY, 20 JANUARY

10.59: Got to the studio with a minute to spare.

Mind you, I had to, as I'd booked an ITV camera crew to film us
at work.

TV is obviously a very important part of this: if we can get some
substantial TV coverage, then we will almost certainly have a guar-

anteed hit. But it's not as easy as it sounds. We can't do this story on *Tonight*, because it's a current affairs programme and this isn't a current affairs story. If we get through to Estonia, however, the ITV bigwigs have said they might be interested in a big documentary. So we are filming a few bits here and there just in case that happens. The crew did shots of me chatting to Steve and playing the bass. However, I am under no illusions about me ending up on the final mix: I am pretty sure Steve is planning to do what we call in TV 'a strawberry filter' job on me. (This is when you carry out an interview with someone for TV knowing full well you're not going to use it but you don't want the interviewee to know that. The sign that this is happening is when the producer says to the cameraman: 'Use a strawberry filter on this one, mate.' Strawberry filters don't exist. But of course the interviewee doesn't know that, sounds suitably impressed and thinks he is getting special treatment.)

12.34: Hank's guitar parts arrived on the computer from the USA. They sounded fab, despite Pete's worries, expressed to me sotto voce yesterday, that 'Hank won't be able to handle it'.

13.45: Pete finished his pork pie and went home for his rest. (He sleeps every day from 3 to 5 p.m.)

14.46: Getting incredibly bored and tired listening to the same old snatches of the song repeated over and over again but feel I can't go home as Jackie hasn't done her vocals yet and I want to hang around and give her moral support.

15.43: Made what may well turn out to be my only contribution to the recording when I accidentally spilled a glass of water over some very expensive recording equipment.

18.54: Stopped for some nosh and a rant from Steve about how appalling it is that the government don't back the British music industry more. If they gave tax breaks for studio equipment and forced Radio 1 to play more home-grown music, he said, the exchequer could earn millions. Something certainly needs to be done: twenty years ago, the American charts were full of British acts. This year, for the first time ever, there was a period when there were no British artists at all in their top fifty.

Steve seems to be getting more expansive and enthusiastic about this project, which is great. He is also getting me very excited despite my best efforts not to count poultry. 'If this wins in Estonia,' he said, 'we will have to have a Surf 'n' Turf album lined up and ready to go. We would have to start recording it the day after the contest and have it in the shops within a month. It could have a few cover songs on it and a few written by Pete, or whatever. You don't get many opportunities like that in this business, you know . . . If it happens, we have got to take advantage. I mean, it could really fly . . . look at that Jane Macdonald. You lot are like her, except it's a better story. She's a cruise singer; you lot are a wedding band. It's great.'

Oh, God. As someone once said, it's not the despair I can't handle, it's the hope.

22.35: Jackie has finally done her vocals. After singing the first line there was a slight pause while Steve considered what he'd just heard. We all waited for his verdict, a bit like those 'Man from Del Monte' adverts.

'That was superb. You are a professional. Thank you.'

After that we all went home. Steve wants me to come round tomorrow afternoon to hear the finished track.

MONDAY, 21 JANUARY

16.08: Have just heard the finished version. Steve insisted on playing it to me on small speakers so as to replicate the effect of hearing it on the radio. My verdict? Goodness me. We've made a great pop song. (Well, Steve, Jackie, et al. have anyway.) I would say that, wouldn't I? But I know a good pop song when I hear it, and this – now – is it. It's bright, fizzy, happy and bouncy. It's dead catchy, and you smile as soon as you hear it. I am beside myself. In fact, I have just done an impersonation of that Mr Shakeyhands character on *Banzai* on Channel 4 and shaken Steve's hand for three minutes. He is smiling too, and looks proud, which is great. The funny thing is, looking back a few months, I told Pete that we should enter his other song, and not this one, for the contest, but he insisted on this one going forward too. I'm glad he did.

We have made a perfect *Eurovision* song, the sort of tune that you could happily play in an old people's home or a primary school. The lyrics are simple and repetitive and, as Steve pointed out to me just after he played it, it possesses many of the cunning technical tricks that pop songs must have if they are to have a chance of being a hit, for instance:

1) There is a key change halfway through.
2) It sounds very simple. But in reality it isn't. According to Steve, 'There are a couple of clever chords in there that you wouldn't normally find in your average pop tune'. In this respect, he said, we have something in common with Abba. (Blimey!) Their songs sounded simple, he said, but they were in fact relatively complex when you started analysing them harmonically (not something I've ever done). Mind you, if the music is deceptively simple, the lyrics, which basically involve Jackie singing 'I Give In' over and over again aren't. But this is a contest that rewards simplicity – as Teach-In, from Holland, found in 1975 when they won *Eurovision* with a song that went: 'There will be no sorrow, when you see tomorrow, when you sing a song that goes ding, ding-a-dong.'
3) (Important one, this.) It is very loud. According to Steve, the louder a pop song is, the better. Especially a *Eurovision* one. This is because most pop songs get heard on crappy speakers, which generally can't do justice to quiet bits. It's about creating a big, fat sound. Our song, he says, has loads of noise in it, practically all the way through. People respond better to loudness, Steve says. That's why the adverts on TV and radio are, apparently, played at a higher volume than the bits in between them. Hold on a minute, I said; our song isn't going to be any louder than the rest of the Euro entries, though, is it? The bods at the BBC will play them all at the same level,

won't they? Yes, said Steve. But ours will sound louder because we've packed so much in, throughout the song: there are no troughs, just lots of peaks. Crumbs.

4) It has lots of signposts in it, apparently. These are little musical tricks that take the listener by the hand (or rather ear) without them even realizing it and guide them gently through the track to make it as pleasurable and comfortable an experience as possible. The journey from our verse to our chorus is signposted, according to Steve. The listeners will subconsciously prepare for the chorus, he says, when they hear the bass getting a bit more busy and the drums building up to a little crescendo, or 'fill', as it's called. This way, they won't be surprised by the chorus; they'll be subconsciously longing for it. I hope he's right.

5) It has lots of sweet-sounding harmonies in it.

6) It has a key moment, i.e. a bit near the end when the main instruments stop playing and all you can hear are vocals and handclaps.

7) It is safe and not too cutting edge. As, indeed, one would expect from Surf 'n' Turf.

Blimey! I didn't know so much thought went into such ephemeral things as pop ditties. I'm also quite proud of Pete. He is good at something. Really good. He can write catchy pop songs. Trouble is, every time I tell him this, he tells me to stop being so condescending. He keeps telling me he is a jack of all trades. Or, as he puts it on the white photocopied bits of A4 paper that he sticks in the windows of the pubs he plays, he is 'London's premier all-round entertainer'.

I'm not sure the blokes from trading standards would agree with that, but he has at least earned a living out of it, which is more than lots of other so-called musicians have managed. And that is a real achievement. As he keeps telling me.

'Yes, that is correct,' I tried telling him the other day in one of those rare moments when he actually drew breath in between the ranting. 'You have made more from performing than songwriting. But the fact is, if this works out, you could end up making a thousand times more money out of writing than you ever have out of playing. So shut up.'

All he needs now is luck . . . and a local Svengali.

16.43: Steve has just played it down the phone to Hank in the USA, who said, 'Man, I can't believe how good that sounds.'

17.09: Have just dropped the DAT tape off at the studios of Steve's mate Dick, who is doing the final CD master version. This is the musical equivalent of dotting the i's and crossing the t's. Dick is a very nice bloke, and I'm not just saying that because he's done me a special deal (call Richard Beetham at 360 Mastering on 020 7385 6161 for details).

18.09: Have just got the final CD off Dick and nipped round the corner to his mate, Simon Payne, who has just very generously run me off ten CD copies, with superb graphics and lettering, for free. In return for a mention in this book.

Done, mate. (Call Mediadisc on 020 7385 2299 or 07973 558515 for more details.)

TUESDAY, 22 JANUARY

09.12: Oh, my word. We are in the papers, big style. First off there is nice Emily Smith's piece in the *Sun*, headlined 'TV John Bids for Euro Glory'. Then there is a big piece on page three of *The Times*, headlined 'ITV Man Spoofs Eurovision Contest'. It says that I have been trying to 'scam the music industry' and that I have entered a 'spoof track' in to the contest. H'm. This is not true. *The Times*, in classic journo fashion, have not let the facts get in the way of a good story. What I have done is not a spoof, which is defined in the dictionary as 'a good-natured deception'. There is no deceit involved here at all. I am deadly serious about this: my tongue is nowhere near my cheek. And, anyway, how can you parody something that is beyond parody? Mind you, who cares? Any publicity, as we in the music biz like to say, is good publicity.

12.00: The bandwagon is rolling. I have had calls from Radio Scotland, Irish National Radio and various newspapers and magazines asking me to do interviews. BBC Choice want me to go on their *Liquid News* show, which hardly anyone watches, but who cares? This is fine, but I now need to turn this publicity to my advantage and make the frigging song a hit.

14.32: Have just been to BBC Television Centre at White City and dropped the CD off to Kevin Bishop, Head of Mainstream Entertainment or Whatever. He played it and looked quite impressed but seemed to be making an effort not to say too much so he wouldn't be accused of favouritism. I asked him if we were in danger of harming our chances with all this publicity. Well, he said: former Page Three Stunna Sam Fox made the shortlist a few years ago and got loads of PR and it actually backfired on her as she came seventh out of eight. Blimey. I'm scared now. Talking to him, it was clear that the BBC are, as I suspected, rather pleased with all the publicity. It means that the contest is getting talked about again, which is exactly what they want. In fact, Paul Walters, Terry Wogan's producer, is going on Radio 5 Live this afternoon to talk about the 'Spoof' story in *The Times*. I hope he doesn't take too long because I'm supposed to be seeing him at Radio 2 HQ later this afternoon to drop off a copy of the song for him to play on the radio next week.

18.05: Just met the aforementioned Paul Walters. Very friendly, very clubbable. I played him the song, which he seemed to like.

'It's a glorious piece of tosh, that's what it is, Jonathan.'

That'll do me, I said.

We started talking about the 'Spoof' story in *The Times* and he told me that someone had actually tried to write a joke song this time round, and that it had nearly got through: apparently, it was a very good tune, but the lyrics made some of the judges suspicious.

One line said 'I love you, you're like my fluffy bunny' and another part of the lyric mentioned 'being stuck together like superglue'. The judges had the longest discussion in the history of the contest but in the end voted – narrowly – to eliminate it. It then turned out that the thing had been sent in as a piss-take by Chris Moyles, the Radio 1 DJ. It was a wise move rejecting the song. It would have been embarrassing if a tune deliberately written as a joke made it to the UK finals, even in a contest as heroically naff as this one.

There's an important point to be made here: we all know *Eurovision* is cheesy, but any song that wants to represent the UK shouldn't whiff too much of Cheddar. As Steve Levine said in the studio the other day, any successful *Eurovision* song has to walk the tightrope between cheese and cool. It needs to straddle the divide between being a good pop song, but one that is also suitable for *Eurovision*. Ours seems to have done that, so far at least. Chris Moyles, on the other hand, has fallen off the tightrope and into a big vat of Gorgonzola.

WEDNESDAY, 23 JANUARY

09.34: More snow on the snowball. Channel 4 have just rung up and want Surf 'n' Turf to play live, throughout tomorrow morning's *Big Breakfast*. In the space of a few weeks we will have gone from playing in front of an audience of three (at a charity gig we did last month) to hundreds of thousands.

12.35: Not yet, we won't. The musical traffic wardens at the EBU and the BBC have struck. The rules state that the song 'May not be performed or broadcast in public before the *Song for Europe* contest takes place'.

Not to worry: Channel 4 have said they will get us on the show as soon as possible, musical traffic wardens permitting.

21.00: Britain is going Surf 'n' Turf crazy! Apparently, Chris Tarrant was going on about us this morning on Capital Radio (he said I was Robin to Trevor McDonald's Batman, which is a new one on me), as were Mark and Lard on their show on Radio 1 this afternoon. The *Guardian* ran a piece about us this morning too, and a famous bloke from Ireland, Pat Kenney, is talking about inviting us on to his programme, *The Late Late Show*, which is the biggest thing on TV over there.

What's more, all these radio and TV stations are begging me to let them play the record, but for the reasons described above, I can't. Yet. But when we do, and when people hear how fab it is, they will hopefully want to buy it. And then we will be in with a chance of having a hit.

Which is why I have just sent the following e-mail to Clive Black:

To: Clive Black
From: jmaitland@ukgateway.net
Sent: 23 January 2002
Subject: Let's Strike While The Iron Is Hot.

Clivey baby!
There seems to be a window of opportunity opening here and I wonder if we should be thinking of jumping through it. Should we be thinking about releasing Surf 'n' Turf's Euro song as a single, as soon as we can, to take advantage of all the PR we are getting?
I know we are supposed to be meeting soon to discuss the Dale Winton project but why don't we have a pre-meeting meeting to discuss this as well?
Rock on
Jonathan
PS: I am getting very excited

One of the things exciting me most, though, is the fact that other people's talents are now getting recognized, or at least starting to: it's great to see people telling Jackie how fantastic her voice is. Now she is in with a chance of finding a proper, substantial audience. She actually came close to 'making it in the business' in the 1980s, when she had a deal with a big record company all lined up, but unfortunately the company went bankrupt, and the momentum (momentum is very important in this business, as I'm learning) was lost. But that didn't make her bitter: she still loves singing, even if it's a shitty Surf 'n' Turf three-in-the-audience gig.

'All I want to do is sing, Jonny,' she keeps telling me, during our thrice-daily phone calls.

'And I'm giving you what you want, Jackie! This is what you've always wanted!' I keep telling her, in response.

'Yes!' she has started saying back. 'You are the local Svengali!'

As for Pete's talents getting recognized, well there's a slight problem here. He is not as happy as he should be, and I don't blame him, as his songwriting ability isn't getting as much attention as it should. That is because I, to be blunt, am stealing the credit. I feel bad about that. But I've had to do it, to make the story better. After all, 'Self-Confessed Crap Musician and ITV Man Pens Euro Song' is a better story than 'Self-Confessed Crap Musician and ITV Man's Brother Pens Euro Song'. And the better the story, the more publicity. And the more publicity, the more records shifted (hopefully). Pete understands this but is still getting increasingly resentful at opening the papers and having to read articles about how his younger brother has penned or co-penned a song which was in fact wholly written by him. And I don't blame him. Which is why I have promised him I will try to put the record straight as soon as possible. In fact, when I do, it might even help. I mean, 'ITV Man Confesses: "I didn't write Euro song, my brother did"' might be worth another valuable headline or two. But simmering sibling rivalries aside, something wonderful is happening with my brother. He might – just might – be starting to fulfil his potential.

THURSDAY, 24 JANUARY

Today I joined the Musicians' Union, which is as close as I'm ever going to get to being a proper musician. That's not why I did it, mind you. If we get to play the song on the telly we can get paid only if we are fully paid-up members.

There was a section on the registration form which said 'Please tell us how much you make from music each year' and gave four choices: £7500 or less, £7501–£15,000, £15,001–£25,000 and over £25,000. As someone who made just 400 quid out of gigs last year, but spent at least three times that on equipment, that was an easy one. Mind you, my musical income this year should be more healthy, as someone from the BBC has just rung and asked me for the names and addresses of everyone involved in the track. Apparently, we can expect royalty cheques of anything up to £300 each once the songs have been played on the radio next week. We are earning money from our song! OK, so it's not exactly being delivered in wheelbarrows, but it's a start.

That same BBC person also told me some big news. Well, big *Eurovision* news. Apparently, someone from *Pop Idol*, the TV show of the moment, is about to enter the race and sing one of the other songs. He wouldn't give away the identity; he just said that it was a girl and that she had been voted off the show a couple of weeks ago. I can't help feeling sorry for the person she's replacing, though. Imagine having something like that taken away from you at the last moment. Mind you, I don't want to tempt fate: if we make it through to the final four, the BBC could still decide to replace the lot of us with a band of dancing bimbos. I'd like to see them try, though.

I also had another Noel and Liam Gallagher/Ray and Dave Davies-style dust-up with Pete today. He thinks the final version of the track (he got it in the post today) is, quote, 'too modern, full of that electronic-y jiggery-pokery stuff'.

No, it's not, I told him. It's just that you're so stuck in the 1960s, anything that uses more than a plug and a couple of leads scares you off.

Everyone I've played it down the phone to (around sixty so far and growing by the day), I said, thinks it's great. Jackie thinks it's great. The BBC lot I played it to seemed pretty impressed as well. 'If you had produced it, it would have sounded shit,' I said. 'You're a writer, not a producer. You have got to realize what you're good at and what you're not good at.'

The trouble is, if we get knocked out a week tomorrow, when Radio 2 listeners vote for the final four to go on TV, I am worried that Pete will go round saying: 'Huh! Told you so!' In which case I will emigrate.

FRIDAY, 25 JANUARY

19.35: Have just finished appearing on *Liquid News*, an entertainment show on BBC Choice, a digital channel which is a complete waste of licence-payers' money and which hardly anyone watches.

The presenter, Christopher Price, who is large, bald and camply witty (Russell Grant meets Kojak meets Kenneth Williams), kept saying what a 'momentous' event it was that we'd made it to the last eight. (I'm still trying to work out whether he was taking the piss.)

He then did a live link-up with a BBC reporter in Estonia who was standing in the very auditorium where the contest will be held in May. It was all blue and plasticky, a bit like Loftus Road, where Queen's Park Rangers play. The reporter said that Estonians were voting for their winning entry this weekend and that they were all taking it very seriously. Christopher then cued in some footage, shot on a small camcorder by Matt's brother, of that appalling charity gig we did (Turf Aid) at the Irish Centre in Hammersmith, i.e. the one when Rocking Bob's band blew the speakers up and Del Amitri very nearly refused to play. We looked and sounded appalling. Or at least I did. I resembled someone who had just come round after being smashed repeatedly over the head with a cricket bat. (Six pints of very strong and very cheap lager and no packets of crisps, please.)

Christopher asked about the *Pop Idol* business. It had 'just been announced on the wires', he said, that Jessica Garlick, a recent evictee from the show, was singing one of the other seven songs. What did I think?

Great, I said, quoting the Sam Fox story about her coming seventh. It doesn't really matter who's singing what at this stage, I said; it's all down to the songs, and how they are going to sound on the radio. I hope I'm right, though. *Pop Idol* gets ten million viewers. If *Pop Idol* viewers start voting for her in droves, we're stuffed.

SATURDAY, 26 JANUARY

Have just bought a copy of the *Sun*, which informs me that not only has Jessica *Pop Idol* girl entered the race but so has someone called Tricia Penrose, who plays a barmaid in the hit ITV show *Heartbeat*. Blimey. Things are really hotting up now. *Heartbeat* gets ten million viewers too.

SUNDAY, 27 JANUARY

Got an e-mail from Stephen Budd, my cousin in the music bizzo today. He was asking whether, if we got knocked out this Friday, I would want to rerecord the song with another (i.e. younger and more famous) singer. I don't think so. I just couldn't bear to replace Jackie. I'd rather lose the chance of the song being a hit altogether than have that happen. I know you have to be brutal in this business, as the Beatles proved when they got rid of Pete Best, their original drummer: they replaced him with Ringo just before their first hit. Best went on to become a butcher and missed out on seventeen trillion pounds. But I do not want to do a Pete Best on Jackie. I mean, integrity is something I value very highly. In fact, I'm prepared to pay a lot of money for it.

MONDAY, 28 JANUARY. THE BIG WEEK

This is the week that Radio 2 play all eight of the shortlisted songs. Every day, Terry Wogan and Ken Bruce will play a couple each. By the end of the week, all the songs will have been played three times. The climax will come this Friday morning, when the results are announced. People keep asking me if I'm going to 'rig' the vote. Of course I'm not. I couldn't even if I wanted to, as the BBC are bound, I assume, to have systems in place to prevent such a thing from happening. But I am, however, going to 'mobilize' a few voters, in the same way that politicians do in key marginal constituencies.

The BBC, cunning foxes that they are, will not be announcing the relevant telephone numbers for voters to ring until the very last moment, i.e. 9 a.m. this Friday. The lines will then stay open for two hours, and the BBC will announce the names of the last four songs in the contest at 11.15 a.m., live, on Radio 2. To that end I have written down a list of friends whom I intend to call at one minute past nine this Friday morning, informing them of the number to ring. Mind you, the timing is unfortunate, as a number of them will be on the train to work at that time.

In a way I wish I didn't have to do this: I would prefer a level playing field. But I'm pretty sure the people behind the other seven songs will be planning similar campaigns, so it would be silly not to get some sort of a bandwagon rolling. In fact, the more I think about it, the more I realize that we would be at a distinct disadvantage if we didn't do something like this. Each 'act' is going to be able to call on loads of friends/family/people they've just met down the pub, etc., so if we want to compete on equal terms we've got to get lobbying.

Then, of course, there is the Internet. Surprisingly, e-votes are already being allowed via the BBC's *Eurovision* website. I thought Internet voting would be forbidden until 9 a.m. this Friday, when the phone voting starts. But this is not the case: the e-lines are open now.

That is why I have just e-mailed seventy people with the relevant link – i.e. the BBC website address where the *Eurovision* voting form can be found – and asked them, politely, to consider voting for us. It's quite simple: all they have to do is click on the link, click on our song, listen to it, and then, if they want to vote for us, press SUBMIT, and, hey presto . . . one vote for Surf 'n' Turf.

Actually, the potential of this pyramid-voting scheme is quite awesome, as the Internet is so efficient at spreading the word. If everyone I've sent e-mails to sends e-mails to ten of their friends, and if all of those ten friends, in turn, pass the word on to ten of their friends, then in theory we could eventually end up lobbying the entire population of planet earth.

Mind you, it doesn't matter if we don't win this stage: coming in the top four is all that counts. Agonizingly, a handful of votes can swing it. Last year, the gap between the songs that came fifth (disaster, knocked out) and fourth (triumph, through to the televised final) was just a few hundred.

Interestingly, some countries (i.e. Ireland) don't let the public vote at all. The whole thing is decided by a panel of judges, from start to finish. I think I prefer this way, though. More democratic.

TUESDAY, 29 JANUARY

Today I heard our song on the radio for the first time. Ken Bruce played it on Radio 2 at 10.32 a.m. 'It's that time of year again,' he said, and then, trying to sound as neutral as possible, he declared: 'This is called "I Give In". It's written by Jonathan Maitland, Jackie Collins and Peter Maitland, and it's performed by Surf 'n' Turf.'

Then he played the song.

God, it sounded so *Eurovision*. As *Eurovision* as it is possible to be.

Ohmigod. What if the punters think it's *too Eurovision*?

The other song from the eight that he played was a friendly-sounding boy band ballad thing. It was really quite good. Earlier this morning I heard Terry Wogan play two others, a power ballad, which I think was sung by that *Pop Idol* evictee Jessica Garlick, and a rather pleasant up-tempo poppy thing that could have been done by the Corrs. All of them sounded like potential winners to me. Oh, dear. I am getting very nervous. This is a bloody lottery.

WEDNESDAY, 30 JANUARY

Someone sent me an e-mail today. It came from a friend of one of the other contestants. It was pretty much the same as the e-mail I've been sending out: it had the link to the BBC *Eurovision* website on it, and it was politely suggesting that the recipient, i.e. me, might like to vote for one of the other songs.

As I thought . . . they're all at it. This could get dirty.

I also met a mate of mine – who shall remain anonymous, for legal reasons – for lunch near the BBC at Oxford Circus. He suggested getting a computer hacker to infiltrate the BBC's web systems. He knew someone, he said, who could create thousands of false web addresses, each of which would count as a legitimate vote. 'It can easily be done,' he told me.

H'm.

'Vote mobilization' is one thing, but this would be straight-up cheating. Last time I cheated was in a pub quiz in 1996 when I wanted to remember which actor played Captain Peacock in *Are You Being Served?* but couldn't and so used my mobile to find out. And I felt bad enough about that. No. I couldn't do it: I haven't got the balls. (It was Frank Thornton, by the way.)

After we'd parted, I nipped in to the foyer of the BBC at Portland Place to make a call on my mobile. And there, in a chair, was Mark Nevin. Serendipity or what? Mark, who is quite shy and has thinning blond hair worn in Bobby Charlton-style comb-over fashion, wrote a song called 'Perfect', for Fairground Attraction. It got to number one. The song is a classic. It is a standard, known and loved and recognized the world over. It makes people feel happy; it is magic in a bottle. It is special. So much so that it is now an integral part of the Surf 'n' Turf wedding set.

This was an opportunity I was not going to miss. I quickly explained what was happening and played him our song on the mini-portable CD player thing that I now carry round with me at all times.

He smiled as he heard it. 'Very *Eurovision*, isn't it?'

I had to ask him The Question. What made 'Perfect' such a good pop song? Was it the guitar solo? Eddi Reader's lovely clear voice? What?

Well, he said gracefully, showing not a hint of boredom at having to answer a question that he must have been asked a million times, it was a combination of things, a happy accident. Eddi's voice, a great sound, catchy tune, and most of all a sentiment everyone could associate with.

He has a point. I mean, I don't want half-hearted love affairs. I want someone who really cares.

Does he ever get sick of the song? No way, he said. Not when he sees the cheques that keep coming through the post.

21.34: Have just checked my e-mails. A bloke from Australia whom I struck up an e-mail friendship with, following my last book, wants to know if he should e-mail all his pals in Australia and tell them to vote for me.

21.46: Pete has just rung. He heard his record played on the radio for the first time this morning. He said he cried when he heard it.

22.00: There are now just over thirty-seven hours to go until they announce the results of the vote.

THURSDAY, 31 JANUARY

11.15: Twenty-four hours to go.

12.15: Twenty-three hours to go. Fortunately, I have something to take my mind off things. A bit. On *Tonight* tonight we are doing a report about the apathy surrounding the Queen's Golden Jubilee celebrations, and I'm presenting it. So I am in the office, writing the script and getting ready to do the commentary.

15.20: Have just remembered. I need to ring Uri Geller to get him to do his thought vibe thing.

15.34: Have just stuck my mobile to a speaker in the office and played the song to Uri, who listened to it on his mobile.

'It riilllly sounds much better now, Jonathan. I will be thinking very strongly of you tomorrow. If you want, I will design the cover of your record sleeve for you. I did Michael Jackson's, you know. Did you know that? By the way, make sure you tell the press that I am involved.'

Halfway through this pantomime I noticed Trevor (as in Sir Trevor McDonald) over the other side of the office. He was pouring a glass of champagne for Louise, a production assistant, whose birthday it was. While he was joining in the chorus of 'Happy Birthday', I saw him pointing at me and chuckling.

17.45: I can't bear the thought of having to wait another eighteen hours until we know our fate. I am feeling sick. So is Jackie, whom I have just rung. My brother claims he's not bothered, but I know he is. I am meeting some friends tonight, which should help stop my brain imploding.

23.15: On my way back from the pub, mildly out of it. Twelve hours to go.

23.56: Home now. Set the alarm for seven tomorrow morning. Eleven hours nineteen minutes to go.

FRIDAY, 1 FEBRUARY. THE BIGGEST DAY YET

05.32: What a surprise. Have woken up early.

08.32: Ken Bruce has joined Terry Wogan on air and they are playing all eight songs before the lines open.

08.43: They have just played our song and announced the number to call if you want to vote for Surf 'n' Turf: 09011 161205. In order to hit the ground running I have just left messages on three friends' mobiles telling them to ring 09011 161205 – if they want to, of course – when the phone lines open at nine o'clock.

09.00: The lines are open. I have cast my vote. I tried voting on my mobile too, but the ruddy thing bars calls to numbers starting with 09011.

09.12: God forgive me! I have pressed REDIAL about six times. That's 25p a call. I've spent nearly £1.50 already. And I've just realized it might well be wasted money: the people running phone votes have technology which I'm told can spot it if you redial. Oh, well. Time for another cigarette.

10.05: Pete has just turned up. He always makes my blood pressure rise, even when I'm calmer than a Buddhist, so the sight of him on my doorstep gibbering away at a thousand words per minute has had double the usual effect.

10.09: Pete and I are arguing. He keeps asking me what time it is, and I keep telling him. Then, a minute later, he keeps asking me what the time is again. I have told him to shut up. He does . . . for a second, then starts again, like a jack-in-the-box.

10.23: Jackie is here, thank God. Pete likes her a lot, so he tends to moderate his behaviour a bit when she's around.

10.46: I am starting to get text messages from people asking me how I am. I am sending the same response out to everyone: 'Dying.'

11.00: The lines are closed. The result is being read out in fifteen minutes.

11.08: Seven minutes to go. One more song after this one, then we will hear.

11.11: Jackie says she has had a premonition. 'It won't be us. I know we're not going to get through.'

'Don't say that, you silly cow,' I growl.

11.12: They are playing the last song before the announcement. It is 'Beautiful Stranger' by Madonna.

11.13: I light another fag. Jackie's face is buried in her hands.

11.14: I haven't seen Pete this quiet. Ever.

11.15: Here we go. Ken Bruce is talking.

'And now, ladies and gentlemen, it is time . . . time to announce the final four songs, to go forward in the *Song for Europe* contest. To be fair, I will announce them in alphabetical order. Song number one . . .'

Oh, God, let it be us. Please let it be us.

'"Come Back" by Jessica Garlick . . .'

It's not us! Shit! Hold on . . . 'Come Back' starts with a 'C' . . . our song starts with an 'I'. We're still alive.

'Song number two, "DJ Romeo" . . .' Oh, God. Alphabetical order. That means the next song has to be ours. If it isn't, we're out.

'Song number three—' this is it. Either it's all over or the dream continues '—is . . .'

Please say 'I'. Please.

'"I Give . . ."'

SATURDAY, 2 FEBRUARY

I have a hangover.

PART THREE

★★★★★

I'M SO EXCITED

SUNDAY, 3 FEBRUARY

I can still hear, in my head, the noise that Pete made when Ken Bruce said, '"I Give . . ."' It was like the sound of someone being stabbed, except that it went on for about six minutes. The moment we realized we were through, Pete jumped on me, and Jackie jumped on him. A writhing human pyramid, complete with Pete's strange yelps. A bit like the celebration that follows the winning goal in a penalty shoot-out in a World Cup match. When we got up, Pete started marching around the room, both arms aloft, shrieking repeatedly: 'This is the best day of my life!!! This is the best day of my life!!!'

Three different phones started to ring at once: Jackie's mobile, my mobile and my home phone line. The first person to get through was someone from BBC Radio Bristol. I'd done an interview with them earlier in the week, and they wanted a comment, live on air. I was too delirious to talk to them coherently, so I just said, 'I can't speak now, I'm too excited, talk to my brother, he wrote the song', and handed the phone to him. Then I went and hugged Jackie.

Forty-five minutes, two dozen phone calls and two bottles of champagne later I finally slumped into an armchair, smiled and tried to take it all in.

We are through to the final. We are one step away from Estonia, and one billion people. That is roughly one billion people more than we've ever played to, in our lives.

The phone went again. It was Clive Black.

'Congratulations, darling, I'm so pleased for you. It's marvellous. We must get the single out. It's going to be huge in Germany.'

What about the Dale Winton project, I asked him? 'Well, let's see how it goes, but I think we need to concentrate on this for the time being and maybe come back to it. We need to keep our eyes on the ball.'

The phone went again. It was the *Big Breakfast*. Would we go on the show and perform the song on Monday? You bet.

The phone went again. Steve Levine. I'd never heard him this animated before. 'Do you know, Jonathan, it's really spooky. I was thinking only the other day that the weekend we did your track was the twentieth anniversary, to the day, that I did the Culture Club demos that eventually got to number one.' Blimey. I didn't want to say it until now, I said, as I didn't want to tempt fate, but I've always had a bit of a feeling about this whole project.

Steve told me that from now on we had to play our trump card. 'You guys are the antichrists, compared with all the other acts,' he said. 'They are professional singers, and musicians, and you lot are just a wedding band. You have to play on that. People will like you for it.'

I know, I said. Of course we will play on it. It does, after all, have the merit of being true. Then Steve pointed out that there was some work to be done. We need a stylist. A choreographer (eek). And most important of all, we need two female backing singers. Jackie did all the vocals, lead and backing, on the recorded track. But when we do the real thing, on 3 March at Television Centre for the BBC, all vocals will have to be live. Jackie will obviously be able to sing only the lead vocal, so she is going to need two female backup singers to help her out.

Steve said he had two suitable women in mind who, if they were up for it, would be perfect. Great, I said, give them a ring.

Afterwards I realized that that might leave us with some tough decisions. The rules state that on 3 March, and in Estonia (if we get that far), only six people can be on stage. If we have three girl singers – and we've got to – that means that there will be room for only three musicians. That's three out of me, my brother Pete, Matt, Rocking Bob (Matt's financial adviser who lives in Watford) and Pete, our pretty Scottish drummer, one of the original members of Surf 'n' Turf.

Oh, God. I don't want to think about that now.

The phone went again. It was *The Times*. The same bloke who'd done that 'Spoof' story last week. How did I feel?

'Great, but a bit worried, actually, as we've got a wedding gig on 25 May, when the *Eurovision Song Contest* final is due to be held in Estonia, and I'm reluctant to cancel it at the moment as we get so few gigs anyway.' Well, it makes a good story, dunnit? I mean, integrity is something I value very highly (and I am still prepared to pay a lot of money for it) but there are some times, as any pop PR person will tell you, when you just can't let the facts get in the way of a fun-sounding yarn. Blimey.

First, there were six hundred.

Then there were twenty.

Then there were eight.

Now there are four.

Soon, there will be just one.

Will it be us?

MONDAY, 4 FEBRUARY

We performed on the *Big Breakfast* this morning. My brother, who was playing the South Ockendon Ex-Servicemen's Club last night, stayed over in the spare room, and we got picked up by a limo-type car at 5.30 a.m. Because he wanted to stop for tea and toast on the way – much to my annoyance – we got there late, at 6.30 a.m., just thirty minutes before the show started. There was an American theme to the whole thing (not sure why), so they wanted us to perform the American national anthem just after the opening credits.

None of us knew the chords – except for Matt, so he did it on his electric guitar, Jimi Hendrix-style, while we sat around laughing and loads of young girls dressed as cheerleaders jiggled about waving their pompons. Shambolic but fun.

A bit like a Surf 'n' Turf gig, in fact. Before we did the song (we mimed; Jackie sang live), a bloke called Richard Bacon interviewed me. He was very taken by the fact that Surf 'n' Turf could boast not one but two consumer affairs TV presenters (i.e. me and Matt) as well as an independent financial adviser, i.e. Rocking Bob. Yes, I said, invite us to play your wedding and we'll not only sort out your mortgage but see to your dodgy builder problems as well. When we performed the song, the jiggling cheerleaders danced all around us and Richard Bacon got up on the table and started shouting, 'Yes! Yes! Vote for Surf 'n' Turf!', which created just the right atmosphere for the song: a bright, breezy, cramped, energetic, spontaneous party. Unfortunately, on 3 March, when we have to perform it at the BBC, it won't be quite like that. It'll be just us, on a big, bare, stage. Eek.

Talking of 3 March, I am still going through agonies about the band line-up. Pete (as in my brother Pete, not Pete our pretty Scottish drummer) keeps asking me who is going to be in and who is going to be out. He also keeps asking everyone else, which is creating a little bit of tension. My instinct is that the three blokes in the band should be me, Matt and Pete, our pretty Scottish drummer, simply because we were the original members of Surf 'n' Turf and we feel very at ease playing with each other: we forged a good vibe together doing gigs at my local Italian restaurant, Numero Uno (fee: £50 between the four of us and a free lunch), and I feel a loyalty to that original line-up. What's more, that vibe, I hope, comes through when we play. The trouble is, I also feel an immense loyalty to my brother. He has waited more than thirty years for this, and now I am taking it away from him. Not all of it. But some of it. But I have to do what is best for the project, and what is best for the project is also best, in the long run, for my brother.

Fortunately, the most important person of all, Jackie, agrees with me. She is the key in all this, as she has to give the best possible performance. And to do that she has to feel as comfortable as possible. And she feels most comfortable with the three people who used to sit wedged in the corner with her at Numero Uno and get shoved out of the way by resentful Italian waiters as they carried platefuls of pasta out of the kitchen, past us and on to the customers. And what's more, the big cheeses at the BBC *Song for Europe* show also agree that Pete, and us, would be better off if he were cast as the writer behind the band rather than one of its members. As they have pointed out to me, the writers of the other three songs left in the contest aren't going to be on stage either. And what's more, the BBC still want to interview him on TV, as the writer of the song, come the big day on 3 March. So: he might not end up in the spotlight, but he will be illuminated by a fair few light bulbs. Right. That's enough self-justification. The fact is, I am going to have to do a Pete Best on him, i.e. inform him that his services are required backstage, not on stage. He is used to being on stage, though. The prospect is haunting me. What if he throws all his toys out of the pram?

Rocking Bob, on the other hand, is cool about it. He is along for the ride, wherever that may take him. And this morning it took him to an industrial estate in Bow, East London, and the house-cum-studio where the *Big Breakfast* is filmed. Me and Matt keep telling him that he should put a new slogan on his business cards: 'Mortgages: the New Rock 'n' Roll.'

Constant scanning, meanwhile, of the BBC's *Eurovision* website shows an encouraging level of burgeoning support for the song. One punter, from Oxford, put up a message saying: 'My heart says vote for Jessica Garlick but my head says Surf 'n' Turf. This is a classic Euro tune. I haven't had such a good feeling about a song since Katrina and the Waves won in 1997.' Another bloke, from Lithuania, posted a message saying: 'Surf 'n' Turf are great, man!! You guys rock!!!' I don't think he was taking the piss, either. The further east you go, the less ironic they are about *Eurovision*.

As far as the two female backing singers are concerned, we are sorted. I spoke to Natasha and Belle today (both suggested by

Steve Levine) and they are well up for it. Natasha told me to look at a pop video on the Internet. In it, she did a pole dance. Crumbs. She will have to tone it down a bit for us: we want to be fun sexy, not dangerously sexy. I mean, we don't want to alienate people. The show on 3 March is, after all, going out on a Sunday afternoon when there will be lots of kids and mums and dads watching.

TUESDAY, 5 FEBRUARY

08.17: I am worried about our choreography. I can't dance. But I know a man who can: Ben, the lead singer from Curiosity Killed the Cat. I, you will remember, bumped into him on the train when I was on the way to Brighton to see him perform in a 1980s revival gig. I have left a message on his mobile.

09.03: Just got an e-mail from Graham Sharpe, the bloke at William Hill. He was the bloke I placed the bet with, i.e. £100 at 50–1, on Surf 'n' Turf to get to number one.

From: pressoffice@williamhill.co.uk

To: jmaitland@ukgateway.net

Sent: 04 February 2002

Subject: I'm Not Nervous No Really I'm Not

Jonathan

Bafflingly enough, some people actually want to back your creation to be the UK entry for Eurovision. Not having had the pleasure of hearing the offending piece of work, I would be grateful if you could send me a copy.

By the way, I intend to cast 10,000 votes for each of the three other entries.

Regards,

Graham Sharpe

Media Relations Director

10.09: Belle, one of the backing singers, just came round to pick up a tape of the song. She is small, sweet, blonde and pretty.

10.24: I am really worrying about the dancing issue. Ben from Curiosity still hasn't called back, so I've left him another message. Oh, dear. Now he probably thinks I'm a mad stalker. The fact is, me and Matt can't just stand there on stage like statues. But we do have a choice. We could sway a bit, or we could do a full Bucks Fizz/Brotherhood of Man heavy on the Edam dance routine. Or we could do a quasi-dance routine. A bit like the one the Shadows did for 'Let Me Be the One', the UK *Eurovision* entry in 1975. They simply bent their knees a bit in time to the music, like comedy coppers. It looked a bit stupid.

I think I favour the 'swaying a bit and looking like we're having a good time' option, which, hopefully, we will be: I know I'll be nervous and a bit self-conscious (I am forty, after all) but when I play music – or rather attempt to – I can't stop myself from having a good time.

12.34: Just spoke to Dominic Smith, the BBC producer of the 3 March show, who has advised us to get a stylist. This is essential. So much will depend on our look. Jackie in particular needs to look the best she can, as the camera will be on her most of the time. One false move fashion-wise – i.e. a naff top – and it could be all over for us. She also needs advice on hair and make-up and all that stuff. The rest of us need to sort out our clothes. Or at least I do. I am no fashion plate. After one televised sartorial disaster (shirt hanging out, creases in jacket), my boss at *Tonight* accused me of looking like a *Big Issue* salesman and warned me, threateningly, not to appear on TV looking like that again. But I don't want to be made into something I'm not. That means no glittery jacket and no naff white jumpsuit and high boots. It also rules out Steve Levine's suggestion of a turtleneck jumper and blazer. I don't want to look like a prat.

As for the overall look, I think we need to go with the grain of what we've got, i.e. the shambolic pub/wedding band look. Not too smart or stylized, but not too *Big Issue* either.

13.53: Have just got a call from *The John Daly Show*, a Parkinson/Graham Norton hybrid chat show which, the producer told me, gets huge ratings on BBC Northern Ireland. They want me and Jackie to fly over there tomorrow morning. They want me to be interviewed by the host and then, at the end of the show, sing a famous *Eurovision* song.

Me? Sing?

Not a good idea, I told them. I am only good for a bad imitation of a drunken, out-of-tune pub singer, at best. It would leave people watching with the idea that we are a joke, which we are not. We are fun, but we ain't a spoof. Fortunately, the producer of the show agreed and so Jackie is now going to sing 'I Give In', backed by the house band, instead. This is going to be fun!

15.56: Arse. No, it isn't. Just got a call from Carl, in the *Tonight* office. The show want me to do a report, now, on carjacking. This is the story of the moment: last week a twenty-five-year-old estate agent was stabbed to death by people who were trying to nick his car and only the other day a forty-one-year-old woman was punched unconscious by a gang who stole her Mercedes. Most unpleasant.

I asked Carl to ask the editor if one of the other reporters on *Tonight* could possibly do it instead of me, so I could do *The John Daly Show*.

15.58: The answer is no. Fair enough. This is what *Tonight* pay me for: to be available to work at the drop of a hat at moments like this. I have rung *The John Daly Show* to tell them the news.

I knew this would happen eventually. The twin pressures of trying to win the *Eurovision Song Contest* in my spare time and being a full-time reporter on a twice-weekly TV current affairs show were bound to come into conflict at some stage.

16.02: Now seems the right time to do what a man's got to do. I am going to phone my brother. I can't let the uncertainty and the tension over the line-up of the band carry on any longer. I have lit a fag, picked up the mobile and am about to take a walk on Wandsworth Common. (My preferred routine for those difficult phone calls.)

16.55: Have just got back. I got through to him (or rather his

wife Jane, who handed me over) halfway down the path that leads
to the kiddies' swings.

'Hi.'

'Hi.'

As usual, before I could say anything, he started jabbering away.
'Yeah, I saw the vid of us on the *Big Breakfast* this morning and it
was good, but Jane said I looked a bit old and gnarled and I just
don't look right and Pete the drummer looks great and . . .'

'Well, yeah, funny you should say that, coz I was thinking the
same thing and I reckon it should be me, Matt and Pete the drummer backing the girls.'

'Yeah, fine.'

'You're not pissed off then?'

'I'm quite relieved, actually.'

Then, in typical fashion – i.e. worried about the minutiae rather
than the big picture – he moved on to the subject that was really
causing him concern. 'What about parking on 3 March? Will I be
able to park? Are there parking restrictions? I need to know. Let me
know as soon as possible.'

Phew!

17.02: Just got a call from Ian Levine (no relation to Steve), the
Take That producer with the bizarre Graceland-style house (sauna,
gym, swimming pool, Dalek, lots of pictures of his mum on the
wall) in Ealing. It was a bit of a rant. 'What is happening with Dale
Winton? Why hasn't Clive Black phoned me? Why didn't you get
me to do your *Eurovision* track?' And so on. I managed to fend
him off – just – by saying that the Dale Winton thing could still
happen; it was just a question of whether the horse that I'm currently on – i.e. the *Eurovision* one – comes in. He didn't sound too
happy. I am feeling a bit besieged. It's all getting a bit serious. I
mean, it's only *Eurovision*.

WEDNESDAY, 6 FEBRUARY

Am off to Buckhurst Hill in North London to do the carjacking
interview. Have sent a grovelling e-mail to *The John Daly Show*

apologizing for mucking them about. It may be a blessing in disguise, though, as there may be a slot available for us on the same show in two weeks' time. That would be much better timing, as it would go out only a few days before 3 March, when the need for positive publicity will be at its greatest.

I am also getting calls from all over the shop enquiring about tickets for the big day at BBC Television Centre. I could get rid of 150 just like that. Unfortunately, the BBC have told me that I can only have fifteen. The reason is that the thing is being filmed in the *Top of the Pops* studio, which holds just 300 people. Once they've invited members of the press, music biz executives and the like, there won't be many tickets to go round. Apparently, about 130 were available to the public, but they got snapped up within ten minutes of the phone lines opening.

There has also been a major development as far as our competitors are concerned: one of the other three songs has fallen foul of those notorious EBU/BBC regulations and been chucked out of the competition. It has come to light (m'lud) that 'Never in a Million Years' by Zee (one of Culture Club's backing singers) has in fact been available commercially, to the record-buying public, in the past. It was on a CD compilation of Hungarian ambient dance music two years ago. This is against the rules. All songs entered in the competition have to be unsullied by previous commercial release. Poor old Zee. The Hungarian ambient dance album which contained the offending track sold only 2000 copies, so it would probably have earned her enough to buy a round of bacon sandwiches for everybody: as a result of which she has now potentially lost out on a million quid or more.

I wonder how she's feeling at this moment. She is being replaced by a song called 'Every Step of the Way', the boy band-sounding thing. This could be dangerous for us. When I heard 'Every Step of the Way' and realized it was likely to be performed by a tasty-looking bunch of pubescents, the alarm bells went off immediately. What chance would we have of winning the kiddy vote against a boy band? I breathed a sigh of relief when the track didn't get through. Now it's back in. My brother is worried that 'Every Step of the Way' could do what Denmark did in the European Football Championships a few years ago: they didn't qualify for the finals, but then got included at the last minute due to another country being chucked out (maybe they'd released an ambient dance album in Hungary too). The Danes then went on to win the competition after being let in through the back door. Could a similar thing happen here? We shall see. Zee's track – a strange-sounding disco thing – didn't, to my mind, stand much of a chance. I reckon her replacement does. Eek!

THURSDAY, 7 FEBRUARY

09.12: This whole thing is nothing if not stressful. Am now late for work and have one ear hanging by a thread, having just had to withstand a good twenty minutes' worth of ranting from my brother. It started badly and got worse.

'RIGHT LISTEN TO ME WE ARE GOING TO HAVE A BIG ARGUMENT NOW RIGHT BUT I DON'T CARE I KNOW I SAID YOU COULD HAVE A SHARE OF THE SONG RIGHT BUT I WANT EVERYTHING I'M SICK OF BEING LEFT OUT OF ALL THE DECISIONS YOU SAID I COULDN'T BE IN THE BAND YOU DIDN'T EVEN ASK ME WHO I THOUGHT SHOULD BE IN THE BAND . . .'

He drew breath for a millisecond, so I nipped in. 'Look, if I asked you what you wanted, you would want to sing it, play bass and guitar and drums, and do all the backing vocals. And produce it. We have to do what's best for the project and having a forty-eight-year-old pub musician looking like a fish out of water on stage isn't best for the project. What do you want? Tell me what you want?'

'CONTROL! I WANT CONTROL!'

Aha. This is what it's all about. It's what it's always been about with Pete: he has to control every situation he's in, or else he's not happy. Every time he walks into a room he turns the TV down, adjusts the lighting and heating, and then hijacks whatever conversation is going on. A lot of people find it hugely entertaining. I don't. Probably because I'm a bit like that myself.

It turned out that some old friends of his, who were in a band with him in the early 1970s, had been round to his place the night before. This was the band I wrote about a few months ago: the one that nearly got signed up by ace songwriters Bill Martin and Phil Coulter but got snubbed at the last moment for a group called Slik, who subsequently went to number one with 'Forever and Ever'. His ex-band mates, who now work in the music biz, had – surprise, surprise – been waving pieces of paper under his nose, asking him to enter into a publishing agreement with them vis-à-vis 'I Give In'. Their publishing agreement – apart from benefiting them, of course – differs from the one I have signed in one crucial respect. My one says the song was written by me, Pete and Jackie. The one Pete is threatening to sign says it has been written a hundred per cent by him. Which it was, of course. But when I phoned him up all those months ago, we very clearly agreed to give a writing credit to me and Jackie as well, i.e. split the song three ways, in return for me financing the whole project and Jackie singing on it.

Fortunately, he hasn't signed anything – yet. If he does, that would be a problem. Because I have already signed a publishing agreement with our cousin, Stephen Budd, who is a big cheese in the music biz. If Pete signed a different agreement, I said, we could conceivably end up battling it out in court. I told him he was like a madman running amok at a party with a loaded gun in his hand. If he wasn't careful, the only person he'd end up shooting would be himself. I managed to calm him down, gradually. I explained that I understood his frustration. This is how it happens in business, I told him. People often give away large chunks of their company (or in this case their song) to other people. The good thing about that is that those people who've taken a chunk then go on to work as hard as they can to make the company (or indeed the song) become a success. Consider yourself lucky, I said. Some songwriters end up signing away the rights to virtually all their songs, forever, without even realizing it. (One particularly tragic case involved two guys called Pete Ham and Tommy Evans, from a group called Badfinger. Pete and Tommy wrote the all-time classic 'Without You', which has been covered by Nilsson, Mariah Carey and about a hundred others. They got ripped off so badly they ended up penniless, and killed themselves.)

OK, I said, you've given away a fair bit of your first song. But all your other songs are yours. You can do with them what you like. And if you really feel that bad about things, you can have my share.

'This isn't about money,' he said. 'It's about control.'

'Look, we haven't done too badly so far. You have got to let other people do what they do. You can't control everything. You've tried to control everything in the past, and look where it's got you.'

'OK, but if you annoy me I'm warning you I'll sign this piece of paper.'

'Stop acting like our mother.'

He laughed. I laughed. He only wanted to wind me up, I think. And he's succeeded. It might not have been about money then, that spat between me and Pete, but it could easily have been. The potential sums involved in writing a successful pop song are huge. Take Cat Stevens, for example. He hasn't recorded anything for more than twenty years, and yet last year alone he earned £1.2 million from his back catalogue, i.e. 'Wild World', 'Matthew and Son' and the rest. There's money in pop. Potentially.

14.57: Have just got a bit paranoid. One of the *Tonight* producers has just said to me: 'Jonny, it's so great that you're doing this; you obviously don't care about your career.' Oh, no! Have I ruined my credibility as a TV reporter by doing the *Eurovision* thing? Have I sold my TV soul for a pot of *Euro* stew? Will anyone ever take me seriously again?

15.02: Maybe I'm overreacting. Credibility, on TV, is a much-overrated thing. I'm not sure viewers care whether or not the person talking to them has credibility; they do care, however, if the person isn't actually talking to them, but at them. If any of the viewers who see my reports know – or give a monkey's – about what I'm doing in my spare time, I would have thought that was a plus, as in 'At least he's a normal bloke having fun'. A number of the reporters you see on TV look like they spend all their spare time doing precisely what they do when they're on the telly, i.e. standing bolt upright, talking in that strange repetitive singsong way, and looking like they've got a pole stuck up their arses. Which doesn't exactly endear them, or their reports, to the viewer. The only people who really matter in these situations, though, are The Big TV Cheeses. And fortunately, my ultimate Big TV Cheese, Steve Anderson, who is Head of News, Current Affairs, Arts and Religion at ITV (titles are almost as important at ITV as they are the BBC, you know), is cool about the whole thing.

Actually, he's more than that. He keeps giving me advice on how we should present ourselves on the big day and has taken to calling himself Colonel Tom Parker whenever he calls up. (Colonel Tom was Elvis's manager and the ultimate local Svengali.) The other day a reporter from the *Guardian* asked him what he thought about the whole thing, and he said: 'I don't care if Jonny sings as long as it's on the BBC. Estonia is definitely the best place for his talents.' Praise the Lord. A Big Cheese with a sense of humour.

16.43: Have got a bit paranoid again. This time about the *Euro* opposition. Level Best, the boy band lot who are doing 'Every Step of the Way', could cruise it, I feel.

16.54: Have just had a thought. The late entry of the boy band could be to our advantage. Maybe the kiddy vote, which previously looked like it was going a hundred per cent to Jessica Garlick (because she was on *Pop Idol* and kids loved it) will now be split, i.e. between her and the boy band lot. That might leave us in a good position to steam in through the middle and win. A bit like a left-wing Lib Dem candidate who wins a by-election on account of the right-wing vote getting split between New Labour and the Conservatives. Just a thought.

17.42: Yet another strange quirk of fate. I have just got an e-mail from Bill Martin. The same Bill Martin who turned Pete's band down all those years ago when their nostrils were, agonizingly, beginning to sniff a whiff of success.

From: Bill Martin
To: jmaitland@ukgateway.net
Sent: 05 February 2002
Importance: High

Dear Jonathan
In the words of my old immortal song, 'CONGRATULATIONS' on getting to the last four.*
As you can see by my short history attached, I have won *Eurovision* a few times! There is more to winning the *Euro* than the song.
I am involved with the major publisher Sony and apart from everything else I look after the following catalogues: the Beatles, Dylan, Neil Diamond, David Gates, etc. Please give me a call on the numbers attached: I am sure it will be in your interest!**
Best wishes
Bill Martin

18.56: Read Bill Martin's CV on the train. Blimey. He's won three Ivor Novello awards, been named Songwriter of the Year, he was Scotland's Songwriter of the Decade, no less, in the 1980s, and wrote 'Congratulations' (immortal, really immortal), 'Puppet on a String' (won *Eurovision* in 1967), 'All Kinds of Everything' (won *Eurovision* in 1970), 'My Boy' and a load of stuff for the Bay City Rollers.

---

*I keep rereading this opening sentence. 'Immortal' – he's not modest, is he? Then again, I suppose he's just trying to set out his stall. Not that he needs to with me. As someone once said, 'Modesty is only for those who can afford to be modest'. Bill can afford not to be modest.

**I think it might have been slightly more accurate to have added the words 'and mine' in here. Still, I'll call him anyway.

19.34: Called Bill Martin.

'Hi, Bill. It's Jonathan.'

'Hi, how are you?'

'Very excited. You might remember my brother. You almost signed him up about twenty-five years ago.'

'Oh, really? What was the group's name?'

'Surrender.'

'Oh, yes. I remember.'

'So. Can you give me a bit of advice on how to win *Eurovision* then?'

'Well, yes, but there's got to be something in it for me. I mean, have you got a publisher?'

'Yeah, my cousin. Stephen Budd Management. I've done a deal with him and I'm not gonna just tear it up.'

'Well, I'd like to see the contract.'

H'm. Why not? There's no way in a million years I would renege on the deal with my cousin. But in the interests of journalism . . . and this book . . . and having fun . . . and meeting the man who wrote the immortal song 'Congratulations' . . . I feel I should.

FRIDAY, 8 FEBRUARY

Tomorrow we are shooting the pop video for 'I Give In'. It's pretty low budget. We have managed to keep the costs down because the cameraman, producer, director, editor and general wielder of the megaphone are all the same person, i.e. Jackie's husband John, and he is doing it for nothing. We are shooting it like a wedding video: we're going to be the wedding band and we have invited a few pals and their kids along to be the guests. My mate Nickie, who has been begging me for years to get her on TV, will play the part of the bride. When I told her she could be in the video, she let out the scream of someone who had just won the final on *Pop Idol*. She has spent the last few days dusting off her old wedding dress and e-mailing me about tomorrow. Her groom will be a friend of a friend whom I've never met, called Ziad. Apparently, he is small, charismatic and good at throwing shapes.

Things are chugging along nicely on the publicity front too. Matt's new series on dodgy builders starts on BBC1 tonight (it's basically *House of Horrors* with knobs on), and so he has been plugging our song in all his interviews.

SATURDAY, 9 FEBRUARY

Have just returned from a primary school in Stoke Newington, the venue of the video for 'I Give In'. John, Jackie's husband, is a member of the Parent Teacher Association there and so we got the place for free. Just as important, we got the use of a jib (a ruddy great crane thing with a camera stuck on the end of it) for nothing as well. A jib can turn visual water into wine: thanks to its ability to sway, swoop and dive, it can take what would previously have been a static, unimaginative shot and turn it into a groovy, panoramic, swirly one.

With fifteen kids between the ages of three and eleven wandering around, the day was never going to be straightforward and so it proved when Tommy, Matt's one-year-old, chundered up his rusks before the cameras had even started rolling. Very rock 'n' roll. Equally incongruous was the sight and sound of Ivo, a round-faced ginger-haired gap-toothed eight-year-old, playing 'God Save the Queen' on his trumpet, loudly and repeatedly, for twenty-five minutes. But given that Princess Margaret died this morning at 6.30 a.m., what could be more appropriate? I was worried that I might get a call from the office about that, but I needn't have worried: Steve Anderson, Head of News, Current Affairs, Arts and Religion at ITV (sorry, I have a thing about titles), who'd turned up hoping to secure a starring role in the video for his little girl Amy, told me that ITV weren't going big on the story. They were going to fill the news with it, he said, but nothing more tonight. Especially since tonight is the Grand Finale of *Pop Idol*, which twelve million people are expected to watch: they wouldn't be too chuffed if it got replaced by an hour-long profile of Charlie's aunt.

The shoot was fun and the sandwiches excellent, but by 3.31 p.m., five hours and thirty-eight takes in, the energy levels

were dropping a bit. Trying to look happy for that long, even when
you are, is tiring.

Thankfully, at 3.43 p.m., John called it a day. The highlight of
the shoot was the dancing. Nickie, the not-very-reluctant bride,
had brought her mum and dad and a couple of friends of theirs
along, and they put on a magnificent display of granddad-down-
the-disco footwork. You know the moves: liberal use of the arms
and elbows and an uninhibited (or at least what passes for uninhibited in the suburbs of Surrey) shuffling from the left foot to the
right foot and back again, occasionally in time to the music. One of
these – ahem – 'mature' dancers, a bloke called Colin, didn't seem
entirely *au fait* with exactly what was going on, or what it was all
about. He kept asking where the pub was and at one stage asked,
loudly, 'Is this for *Pop Idol* then?'

At the end I paid John's two mates fifty quid each for helping us
out. Once you take sandwiches and other incidentals – like editing – into account, this video will have cost me £247 by the time
it's finished. Which reminds me. A full list of accounts re this project will be drawn up at the end of this book. At the moment I am
showing a loss of around £1500. But if we get through on 3 March
that could change very quickly.

SUNDAY, 10 FEBRUARY

At last: a *Eurovision*-free day. Am going to the Valley to see
Charlton, my team, whup Manchester United. Hopefully, I will be
able to think about something else for a change. It's going to be
hard, though. The tune to 'I Give In' now plays in my head so
automatically and so repeatedly, at the most unexpected times,
that I have come to hate it. I can't bear it. It's a form of madness.
If it gets any worse I may need to see a shrink.

MONDAY, 11 FEBRUARY

10.32: Got interviewed by a twenty-six-year-old from the *Guardian*
called Emma today. Let's hope a) that the article is favourable and
b) that lots of people who read it will then be convinced to vote for

us on 3 March. Halfway through our chat, Emma started humming something. I suddenly realized it was our song, which I'd played her at the start of the interview.

'You're humming our tune,' I told her.

'Oh, my God!' she said, blushing. 'You're right, I am. I can't believe it!'

Our song may not be a classic but it is catchy.

13.46: Another interview, this time conducted by me. It was for *Tonight*, and it was with a bearded Professor of Transport Studies at London University, about traffic congestion. Rock and roll!

15.45: Another *Eurovision* interview, with Independent Radio News. I just hope people will hear all this stuff and vote for us as a result. My worry is that all this PR won't make any difference at all.

16.42: Yet another *Eurovision* interview, this time with Mike Ward from the *Daily Star*. He loves the contest and has covered it in depth for the last three years. He reckons it's between us and Jessica Garlick who goes through on 3 March. Mind you, last year he gave the Estonian entry 'nul points' in his pre-contest round-up and it went on to win the whole thing.

17.23: I am depressed. Jessica Garlick is going to walk it. Matt has been on the phone telling me that the *Pop Idol* finalists Will and Gareth have been on TV (well, ITV2) urging everyone to vote for her. What chance do we have against a Will- and Gareth-endorsed candidate? Thirteen million people watched *Pop Idol* over the weekend, and nearly nine million votes were cast for Will and Gareth. They are the heroes of the moment. What they say goes. We are shafted.

17.35: Phoned Matt back and told him how pissed off I was. He told me not to take it so seriously and that in this game anything can happen. Look at Will and Gareth, he said. Everyone thought Gareth was going to win by a mile, but he didn't. And if you spend your whole time worrying about the voting you'll end up looking worried on the big day, which is precisely what we don't want. We want to look like we're enjoying it. And anyway the *Eurovision* voting public might be less susceptible to the charms of Will and Gareth than you think. OK, he has a point. But I'd rather be in Jessica's shoes than ours. She has 'sympathy vote' written all over her. And she can sing. And her song's not bad either.

17.46: I have decided I need more PR, so I have e-mailed *Gay Times* offering to bend over backwards, as it were, for some coverage in their rag. Apparently, the gay vote is crucial in *Eurovision*.

17.55: Have just got home after seeing Bill 'Congratulations' Martin. We met in the lobby of a hotel in Knightsbridge. He strode in wearing a navy-blue velvet suit and a purple shirt and tie. He was very well preserved and smiled a lot. But then he has a lot to smile about. He is a millionaire several times over, thanks to his songwriting, and publishing and property deals. His hair is thick and silvery, a bit like Leslie Neilsen's, the star of the *Naked Gun* films. I pointed this out to him. 'I know. He copied me.'

His mobile went off within seconds of our introductory handshake. I recognized the ring tone immediately. It was 'Congratulations'.

'Don't tell me, Bill,' I said. 'You get money from royalties every time your phone rings.'

'Absolutely. I do.' Another smile.

We adjourned to a pub around the corner. He bought the drinks. He had a soft one. He never drinks between 1 January and 14 February, he said.

It turns out he (like Muff Winwood) was a judge on the panel that selected the final twenty songs. He knew ours would get through, he said, because it was catchy. Suddenly, 'Congratulations' started playing again. He went outside to answer it and came back within three minutes.

'That was Suzi Quatro, asking me what I thought of her album.'

'Well, what do you think of it?'

'Well, if this is going in your book, just say I think it could do very well in Germany.'

We looked at each other. Silence.

'Well?' he said.

'What?'

'I don't give advice, you know. Where's your agreement?'

I handed it to him. He read it carefully. 'You've signed it, but has your cousin?'

'Yes.'

'Well, then. There's not much point in my trying to get involved, is there?'

No, I said, I suppose not. I can't really renege on a deal with my cousin.

Time for a change of subject.

You wrote so many hits, Bill, I said. What's the secret?

'It's very simple. Simplicity. Go for the jugular every time. We knew we would win with "Puppet on a String" because it was so direct, so catchy.'

Could you write another number-one hit now, to order, if you wanted to?

'Of course we could.'

'Why don't you, then?'

'Because the industry is so ageist. No young band wants old codgers like us to be associated with them.'

'Go on, give me some advice.'

'Why should I?'

'Because I don't know what I'm doing and I'm a nice person.'

'I tell you what. If you get through on 3 March I'll take you to lunch and give you some advice on how to win it. If you don't get through I'll take you to lunch anyway and tell you where you went wrong. Because you've already made some mistakes.'

'Bill, that would be wonderful. Thank you.'

'Right. I've got to go now,' he said, looking at his watch for the third time in our seventeen-minute chat. 'I'm doing a deal, with the Americans, to do with Dan Dare. Twenty million quid. Very exciting.' And off he went. As I walked away to hail a taxi I heard 'Congratulations' ringing out once more.

TUESDAY, 12 FEBRUARY

Went to Birmingham today to interview a young mother of two about traffic problems in Walsall. I made her promise to vote for us on 3 March. She said she would and, what's more, she would get everyone at her mother-and-toddler group to do likewise. I feel like I'm standing for Parliament. Every vote counts, I kept telling her.

Another vote-harvesting idea has come to me. The day before 3 March, my team, Charlton, are playing Chelsea, and 25,000 fans will be there. That's 25,000 potential votes. I rang the head of media relations at the club, Mick Everett, and asked if I could go on the pitch at half-time and have the song played over the loudspeakers. I was expecting him to tell me, politely, to get stuffed.

'We'd love to do that for you, Jonathan. No problem. Send me the CD and we'll sort it.'

Woof!

Steve Anderson, aka Colonel Tom Parker, the Head of News, Current Affairs, Arts and Religion at ITV (this must come under the 'Arts' bit of his brief), has also come up with an interesting idea. He reckons I should go on National Hospital Radio and tell all the patients listening: 'Vote for us . . . and you'll get better.'

WEDNESDAY, 13 FEBRUARY

Today we did some publicity pictures for the BBC. They were taken at a studio in Ladbroke Grove. Pete, our pretty Scottish drummer, couldn't turn up as he is working on a building site at the moment. And Matt was doing some filming, so it was just me, Jackie and the two backing singers, Natasha and Belle. When I got there, the two presenters of the show on 3 March, Claire Sweeney (of *Celebrity Big Brother* fame) and Christopher Price (large, camp, bald, witty), the bloke who interviewed me on BBC Choice's *Liquid News* show a few weeks back, were having their shots taken. In a room adjoining the photographic studio, a large buffet of quiche, pasta and salad had been laid out and there, at the table, partaking of one of those dinky little chocolate bars (a mini-Toffee Crisp, I think it was) was a young, lithe (damn him) and pretty lad called Jamie. Jamie is Level Best, i.e. the bloke who sang on that boy band-sounding thing. It turns out that there is, in fact, no boy band: it was just Jamie on the track. I asked him how he felt when he didn't make the final four, first time round, and how he felt when he heard, a week later, that he'd been reinstated due to Zee's unfortunate Hungarian incident. 'Absolutely gutted,' he replied in a soft Geordie accent (he's from Middlesbrough). 'But then when they phoned me, like, a week later, like, I couldn't contain meself . . . me mates say it's a bit like Denmark, the footie team, they got into European Championships like me, like, at the last minute . . . and they won!' You don't need to tell me that, mate, I thought. My brother has been making the same doom-laden analogy every day for the last week, and the awful thing is that I can just see it happening.

Jamie was wearing a tight black T-shirt and a pair of jeans that looked like they'd just lost an argument with a hay-threshing machine. A good look for him, but definitely not for us. He was extremely well mannered. He is a wannabe. But a nice one. At the moment, at least. The acid test comes six months after a wannabe has made it: that is when they tend to start thinking that it's all real. That's when they start to a) believe their own PR, b) think they can do other people's jobs better than them and c) send back the bacon sandwiches. Jamie has had several goes at fame. He tried to win *Soapstars*, the ITV show that rewarded 'ordinary people' with roles on *Emmerdale*, but he didn't make it. He had a go at *Pop Idol* too, but that didn't work out either. At the moment he is being supported by his mum and her boyfriend, who run a restaurant together. 'If I don't win this, like, I'm joost gonna keep on trying and trying again, like. I'm not giving up, like.' Blimey. This is his whole life. If it doesn't work out – and, let's face it, it probably won't, as only a tiny fraction of kids make it, and even when they do they get only about seven minutes in the spotlight – how will he cope? It's OK for me: I have another career. I'm not doing this because I want to be a famous pop star – I couldn't think of anything more embarrassing – but because a) I want to write a book, b) I like a challenge, c) I want to see how it all works and d) all I want to do is have a little fun before I die, as Sheryl Crow would say.

THURSDAY, 14 FEBRUARY

I have made some money from 'I Give In'! Well, kind of. The BBC sent me a form today telling me that the song has earned 620 quid in royalty payments thanks to the three plays it received on Radio 2. This is wonderful. My share of the proceeds is about 90 quid, as I am listed as one of the seven musicians who played on the song. Trouble is, I don't know if I did. I plucked a few bass strings in the studio on one of the days it was being recorded, but I can't really be sure if a single note of mine made it on to the final track. I'm in illustrious company on this one, mind you. Simon Cowell, the camp, black-haired, publicity-loving record executive who was a judge on *Pop Idol*, tells the story about how he used to play the triangle very softly at the back of the studio when famous songs were being recorded. Technically, as he was 'on the track' – i.e. one-millionth of a decibel of his contribution made the final cut, and anyone with ears like Dumbo, who listened very closely, will confirm that – he qualified for a royalty payment.

Talking of playing on the track: to my shame I still haven't learned the exact notes to 'my' song. I must get someone to teach them to me. I know we're only miming to the music, but if an eagle-eyed musician spots me thwacking the wrong bit of the fret-board, what little musical credibility I have will evaporate.

At midday today I was supposed to meet Katrina, of Katrina and the Waves fame, at the ITN studios in Gray's Inn Road, near King's Cross. She's been there and done that (won the whole shebang in '97, remember), so I wanted her advice. Fifteen minutes after she was due to show, I called her at home. She picked up the phone.

'Sorry, I can't make it. I'm flying to America tomorrow and I'll be back on 2 March.' Oh, dear. She might have called.

This evening I had a chat with my cousin Stephen Budd, the big cheese in the music biz, who is handling all the publishing stuff for us. He is putting almost as much time, energy and adrenaline into this as I am. 'We need the *News of the World* to back us,' he kept saying. 'We really need them. If we can just get them to come out for us on the day of 3 March . . . I've got it. This should do it. Why don't you ring them and offer them a share of the profits of the record? They'll love it.'

Nice idea, I said . . . but dangerous. In fact, it's more than that. It's a potential cataclysmic disaster. How would he feel, I asked, about a newspaper headline that screamed 'ITV Man Tries to Bribe *News of the World* to Back Euro Song'?

Good point, he said. But it's great to have Stephen in our corner. He is an ideas machine. His (other) latest one is to try to get Victoria and David Beckham to record a message of support for our song, which would then be played on the TV show on 3 March.

Fantastic, I said. If you can get them I will perform sexual favours on you. We have to get someone famous to support us, though, Posh and Becks or no Posh and Becks. This is because the producers of the *Song for Europe* programme want each of the four songs to have a celebrity backer. At first I thought of Anne Robinson. Then I thought again. Trevor McDonald? Not his bag, really. Our best bet, I think, is Alistair (as in McGowan) and his comedy partner Ronni. Hopefully, they will be able to do it as Posh and Becks, whom they take off marvellously. Then, if we get the real things to do likewise as well, it could look pretty good.

Jessica *Pop Idol* looks like she's going to get Will and Gareth, the two finalists, to be her backers, which is worrying me as they could run for President and Prime Minister respectively at the moment and get in. I am practising my look for when they read out the results on the big day, and we realize that no, we haven't won, but

146 JONATHAN MAITLAND

Jessica has. It's my smile-through-the-pain look. But having looked at it a few times I realize it could also be the look of someone who is actively battling constipation. Instead, I have decided I will just bury my head in my hands the whole time so no one will be able to see the bitterness, envy, resentment and grief on my face when we don't get through.

Bloody hell. What is happening to me? Why am I taking this all so seriously? It's only *Eurovision*, for goodness' sake. It is *so* unimportant. It is the most trivial, mocked, culturally irrelevant event in the calendar. But it's taken over my mind. I dream about it. I wake up every morning feeling like slugs are crawling around in my belly. It has sucked me in. It is taking over my life . . .

FRIDAY, 15 FEBRUARY

09.23: Arse. Alistair and Ronni can't do a message of support for us. They are currently being worked like dogs on their new show (starting at 5 a.m., finishing at 11 p.m.) and every minute of the next two weeks has already been accounted for. To do something as simple as this would still take about an hour and throw a large spanner in their schedule. I spoke to Alistair about it last night when I phoned him with a Scrabble query. We are big Scrabble chums, you see, and last Christmas I got him the official Scrabble dictionary, the one with all the Scrabble words in the world in it. Someone had put down 'fishpeg' and was claiming ninety points for it so I called Alistair for an adjudication. After he'd told me the good news – that 'fishpeg' wasn't allowed – he explained how he really wanted to help, but couldn't. So now we need someone else. I have asked Steve Levine if he can get Boy George to do something for us as he is big mates with him. (Steve produced all George's biggest hits in the early 1980s.)

09.45: Double arse. The BBC researcher on the *Song for Europe* programme says Boy George would not be acceptable as 'It needs to be someone whom the public would associate with you, Jonathan'. Understandably, they don't instantly associate me with

George. The researcher made another suggestion. 'What about Anne Robinson?'

No way. What kind of effect is it going to have if someone who's always winning those 'meanest woman on the telly' polls suddenly pops up and says, 'Vote for Surf 'n' Turf'? It would be like getting a character reference from Joseph Stalin.

09.48: Just rang Downing Street and asked if Tony Blair could do the honours. You've got to aim high, haven't you? I mean, I have met him. And although we didn't exactly bond, we did at least talk about music for a bit. You never know . . .

09.52: I feel I might need a plan B so have put in a call to Sir Trevor McDonald's secretary. I just can't see him saying yes, but then again don't ask, don't get.

09.56: I was at college with Rory Bremner. Maybe he could do it, dressed up as Tony Blair. It could be quite funny. Have left a message with the production assistant on his show. As Steve Levine says, we have got to trump Jessica Garlick's two aces, i.e. the two *Pop Idol* blokes who will be endorsing her song. And there aren't that many suitable trump cards around. The Prime Minster is one, obviously. Mind you, so is the Queen. But we've got to be realistic. Trevor would be good . . . when he speaks, the nation listens. Rory might work too. But no one has said yes yet. At this rate we might have to beg that bloke from the Swinging Blue Jeans who turned down that wedding gig last year to do it.

SATURDAY, 16 FEBRUARY

No reply from Rory Bremner's office, so I have gone one step further and tracked down his mobile number and left a message on it. Some might say I've got a bit of a cheek asking someone for a favour on the basis that we went to the same college more than twenty years ago . . . and they'd be right. But I have the wind in my sails right now. I have also been advised by 10 Downing Street, no less, to put in a written request to the real thing, so have just sent the following:

Dear Tony

Hello, Jonathan Maitland here. We met when I interviewed you for *Tonight* last year and we spoke about, among other things, the Chinese Premier's singing ability, what a great band Free were and (by the by) politics.

This is an unusual request but, given our mutual fondness for music, a not unreasonable one, I hope. My band, Surf 'n' Turf, find themselves in the finals of the *Song for Europe*, and one step away from the *Eurovision Song Contest* on 25 May.

The BBC wants a well-known person endorsing our song, 'I Give In', a copy of which is enclosed, and I was wondering if you could do the honours for us.

I know you're busy, but it would, I think, be great if you could help out as a) you could crack a gag along the lines of 'Europe is a crucial issue and never more so than now and Surf 'n' Turf's Euro-vision is very much my own, so vote for them', b) it would show you're prepared to have a laugh every now and then and c) who knows? There might even be a few votes in it (for you as well as us).

All the best

Jonathan Maitland

PS: If you can't do it, do at least let me know what you think of the song.

MONDAY, 18 FEBRUARY

No reply from Sir Trevor (I think he's trying to avoid me), Rory Bremner or the Prime Minister. Yet.

One of our opponents, Tricia Penrose, the barmaid in *Heartbeat*, was on the Lorraine Kelly show on ITV this morning doing her song, 'DJ Romeo'. This, as Steve Levine has just pointed out to me in an e-mail, is just not fair. If she can get on that show, then so should we. When General Elections occur, there is a law – the Representation of the People Act – which obliges all broadcasters to give each of the political parties equal airtime.

This law, I feel, should apply to the four remaining acts in the *Song for Europe* contest. Unfortunately, there isn't time to rush the relevant legislation through Parliament, so I have rung up the Lorraine people myself and made out a strong case for our inclusion on the show next week. They have said they will get back to me. That, as we all know, is TV shorthand for 'Piss off'.

TUESDAY, 19 FEBRUARY

Spoke to my brother. He went to see Steve Levine on his own last night to play him some of his other songs. Steve told him bluntly that if we miss out on 3 March it will be all over. But if we make it, there will be a window of opportunity, and some of Pete's songs might be very useful in helping us leap through it. He also told Pete, much to his bemusement/delight, that he was a valuable musical commodity. Bands these days are desperate to play in the style of late '60s/early '70s musicians, apparently, but they can't. And they can't find anyone else who can, either. But Pete, said Steve, is like a time capsule: he plays in exactly the same way now as he did when he was seventeen, in 1971. That could come in very useful one day, Steve told him.

Pete has a new worry about 3 March. He likes his sleep, and he knows he won't be able to have his daily 3 p.m. to 5 p.m. nap, as the TV show goes out right in the middle of it, i.e. at 4.35 p.m. I told him he could go right ahead and take a nap anyway, but it might not look too good. In fact, he said, he will be doubly knackered that day, as he has a gig at the Royal Oriental Phoenix (a Chinese restaurant in Epsom Downs) the night before which he doesn't think will end until 2 a.m.

But apart from that he is in an upbeat mood – thank God – at the moment. This may have something to do with the fact that he has now achieved MLC(T) status: as in Minor Local Celebrity (Temporary). At one of his gigs the other night a punter said to him: "'Ere, you dun awright, incha? Your song got threw that *Yurrervishen* thing, dinnit?' This is good. I am pleased for him. Recognition – of sorts – at last.

Anyway. Back to the search for a celebrity backer. I keep ringing Sir Trev's secretary, but he always seems to be out. She has suggested sending him an e-mail – hence the following:

From: jmaitland@ukgatewaynet
To: Trevor McDonald
Sent: 19 February 2002
Subject: My Euro Vision

Trevor!

Hi, hope you're well. As you may know, I'm one step away from representing the UK at the *Eurovision Song Contest*.

The BBC want a well-known person who I'm linked with to record a good luck message, to be broadcast on TV on 3 March, when the final vote takes place. I would quite understand if you have neither the time nor the inclination to get involved but if you could I'd be well chuffed and would present you with the latest copy of *Wisden's Almanack* as a sign of my gratitude. (OK, it's a bribe.)

Cheers

Jonny

WEDNESDAY, 20 FEBRUARY

22.43: Have just got back from doing *The John Daly Show* for the BBC in Northern Ireland, the one I had to cancel because of the carjacking report on *Tonight* a couple of weeks ago. Being a guest on a chat show is the nearest an ordinary person like me will come to getting treated like royalty. It's great. As soon as Jackie and I got off the plane at Belfast Airport, we were greeted by a friendly bloke with an outstretched palm.

'Hi, my name is Damian. I'm from the BBC. I'm really pleased to meet you. Welcome to Belfast. I'm here to take care of you, but I have a slight problem. My car is around the corner, and I'm afraid you'll have to wait here for two minutes while I go and get it.'

And off he ran. And I mean, ran. On the way to the BBC I told Jackie how all the nervous tension and expectancy were playing havoc with my sleep patterns and digestive system. She has been suffering too, it turns out, so much so that she is now taking herbal tranquillizers to keep her calm. We are on drugs!

Once we got to the BBC we were led down a series of corridors by TV person type C, i.e. a good-looking young woman with an ever-present clipboard and a headset. There are always at least four of these on any TV set. As we neared our destination, we heard a familiar tune being played. 'They're playing our song,' said Jackie. The door swung open and there, crouched around a table, were a bass player, a guitarist and two women on vocals, one with striking red hair, practising 'I Give In'. This, it transpired, was the house band for *The John Daly Show*.

Within seconds Jackie was in there, singing with them. Then another good-looking woman with a clipboard and a headset brought in a pair of congas and put them in front of me. After a few enjoyable run-throughs, someone said: 'Niamh won Eurovision, you know.' The woman with the striking red hair looked a bit embarrassed. 'What?' I said. 'Really? When?'

It turned out that Niamh was in fact Niamh Kavanagh, who romped home in 1993 with a ballad called 'In Your Eyes'. According to my current Bible, *The Complete Eurovision Song Contest Companion*, one of the reasons Niamh won was because she was wearing aubergine. This, apparently, is the colour most likely to be worn by *Eurovision* winners, after the staple black and white combos favoured by so many acts. Niamh was twenty-five at the time and working in a bank. Hers was the second Irish *Eurovision* win on the trot. As you may know, the country that wins the contest has to host it the following year. Funnily enough, the year after Niamh triumphed, the Irish – it was alleged – tried desperately hard not to win again, as they were so worried about the cost of staging it for the third time in a row. But if they did have such a plan, it didn't work. They ended up romping home by the highest margin ever recorded. I must talk to you later, I said to Niamh.

Then it was off to our hotel room at the Europa, just down the road from the BBC, where they'd booked us in for the day. If I was in Motley Crue, the depraved nutter heavy metal band made infamous by that book *The Dirt*, I would, of course, have trashed my hotel room. But instead I settled for eating both the complimentary chocolates and leaving the wrappers on the floor. Then it was back to the BBC for rehearsals.

The show took place in a large studio. There was a big chat show-style desk at the front, next to which was a stage, and then seating for about 200 members of the audience at the back. In between the desk and the seating area, hordes of cameramen and young, good-looking women with clipboards and headsets roamed free. It was then I realized what company we were in. The two other musical guests were the Lighthouse Family (inoffensive After Eights-style soul/pop band much favoured by Ford Sierra drivers) and Roland Gift (massively charismatic former lead singer with classy late 1980s pop/soul band Fine Young Cannibals). Blimey! The Lighthouse Family . . . Roland Gift . . . and Surf 'n' Turf. Then there were the chat show guests: Michelle Collins (ex-*EastEnders*, successful actress), Penny Smith (*GMTV* newsreader) and, er, me. Jackie, it turned out, knew blokes in both Roland's band and the Lighthouse Family. She'd worked with each of them, years ago, when she was sniffing the big time.

Before the show they wheeled some nosh into the green room (the room where guests hang out before they're on). Niamh was there. I plonked myself down next to her. She was friendly and very down to earth. She didn't go bonkers when she won *Eurovision*, she said, because she had a taste of all that beforehand: she'd had a big role in the Alan Parker film, *The Commitments*. But she enjoyed the whole thing, she told me, mainly because there were so many parties to go to in the week before the contest. Every country taking part hosts one, and you're expected to put in an appearance at all of them. But beware the Russian one, she said. It's just a bottle of vodka and some fruit. After she won, she went to Nashville and recorded an album produced by Mary Chapin

Carpenter. What advice could she give me? 'Just enjoy it while it lasts. It's fun.'

In the corner I could see Roland Gift helping himself to some quiche. I was over in a shot. 'Aren't you the bloke who did that show on telly in the white van?' he asked me. He was referring to a series called *The Man in the Van*, which involved me getting into, and out of, a white van a lot, and saying 'Hello, I'm the man in the van' to loads of people. I couldn't help being a bit syco-phantic. I told him how great I thought all that Fine Young Cannibals stuff was and how amazingly fresh it still sounds. What was the secret? 'I dunno. Nobody in the music business knows anything. All I know is, when it happens, good pop music just has the power to bypass the intellect and go straight to the emotions. It's not like all that complicated jazz stuff, where people sit around and analyse it all the time. It just works on you straightaway.'

Aha, I said, for possibly the fifteenth time in the last month, that reminds me of the old Noël Coward quote, 'Cheap music is very potent'. I introduced Roland to Jackie. All of a sudden, he looked more animated. Halfway through the conversation, Jackie men-tioned the word 'we'. 'Who's "we"?' asked Roland. 'Are you two married?' No, we laughed. 'Are you married then?' he asked Jackie, with what I thought was a bit of a hungry look.

'Yes. My husband's a cameraman. He shot our video.'

Roland suddenly looked full up and changed the subject.

Just before the show started, I popped into the make-up depart-ment and there, leaning back in a chair, being made up to look like a woman, was the disgraced former Tory MP Neil Hamilton. And standing next to him was his wife, Christine. One of the segments in the show was a 'Guess the Real Woman' contest, judged by Michelle Collins. She had to inspect five people – consisting of four men in drag (one of whom was soon to be Neil Hamilton) and one real woman, i.e. Christine Hamilton – and decide which was the odd one out.

As I waited backstage to go on, I saw Roland Gift, who'd just sung his single, 'It's Only Money'. I whispered, 'You were great, mate. Good luck with it', and he smiled, patted my arm and said, 'Yeah, the same to you'.

During the interview with John Daly (small, hundred per cent bald, friendly), I had Michelle Collins and Penny Smith (who kept butting in and saying how untidy I looked) to my left. I managed to get in a fair few references to the big vote on 3 March before John announced the end of the show.

We performed the song over the closing credits and, encouragingly, the audience started clapping along. Then it was all over, and seconds later we all found ourselves backstage. Michelle Collins asked me if I was hanging around for a drink. No, I said, I've got to get to the airport; my plane leaves in forty-five minutes.

Me and Jackie and Penny Smith shared a cab. When we got to the airport, we found that our plane had been delayed so we sat in the departure lounge next to Neil and Christine Hamilton. Just across from us, the Lighthouse Family sat in a huddle, in the corner, watching a DVD of *Sex in the City* on a small portable DVD player. For some reason I started talking about Vanessa Feltz with Neil Hamilton. But after a few minutes he became distracted when he realized that his wife was now on the other side of the departure lounge in deep conversation with the trumpet player from the Lighthouse Family. Jackie, meanwhile, was on her mobile, talking to her husband John. 'Yeah, we're just having a glass of wine with Neil and Christine Hamilton,' I heard her say, laughing. Blimey. How did I get here?

THURSDAY, 21 FEBRUARY

08.55: Just got a call from a bleary-sounding Miles, the bloke who organized everything for *The John Daly Show* yesterday, thanking me for our contribution. He said the post-programme party had only just finished. At around 5 a.m., apparently. Roland (Gift) was seen getting on very well – as in very well indeed – with Michelle (Collins). Blimey. Welcome to Planet Celebrity!

12.34: Just got back from a full dress rehearsal for 3 March. It was in a small studio, with lots of mirrors on the wall, in Acton. Steve Levine drove me there, with my brother, who made a big fuss about having to sit in the back. He is forty-eight, by the way. Dominic Smith, the producer of *Song for Europe*, was there to greet us. 'Hi, this is Sarah Jane. She's in charge of costumes,' he said, introducing us to an earnest, helpful-looking woman in her thirties. 'And this is Liz. She's in charge of make-up.' Another earnest, helpful-looking woman in her thirties. 'And this is Anne, the production coordinator.' Ditto. 'And this is Alice, our production manager.' Ditto. An earnest, helpful-looking bloke in his thirties, with an earring and tight green army trousers, hove into view. 'This is Kim. He's in charge of staging the whole thing.' Kim eyed me up and down. 'Let's get you into your stage gear and see how you look,' he said. Ten minutes later we were all standing in front of Kim, Dominic, Liz, et al. Jackie had changed into a floral top and black skirt. She looked a bit gypsy-ish, so I asked her how much she charged to tell people's fortunes.

She was wearing her outfit on the advice of Sarah Jane (costumes). In our video, however, which I saw this morning for the first time and which was fab, she was in a pink top and black trousers, which I thought looked better. But I didn't say anything. I wanted to, though: on such seemingly trivial matters do 10,000 votes hang. We ran through the song, and Kim stood there, stroking his chin, looking intense. 'You and Matt need to do something during that little instrumental twiddly bit that keeps cropping up,' he said. What did he have in mind? 'Why don't you both come forward, in time, so that you're standing on either side of Jackie, and then, when the twiddly bit comes, point the necks of your guitars upwards, in unison?'

We gave it a go and got it wrong. Slightly out of time. We did it again and got it wrong again: I came forward too early. Third time lucky, though. It looked good. As in cheesy good. Our little homage to the Bucks Fizz Ripping the Girls' Skirts Off Trick that they pulled when they won with 'Making Your Mind Up' in 1981. Indeed, many *Euro* sages feel it was this that clinched it for them. Could our Pointing-the-Guitars-Skywards Trick do the same for us?

Sarah Jane (costumes) stepped forward. 'The boys look good in black and white,' she said. 'But one of you – either you or Matt, Jonathan – maybe should wear a black bow tie that's come undone around your neck, just to break it up a bit.' Good idea. The devil is in the detail, after all.

Dominic Smith (producer) whispered in my ear. 'Who's that disgruntled-looking bloke in the corner?'

'That's my brother, Pete. He wrote the song.'

'Oh.'

After a couple more goes at the song, it was time for us to vacate the premises. The next rehearsee, Tricia Penrose, the barmaid from *Heartbeat* and the singer of 'DJ Romeo', had arrived. Meanwhile, Sarah Jane (costumes) and Kim (the stager) were studying our pop video, the one in which Jackie wore a frilly pink top. 'I think she looks better in this,' said Kim, pointing at the screen.

'Yeah, so do I, actually,' said Jackie. Sarah Jane nodded in approval. 'Fine. We should go with that then.'

So this is what it's all about: legions of highly paid professionals who advise you on your clothes, your make-up, your dangling bow tie and your cheesy dance steps. Welcome to Planet *Eurovision* . . .

On the way back, in the car, Pete (who insisted on sitting in the front this time) said he'd heard from one of the BBC lot that on 3 March we're due to go on stage third out of the four acts. This is good news. If we went on first, we would miss people who were late switching on. Second is still a bit early. Last, and loads of punters will have already made up their minds. But third . . . third is good!

I wondered aloud to Steve Levine about whether we should have said hello to Tricia Penrose when we saw her in the rehearsal room.

No, he said, this is war now. We've got to unnerve the opposition. We won't do that by being friendly to them. How are we going to unnerve Jessica Garlick, though? I asked. She is the one I fear the most. And do we really want to be mean to her anyway? I mean, she's only a kid. Pete suggested whispering in her ear, just before she goes on stage on the big day, 'Are you sure that's the right key, Jess, love?'

13.45: Have just got an e-mail from a bloke who booked us six months ago for his fortieth. It's our only paid gig so far this year, and it's on 22 June. He wanted to confirm that we were still doing it and asked if we required a deposit. He mentioned the price of the gig – £800 – three times. (This is the most we've ever been paid, but as I pointed out to him at the time he's not getting the basic four-piece, but a seven-piece, i.e. two guitars, drums, bass, vocalist, sax and percussionist. Less Surf 'n' Turf, more Turf, Wind 'n' Fire.) He is obviously worried that we are going to try to put up our prices now that we have achieved *Eurovision* fame/infamy. Don't worry, I e-mailed back, we don't need a deposit and it's still £800. What's more, I told him, you are a bit like the bloke who booked the Beatles for £10 back in 1962, just before they hit the charts. One minute he thought he'd lined up just another local band. The next, he realized he'd got the biggest band in the country playing at his club for next to nothing.

16.10: Am off to Heathrow Airport and thence to Kenya for my best mate Jonny's wedding. It's tomorrow. I'm only going to be there for twenty-four hours. I fly back on Saturday. I was supposed to take the entire week off and have a holiday, but because of this *Eurovision* thing I have had to shorten it to a flying visit.

SATURDAY, 23 FEBRUARY
17.50: Just got back from Kenya. Completely shagged out. My best mate Jonny's wedding took place on a beautiful sandy beach in Mombasa, just below a small clifftop. He had hired a local

choir for the occasion and decked them out in bright green. None
of the guests had a clue what they were singing about as it was all
in Swahili, but they kept mentioning the bride's and groom's
names a lot, as in 'Rachel am-um-po-po, Jonny nan-on-too-too'.
The look on his face when his bride-to-be appeared was worth the
entrance money alone. About two minutes in I gave up and started
crying. About ten minutes later, as if to underline that this was not
your average suburban register office wedding, a camel wandered
past.

During his speech, Jonny thanked me for being his best mate,
got the DJ to play a small burst of 'I Give In' and then asked the
top table to vote. They all held up white cards with '0' on them.
When the dancing started, the DJ played the whole thing three
times, enabling me to demonstrate, air guitar style, the instrument-
pointing-skywards routine that me and Matt perfected in rehearsal
the other day.

MONDAY, 25 FEBRUARY. THE BIG WEEK: THE COUNTDOWN STARTS HERE

09.12: Have just got the following letter:

10 DOWNING STREET
LONDON SW1 2AA

From the Direct Communications Unit

Dear Mr Maitland
The Prime Minister has asked me to thank you for your recent
letter and tape. Mr Blair receives so many requests of this
nature that he has, reluctantly, decided to lend his support
only in cases where he has some close personal connection.
Mr Blair has asked me to send you his good wishes for the
success of your song.
Yours sincerely
Lisa Weller

Oh, well. No great surprise there. At least I got a reply. Which is more than I've got from ninety-nine per cent of the celebs I've approached.

09.45: Have just received the following e-mail:

From: Trevor McDonald
To: jmaitland@ukgateway.net
Sent: 19 February 2002
Subject: Re: My Euro-Vision

Dear Jonny
Love to. Tell me how and when. Love to.
Trevor

This is excellent news. As Steve Anderson, Head of Quite a Lot at ITV, says, 'You should try to get Trevor to do it. When he speaks, the nation listens.' Woof woof! Encouragingly for us, but not for arch rival Jessica Garlick (who is picking up an ominously large amount of support on the BBC's *Eurovision* Internet message boards), it now appears that *Pop Idol* heroes Will and Gareth will not, as we first thought, be sending in a filmed message of support. One of the *Pop Idol* judges, Nici Chapman, will be doing it instead. There is a wild theory doing the rounds in the Surf 'n' Turf camp that this is because Simon Fuller, the bloke who owns most of the rights to *Pop Idol* and is set to make tens of millions from it, doesn't want his two stars to be associated with a potential flop. Fuller, the ultimate local Svengali, may well have surmised, as indeed I have, that no one has ever actually voted *for* Jessica: the only votes she ever got on *Pop Idol* were ones voting her off the show. So it's not as if she's got a huge, proven fan base. Having said that, Matt has pointed out that Jessica is Welsh and can therefore count on the entire population of Wales voting for her, which is a worrying thought. He thinks we should counter the Wales effect by pointing out

that Pete, our pretty Scottish drummer, is Scottish, thereby securing the Scottish vote.

This is the week when I was hoping to hit the PR trail in a big
way. At the moment the only show I have in the bag is Gloria
Hunniford's *Open House*, which will be recorded this Thursday
night. It will then go out on Friday afternoon on Channel 5. The
audience will be in the hundreds of thousands rather than millions, but I'm not complaining. *GMTV* and *This Morning* have
expressed an interest in covering the Surf 'n' Turf story as well, but
so far neither has given us a definite 'yes'. The trouble is, these
shows are in competition with each other, so if one does say 'yes'
the other will automatically say 'no'. Of the two, I am hoping
GMTV will come through, mainly as their ratings are higher: at
around 7.20 a.m., they usually get around a million and a half
people watching.

Press wise, the *Guardian* article still hasn't appeared, which is
good. The closer to 3 March it gets published, the fresher it will be
in the voting public's minds. And the *Daily Mail* are apparently
going to print a large extract from this book, quite possibly the day
before the Big Day. This is good. The *Mail* is the second biggest
selling paper in the UK. What's more, I imagine lots of its readers
will be at home this Sunday afternoon, when the *Song for Europe*
programme is on, trying to work out what to do about all that illegal immigration: so they will be in a good position to vote.

Even more important than PR, though, is the lobbying. The
phone voting lines will be open for just ten minutes on 3 March,
and the BBC are expecting 100,000 votes to be cast. It could be
tight: 500 could swing it. That's why I'm going to spend as much
time as I can this week ringing everyone I've ever met, to beg them
to vote for us. Jackie, Matt, et al. are doing likewise. As indeed, I
have no doubt, will the other three contestants. I'm not looking
forward to this quarter's phone bill.

18.12: The BBC's attention to detail is most impressive. Have
just received the following e-mail:

From: alice.oldfield@bbc.co.uk
To: jmaitland@ukgateway.net
Sent: 25 February 2002
Subject: re: Song for Europe

Dear Jonathan

For the purposes of the programme on 3 March, please could you let us know exactly how you would like Surf 'n' Turf written, i.e. how many apostrophes, and where, and do you want a capital N?

Thanks

Alice

18.15: Have just sent the following e-mail:

From: jmaitland@ukgateway.net
To: alice.oldfield@bbc.co.uk
Sent: 25 February 2002
Subject: re: Song for Europe

Dear Alice

Surf 'n' Turf will do us nicely, thanks! This, I believe, is the way it's spelled on menu boards at Harvester Restaurants (as in those TV adverts where a girl in a green shirt says, 'Hello, sir, have you been to a Harvester before?') and if it's good enough for them it's good enough for us.

Incidentally, you are quite right to attach so much significance to spelling. It can have unexpectedly important consequences. In the '70s, Dionne Warwick changed her name to Dionne Warwicke, on the advice of the eminent astrologer, Linda Goodman. Her career nose-dived from that moment on. In the '80s, she dropped the 'e' and reverted back to the original. Within months she was back at the top of the charts with 'Heartbreaker'.

See you on 3 March

Jonathan

TUESDAY, 26 FEBRUARY

Our lobbying campaign seems to be gathering pace. I say 'seems' as I can't be certain, as unlike General Elections there are no MORI opinion polls being conducted every day, taking the temperature of the electorate. But we appear to be close to securing the votes of sizeable chunks of the population. Mainly thanks to the efforts of John, Jackie's husband.

He has just been on the phone telling me that an army major called Trevor, who is married to his (i.e. John's) mum's first cousin, is going to recommend to his platoon, based in Andover in Hampshire, that they all vote for Surf 'n' Turf this Sunday. The platoon has several hundred people in it. This is very good news as it shows that we may just be capturing the hearts and minds of the voters, which are actually far more important than their ears. That may be due to our story, i.e. 'Crap Wedding Band Has A Go At Eurovision For A Laugh'.

Looking ahead a bit, if we win on 3 March, we will have an even better story on our hands, i.e. 'Crap Wedding Band Makes It To Eurovision Final'. That, in turn, will mean we'll have a good chance of having a hit, and maybe – just maybe – having a number one. Quick, someone. Pour a bucket of water over me before it's too late.

One thing we cannot guarantee is a bit of divine intervention, which is a shame: if we could convince the population that it was God's will that they should vote for Surf 'n' Turf then we would be extremely well placed. Having said that, we do have the next best thing. John (bless him) informs me that some friends of his parents, who are vicars, are going to urge their flocks to cast their votes our way.

If there's one thing I've gleaned from this whole thing it's that John loves his wife. I mean, greater love hath no man than he get on his bike in high winds and driving rain to deliver a pop video of her singing to the HQ of the *Big Breakfast*, so it's guaranteed to get there on time. (He did that this morning.)

WEDNESDAY, 27 FEBRUARY

10.23: Just got a call from Graham Sharpe at William Hill, informing me that Surf 'n' Turf are the joint second favourites to win on
Sunday. Here are the runners and riders in full:

Jessica Garlick: 15–8 (favourite, but only just)
Surf 'n' Turf: 2–1
Level Best: 2–1
Tricia Penrose: 5–1

Poor old Tricia. I suspect the bookies have it right, though. Her
song attempts to be annoyingly catchy: but I reckon it's just annoying.

I am going down the bookies to put £100 on us, but my latest
premonition is that sweet little Jamie, i.e. Level Best, is going to 'do
a Denmark' and win. I was speaking to someone on the exercise
bike next to me at the gym the other day, and she said she liked the
Level Best song so much she wanted to buy it. Eek. Mind you, she
said she was still going to vote for us.

I have also sent out an e-mail to quite a few people, as follows:

From: jmaitland@ukgateway.net
Sent: 27 February 2002
Subject: Eurovision

Hello. As you may know, Surf 'n' Turf are one step away from representing the UK
in this year's *Eurovision Song Contest.* But we need your help in getting us there.
Please strike a blow for proper, melodious Cliff Richard-style pop music by
watching the *Song for Europe* finals on BBC1 this Sunday, 3 March, at 4.35 p.m.,
and voting for us.
Indeed, please encourage – by brute force if necessary – everyone you have ever
met in your life to do likewise. A vote for Surf 'n' Turf is a vote for freedom,
democracy and truth!
Love
Jonny xx

17.26: Nickie, the bride in our pop video, has just left a breathless message on my phone telling me that, a few seconds ago, Judy, of Richard and Judy fame, put out an appeal on the TV for me to ring her now, on the air. Nickie says R and J were interviewing Tricia Penrose (why did they ask her on the show and not us?) on the programme and when she mentioned that I was one of the other finalists Judy looked all puzzled and said something like: 'What's all that about then? Jonathan, if you're out there, give us a ring.' Apparently, Richard said, like he does: 'But that would be just like me being in the *Eurovision* finals.'

Anyway, I have just called the R and J studio and been told by the producer that they will ring me back.

18.01: Arse. They never called back, so I rang them. They told me they couldn't fit me in as they were short on time. Double arse. The PR bang I had planned for this week has turned into a whimper. Tricia Ruddy Penrose, meanwhile, is popping up everywhere. The *Guardian* now tell me that they are planning to run the big interview I did with them after this Sunday, and only if we win. The *Daily Mail*, likewise, aren't going to run anything before the big day. A confused-sounding woman from the Lorraine Kelly show rang me up yesterday but hasn't been heard of since. Which just leaves nice Gloria Hunniford tomorrow and the couple of local radio interviews that I did this morning. Talking of which, the bloke who did the first one – from BBC Radio Northampton – has got me thinking about three very important letters again. As in G, A and Y. He said our song sounds camp, which is good, as *Eurovision* is very big with gays. He reckons the only other threat on that score is sweet little Jamie, i.e. Level Best. The trouble is, Jamie has a higher GAF (Gay Appeal Factor) than we do. We need to do something about this. My only attempt so far – a grovelling e-mail to *Gay Times* – has been met with silence.

18.45: Have just spoken to Matt. He agrees that we need to gay-ify ourselves. He thinks one of us should wear a red hanky in our top jacket pocket, as this, apparently, is an indication that you are – ahem – 'up for it'. I think one of us also needs to have an ear-ring in our right ear, as this is the universally accepted sign that you are homosexual. So, the only question now is this: who wears the hanky and who wears the earring? At the moment it's Matt, and me, respectively. I've told Jackie about this and she is cool about it but worried that whatever we do, sweet little Jamie is going to go down such a bomb with the gays that it won't make much difference anyway. She is also still going on about the herbal tran-quillizers she's taking to stop her getting too nervous. She quoted me the blurb on the side of the packet, which claims they combat 'fear, panic and distress'. Three emotions I am becoming increas-ingly acquainted with, I told her. She too has realized that *Eurovision* is massive with gays: when she said to a gay friend of hers the other day 'Not that many people care about *Eurovision* these days' he immediately got all uppity and said, 'Well, *we* do, actually'.

19.12: Matt has just rung and told me that we have another gig – a wedding – pencilled in for 6 April. He has quoted the bride two prices: one pre-*Song for Europe*, one post. If we win, he has warned her, our rates will skyrocket.

19.46: Matt has rung again, urging me to check out the official *Eurovision* website. It has pictures of all the acts who have made it to the finals in Estonia. Ominously, all but two are solo performers. And even more ominously, one of those non-solo acts – the Slovenian entry – comprises three transsexuals.

THURSDAY, 28 FEBRUARY

We did *Open House with Gloria Hunniford* this evening. This is a show that knows its audience: coffin-dodgers and students. But mainly the former. You only have to see who sponsors the show to work that one out. It's a company that makes cod-liver oil tablets. Hence the first guests: two delightful old buffers who took part in the Great Escape in the Second World War. The real thing, that is, not the film. At one stage the more frail-looking of the pair got so short of breath it seemed there would be only one delightful old buffer left at the end of the interview. Thankfully, he made it through to the end. Just. The next guest was an elderly matron who showed off her collection of obscure Victorian artwork, and then it was us. Gloria, who is – sorry to use the cliché, but it's very apt in this case – a complete pro, was friendly and nice and warm. She was also immaculately turned out. But then Gloria is one of those people who sees it as her job to be immaculately turned out, period. A friend who once went to stay with Gloria's family down in Cornwall told me that they all went to the beach one day. Everyone was dressed in raggedy old shorts and T-shirts and swimming costumes. Except for Gloria, bless her, who stepped gingerly on to the sand in full make-up, high heels, perfectly coiffed hair, and an outfit that wouldn't have been out of place at the Ritz.

Anyway. After the interview, and twenty seconds into our performance of the song, I had a Nightmare Moment. In fact, had it occurred at a different time, i.e. at 4.45 p.m. on 3 March, it could have been even An Excruciatingly Embarrassing Career-Threatening Moment.

We were just launching into the first verse when I felt my guitar strap snap. Ping. Just like that. Or rather, PING! Oh, my God. What do I do? To make things worse, we were just coming up to the twiddly bit, where me and Matt do our Guitars-Pointing-Skywards Trick. My first instinct was to wave my hands in the air, shout 'Stop!' and get everyone to start again. But that would have made me look like a plonker in front of the studio audience. By this time – i.e. half a second after the disaster – my guitar was being held up purely by my left hand, which was clasping the fretboard. The rest of it was slowly travelling south and heading for my knees. All of a sudden I felt an awful lot of the 'fear, panic and distress' which Jackie's natural herbal tranquillizers apparently do so much to combat. But I wasn't really in a position to gulp down three packets' worth, so I quickly hoiked up my guitar with my right hand and then slid it under the bottom guitar string to keep it in position, i.e. airborne. Fine. The guitar was now in the right place, but I couldn't actually play it properly, or at least pretend to (we were miming). What to do? Only one thing for it. Smile, pretend nothing is wrong and try to move the thumb of your right hand about as best you can. And thank your lucky stars that this hasn't happened on the Big Day Itself, live, in front of four million people. The studio audience, thankfully, didn't seem to notice.

Musicians who watch the show go out tomorrow, however, will spot a miming disaster of near Milli Vanilli-esque proportions. (Milli Vanilli were a Grammy-winning duo who were subsequently stripped of their award when it was revealed that they had never actually sung a note on their records, or at their gigs: they were serial mimers. At one such gig the tape broke and the poor guys were left looking a bit stupid.)

Anyway. I am very tired. And there are now less than seventy-two hours to go until You Know What.

FRIDAY, 1 MARCH

12.00: Spent the entire morning at the Clapham Junction Shopping Centre trying to buy stuff that will boost our GAF (Gay Appeal Factor). I tried several pairs of clip-on earrings but couldn't quite bring myself to buy any. They just . . . they just weren't me, darling. Rang Matt, who agreed the three blokes in the band should wear red hankies hanging out of their jacket pockets instead. But couldn't find any red hankies anywhere, so bought a red pillowcase from Arding & Hobbs, which I will cut into three. Hopefully, no one will notice it's a decimated pillowcase. But hopefully lots of the right people will notice that it's red, and hanky-like.

14.32: Just had one of those embarrassing wish-I-could-curl-up-and-die moments at work. A woman – we'll call her Eileen – based in the ITN newsroom asked me how things were going. I told her I needed to mobilize the gay faction. She pointed out an important-looking bloke on the other side of the newsroom. She said he was a leading figure in the gay world and would help me get loads of publicity. I sauntered over. 'Hi. I dunno if you know but I'm in the finals of the Eurovision thing and Eileen said you could help me.'

'Really?'

'Yeah . . . I was wondering if you, with your, you know, er, contacts, could help me, kind of, get on a gay radio station or something.'

'And how would I do that then?'

'Well, Eileen said you were . . . er . . . that you . . . kind of . . . had a lot of tentacles in that world, you know, the gay world . . .'

He let the last two words hang there for a bit while he decided how to react. 'I think you've got the wrong person.'

Meanwhile, back on the other side of the newsroom, I caught sight of Eileen, signalling furiously. As in 'No, not him: *him*.'

Oops. That's one less vote for us on Sunday.

Oh, well. This evening I am going out drinking. To try to forget what's just happened. And what's about to.

SATURDAY, 2 MARCH

I do love Charlton Athletic Football Club. When I phoned Arsenal and asked them if we could play our song at half-time during a recent home match, pointing out that Jackie was a supporter and lived 400 yards away, they were snotty and unhelpful. Charlton, however, were brilliant. Today, during their match against Chelsea, they actually let me go on the pitch to drum up support from the fans. It was an unusual experience. The biggest live audience I've ever performed for, before today, was about 100, at my mate's wedding at the National Liberal Club last September. This afternoon there were 25,900 more than that. The bloke who does the announcements on these occasions is called Brian. He always wears a Charlton shirt on match day, although he is so generously girthed that I suspect it may not be one shirt but three, joined together. At half-time he walked on to the pitch and started bellowing into the microphone.

'ALL RIGHT, EVERYBODY, IT'S THAT TIME OF YEAR AGAIN, EUROVISION, AND I NOW WANT YOU TO MEET

SOMEONE WHO HAS A VERY SPECIAL INTEREST IN THE CONTEST THIS YEAR, CHARLTON FAN AND HOUSE OF HORRORS PRESENTER JONATHAN MAITLAND . . .' His voice echoed around the stadium. Because of the distances involved, there was a delay of two or three seconds before his words reached, and made an impact on, the extremities of the stands. Mind you, it wasn't that much of an impact. There was barely a smattering of applause. Clearly, not that many people were interested.

I walked on to the pitch and stood in Brian's shade. 'JONATHAN, WHAT'S IT ALL ABOUT THEN?'

You don't get much time in these circumstances: there was no point in answering the question. I had to lay out my wares as quickly as possible.

'WELL, BRIAN, I'VE BEEN A CHARLTON FAN FOR MORE THAN THIRTY YEARS NOW. I'VE SUPPORTED THEM MAN AND BOY . . .' Suddenly I felt the atmosphere change. Heads were coming out of programmes. People were actually listening. 'AND I'M COMPETING IN THE SONG FOR EUROPE CONTEST WITH MY BAND SURF 'N' TURF TOMORROW. IT'S ON BBC1 AT 4.35 P.M. AND IF I WIN AND WE GET THROUGH TO THE FINAL OF THE EUROVISION SONG CONTEST IN ESTONIA I PROMISE I'LL WEAR A CHARLTON SHIRT, ON STAGE . . .'

People were doing more than just listening now: they were cheering. In fact, about 20,000 of them were (i.e. nearly everyone in the stadium, bar the Chelsea fans). I had a feeling of mild omnipotence, if there is such a thing. And it wasn't over yet.

'SO IF YOU WANT TO SEE CHARLTON PLAY IN EUROPE, VOTE FOR ME, ALL RIGHT? A VOTE FOR SURF 'N' TURF IS A VOTE FOR CHARLTON.'

Blimey. Now they were applauding and chanting. 'CHAR . . . 'UN!! CHAR . . . 'UN!!'

(Charlton fans are the only ones in the country who actually roar with an accent: a Del Boy/Rodney South-East London one.)

Big Brian asked me what the name of the song was.

'IT'S CALLED "I GIVE IN", AND THE CHELSEA FANS WILL BE SINGING IT BY THE END OF THE MATCH.' More applause, more cheers, and a marvellously malevolent snarling sound emanating from the Chelsea supporters' end.

I walked back to my seat, elated. To have 20,000 people applauding you is a real natural high. I now have some inkling of what rock stars must feel like when they perform in front of thousands of ecstatic fans. No wonder rock stars need help coming down after their gigs. I spent the entire second half buzzing. A few minutes after I'd gone on the pitch I got a text message from Steve Anderson, Head of Quite a Lot at ITV, saying that BBC Radio 5 Live's Ian Payne, the presenter of their Saturday afternoon sports show, had just told his listeners what I'd done and urged them all to vote for us. Ten minutes later, Charlton scored. In the end we won 2–1. Good omen or what!

I have gone through so many phases in the past few weeks. One involved convincing myself that we were going to come second. Another was that we were going to come last, by a mile. But now, for the first time, I feel we have a real chance of winning. I mean, look at the numbers: 100,000 people are expected to vote, so if we can get 40,000 votes, we should win. I reckon that between us – i.e. me, Matt, Jackie, Rocking Bob, et al. – we have more than 1000 people lined up. And they are all, hopefully, going to press REDIAL. I have done an experiment to see how many times you can successfully vote, pressing REDIAL, in ten minutes, which is how long the lines are going to be open for. The answer, if you go at it hammer and tongs, is sixty. So: if our 1000 or so supporters manage to vote 60 times each, that will be 60,000 votes for us. We will be home and dry. Three worries, though: a) Is this cheating? b) What if the BBC smell a rat? c) What if the three other acts do likewise?

Well . . . a) it depends on your definition of cheating. It's certainly not illegal. And anyway, everyone redials: David Beckham admitted to voting seven times for one of the *Pop Idol* finalists. b) I hope not. And even if they do, they might not want to say so, as

they would be admitting that their voting procedures are faulty. c)
They almost certainly will be: it's just a question of which act
rounds up their troops in the most efficient manner.

I am getting very excited now: in less than twenty-four hours we
will know our fate. I am going to a dinner party.

PART FOUR

PART FOUR

★★★★★

THIS IS IT

SUNDAY, 3 MARCH

07.03: I actually got some sleep. I can't believe it. Now I must iron my trousers, i.e. my 'stage trousers'.

09.02: Am now just outside the main reception at BBC Television Centre in Wood Lane, West London, smoking the first of what could be many cigarettes. Matt has found out which dressing room we are in: B.29. The 'B' means it's somewhere in the BBC's notoriously labyrinthine basement. We need to dump our stuff there and go for a bacon sandwich.

09.16: Still looking for dressing room B.29.

09.19: Went past a dressing room, still searching for ours, and heard a familiar sound coming from behind the door. It was Jessica Garlick, doing her vocal exercises. She was singing her song, 'Come Back', unaccompanied. I hate to say it, but it sounded quite good. Worryingly good. It has a very effective moment of drama in the chorus, where she sings 'come back' and then . . . silence. For about two seconds. A bit like 'Stop', which was a big hit for Sam Brown in 1989. For a moment I contemplated knocking on the door and asking her if she was in the right key but thought better of it.

09.23: Still looking for dressing room B.29. Quite amusing, really. In the much-quoted spoof documentary film *Spinal Tap*, an hilarious piss-take of an English heavy metal band's disintegration while on tour in America, there was a great scene where the band were trying to get from dressing room to stage. Trouble was, they were in the bowels of a huge stadium, in Cleveland, Ohio. Each time they thought they were near the stage they broke into a trot and started shouting 'Hello, Cleveland' in readiness for the huge crowd they thought they were just about to face. But they kept taking a wrong turn. On each occasion they ended up in the stadium's underground boiler room, where instead of 10,000 screaming fans they were faced by a bemused-looking attendant wearing blue overalls. Which is why we have now started shouting 'Hello, Cleveland' around the corridors of Television Centre.

09.35: At last. Found the dressing room – it had 'Surf 'n' Turf: Male' on it – and we are now in one of the BBC's many cafés, scoffing bacon sarnies.

Oh, and the entire British Winter Olympic Curling Team have just walked past our table in their tracksuits, with their gold medals around their necks and their curling sticks in their hands. They were guests on *Breakfast with Frost*, which has just come off the air. Only at the BBC.

10.35: Have just finished our first rehearsal, on Stage 2, in Studio 1. The *Top of the Pops* studio. All the greats have performed here. And now we are. Nine months ago we were making arses of ourselves (or at least I was) in front of a few dozen people at Turf Aid, just down the road in Hammersmith. Then, we were just another run-of-the-mill wedding band playing for fun. Now, we are on the same stage as the Beatles, the Stones, the Kinks and Terry Dactyl and the Dinosaurs (who was in fact Jona Lewie in disguise and got to number two in 1972 with 'Seaside Shuffle').

I had a good look at Tricia Penrose and her dancers, who were on after us. Their routine for 'DJ Romeo' was a bit perturbing. Near the end of it, an astonishingly camp-looking dancer with a great body suddenly ripped off his trousers (I think they were held together by Velcro), did a backward somersault, and started gyrating around the stage in tight black Lycra underpants. How on earth are we going to compete with that? If I so much as take my shirt off, people will think there's been an explosion in a blancmange factory. And, anyway, I have my dignity to think about. Last week Sting, who is fifty, decided for some reason to take his shirt off while performing at the Brits. Not a great decision. And as for the backward flip, I can barely touch my toes without pulling something. Oh, dear. There, quite possibly, goes the gay vote. Red hankies or no red hankies.

My brother turned up halfway through our rehearsal and had a long chat with a tall, well-groomed, slightly orange-coloured bloke called Martin, who was dressed in black. He looked a bit like the guy in the Milk Tray adverts. Martin, it turned out, was the writer of 'Come Back', Jessica Garlick's song. Martin told my brother he really liked his song. I felt really pleased for him. Here he was, talking about songwriting with other, proper songwriters. OK, it's only *Eurovision*, but let's not get snobby about it; you've got to start somewhere. And let's not forget that Abba, one of the greatest pop bands of all time, started this way. Who would have thought back in 1975 that a bunch of questionably coiffed and clothed Swedes would, a quarter of a century on, have twenty times more musical credibility than Genesis, Emerson Lake and Palmer, and Yes, put together? It transpires that Milk Tray Martin, an extremely charming man, has tried to win the UK *Song for Europe* contest on no fewer than eight separate occasions. Let's hope that's nine by the end of the afternoon.

11.16: Have just consumed cigarettes numbers four, five and six in the BBC Television Centre garden area. All this hanging around is doing me in. Jackie told me she was worried about the negative comments on the *Eurovision* website about us. One, for example, said simply: 'Surf 'n' Turf are crap.' I told her not to worry. Opinions are like arseholes: everybody's got one.

In an hour we are doing a full run-through of the programme, which will involve me, Jackie and my brother doing a short interview with the co-host, Christopher Price, the large, camp, bald, witty bloke who hosts the BBC Choice show *Liquid News*. Everyone is getting very worried about what my brother will come out with as he is very much the loose cannon in all of this. All morning Steve Levine has been looking at him as if he were an unexploded bomb. With some justification. Recently, we played a disastrous charity gig at which I, against my better judgement, allowed him to play keyboards. There were only eight people in the audience, most of whom stayed seated throughout. They were all, to a man and woman, lefty broadsheet newspaper reader types. At one stage a black man got up to go to the loo. Pete, in Saturday night pub gig mode, said loudly into the microphone as the black man walked past: "Ere, mate, don't go. We've got some Bob Marley later on! Yeah! "No Woman, No Cry"!' Not the most offensive comment in the world, but sufficiently ill judged to induce palpable wincing among band and audience alike. What if he pulls something similar today, on live TV? Steve Levine, Matt and I have decided to try and pre-empt any Pete-inspired disasters by giving him a script for his interview. We have made him promise to repeat it verbatim, whatever question Christopher Price asks him.

14.25: Have just done the full run-through. Pete said his lines magnificently. ('I'd just like to say that I'm not used to this kind of thing, as last night I was playing to diners at a Chinese restaurant, but I've had a great time here and made lots of new friends. This is like a dream come true for me.') There were a few sniggers from the cynics among the crew, but who cares? The people watching this afternoon won't be nearly as battle-hardened. If we could get a bit of syrupy music playing in the background when Pete spouts his stuff for real, it might even be worth a few extra votes.

15.43: A BBC person has just returned all our stage clothes to the dressing room, freshly steamed and ironed. And I have just finished cutting up the red pillowcase from Arding & Hobbs into three bits of hanky-shaped material. Pete, our pretty Scottish drummer, is refusing to wear his, but me and Matt have stuffed them ostentatiously into our top jacket pockets. The show starts in less than three-quarters of an hour. I am going for more cigarettes.

16.15: Have just chain-smoked five in the BBC Television Centre garden area and simultaneously rung half a dozen friends to remind them to vote for us non-stop once the lines open. The audience for the show has arrived. There are now about 300 of them, in a long queue that snakes back from the studio door. Me, Matt and my brother are just a few yards away from the front of the queue, smoking. A couple of very camp-looking blokes in Union Jack hats and tight T-shirts are trying to attract my attention. 'Woo hoo! Jonathan! Good luck!' I thank them: they start singing the chorus to 'I Give In' in return. There are things going on in my stomach. I need to go to the toilet.

16.32: Am still in the toilet. The show starts in three minutes.

16.35: Have just made it. We are now on the air. Am sitting behind Christopher Price, who is sweating a fair bit. They are playing some clips of *Euro* disasters from years gone by, including a fantastic one of a huge, moustached Finnish bloke in a light blue flared suit.

16.40: Jamie has just done his song. I really like it. If we don't win I hope he does.

16.45: Tricia Penrose has just done her song. Her camp backing singer may not have been wearing much (at least not by the time he'd done his trouserless back flip) but she more than made up for it. She had enough metallic bits and pieces on her costume to set off an entire airport's worth of security alarms. She was wearing a pink and silver trouser suit-cum-chainmail kitschfest which clanked so much when she walked that you could hear her coming thirty yards away. Predictably enough, the audience went wild when John Inman Junior ripped his kecks off.

16.49: Matt has just said to me: 'This might be the last time we ever do the song, so let's make sure we enjoy it.' He's right. I'm going to.

16.54: We have just done our bit. We gave it everything. The smiles never left our faces, and there were encouraging cheers every time Matt and I did our pointing-skywards trick with the guitars. It felt good up there. Surprisingly good. One more song to go, then the vote.

16.58: Jessica Garlick has just done her bit. She has a simpering, annoyingly appealing way of looking at the camera. I am concerned that it will win her too many votes. The lines are now open.

17.03: We have just done our interview. My brother said his lines so convincingly that Christopher Price told him he thought he was going to produce a small puppy and start crying. Pete then momentarily lost control and said, 'Actually, I produced one before the programme', which, let's face it, is quite a good toilet joke.

17.15: Claire Sweeney is now on stage. She says the lines have closed and the results are now in. Oh, my God. This is it. The audience have gone quiet. There is a continuous drum roll playing. I am sitting on a sofa at the other end of the studio, next to my brother and the rest of the band. Claire Sweeney is opening the envelope. She says she is going to announce the top three songs in reverse order.

'And in third place, with 8200 votes, is . . .'

Oh please God don't make it us please please don't say it's us. My head is now in my hands. I can't bear to look at anything . . .

'. . . song number one . . .'

Song number one! That's not us! We're still in it! We are song number three! Song number one is Jamie from Level Best . . . He has come third . . . I am looking at him now . . . Just like the song 'Without You' by Badfinger (and Nilsson and Mariah Carey and a hundred others), he is smiling, but in his eyes his sorrow shows.

Oh, Jesus. Claire Sweeney is talking again. 'In second place, with 23,456 votes, is . . .'

I am prepared for second I don't want to come second but hey who would have thought all those months ago that we would come second out of six hundred songs mind you there are no prizes for coming second please don't let it be us please Claire say song four or song two but on no account say song number three coz that's us . . .

'. . . song number two, "DJ Romeo"!'

Jesus! It could actually be us now! It's between us and Jessica Garlick!

You have to be careful, I think, when describing the terminally superficial, unimportant world of show business. I get well hacked off when I read actors describing how 'courageous' someone's performance is. That's bollocks. How can you call someone who is getting paid millions of pounds to pretend to be someone else 'courageous'? That is what you call a fireman who rescues workers from a blazing building, or a passer-by who goes to the aid of someone who is being attacked. There is nothing 'courageous' about parroting a few lines and banking an unfeasibly large cheque afterwards. Obscene, yes, courageous, no. Mind you, having said that, I'd like to make the case for using the word 'brutal' to describe this voting procedure, because at this moment that's exactly what it feels like. Emotionally brutal. In five seconds, we could be on our way to Estonia, the *Eurovision Song Contest* and an audience of one billion people. Or we could be dead. Publicly, humiliatingly, last. Rejected. All of a sudden I feel very sorry for, and protective of, those young kids who were getting voted off *Pop Idol* every week. Kids like Jessica Garlick, in fact. Who is sitting just yards away from me. At least I presume she is. My head is now back in my hands so I can't see anything.

'. . . And in first place . . .'

It's funny how this thing has swallowed me whole. Six months ago I didn't think we had a remote chance of getting down to the last twenty. When we did, I spent the entire time convincing everyone that, hey, we'd done well to get this far, but don't get carried away, we're not going any further. Then we got down to the last eight, and I started getting calls from the likes of Bill Martin, and national newspapers, and I realized that it was quite a big deal. Even so, I told everyone, forget about getting through to the last four, it's been a blast, if it ends tomorrow we'll have done great, no one can take it away from us. Now we are down to the last two. And I so want to win. It's only *Eurovision*, I know. Naff, irrelevant, marginalized, scoffed-at *Eurovision*. But it's still a very big deal.

There are, potentially, millions of pounds at stake here. But more than that I want the fun. And the recognition. And the glory. And the story. Please let it be us. Please let it be song number three, Claire.

'. . . with a massive 67,879 votes . . .'

You know that black and white footage they always show on TV, when they're going through the history of man's earliest attempts to fly? There's one clip that sums up the exact position we're in right now. It's the one where a bloke is running towards the edge of a cliff, wearing giant man-made wings. He runs off the precipice, flapping furiously. For a moment, just a moment, it looks like he might actually defy gravity and fly. That's where we are now: either we are going to soar skywards or plummet into the sea.

'. . . and representing the UK at this year's *Eurovision Song Contest* in Estonia, is . . .'

   Oh, for God's sake, Claire, please say it please say song number three out of the corner of my eye I can see my brother he has got up out of his seat he thinks we've won he's making his way to the winner's podium . . .

   '. . . wait for it . . . song number . . . FOUR!!!!!!!!!!'

MONDAY, 4 MARCH
   MediaGuardian.co.uk

   Broadcast News

   MAITLAND'S SONG FALLS ON DEAF EARS
   By Lisa O'Carroll

   The ITV presenter and journalist Jonathan Maitland has crashed out of the *Eurovision Song Contest* after his stunt entry failed to muster enough votes from viewers in the penultimate round of the annual kitschfest.

His group, which he openly admitted was 'a crap wedding and bar mitzvah band', came last out of the final four performances in yesterday's *Song for Europe* on the BBC.

The competition was won by failed *Pop Idol* contestant Jessica Garlick, who also saw off another TV star – *Heartbeat* actress Tricia Penrose. She collected nearly 68,000 of the 100,000 votes cast.

Maitland was spared his blushes, however, after organizers decided not to announce how many votes his band, Surf 'n' Turf, had achieved.

Bookmakers William Hill also installed Garlick as their favourite to win the contest, at odds of 6–1.

A spokesman added: 'We are slightly relieved that Jonathan Maitland didn't win because he has a bet on with us that he'll have a number-one record this year at odds of 50–1.'

Maitland's fluke appearance on the show was part of a stunt for his new book about how to have a hit single and become a pop star.

Yesterday, insiders attributed his sombre attire – a black suit with red handkerchief – to another stunt.

'He was told the *Eurovision* contest had a big gay following and was banking on the fact that if he wore something pink or red it would appeal to the gay community,' an insider said. 'Clearly, it didn't work.'

PART FIVE

★★★★★

I WILL SURVIVE

I can talk about it now. Just. I can, Jonny Nash-style, see a bit more clearly now that the pain has gone. Actually, it hasn't gone; it's just subsided a little. I still can't bring myself to see the video of the show. I tried the other day, but I had to turn it off after thirty seconds. I felt like a husband who's just gone through an acrimonious divorce trying to force himself to watch the home movie of his wedding. What's the point, when you know there's going to be an unhappy ending? Why put yourself through all that trauma again, voluntarily? Jackie says she finally managed to do it three days ago and found it very cathartic, but I'm not ready to . . . yet. Mind you, there are consolations: we now have a new, impressive and only slightly misleading motto for our Surf 'n' Turf business cards, i.e. 'One of the last two bands left in *Song for Europe* contest 2002'.

Like a car crash victim who is regaining his memory, I have managed to piece together most of what happened after the announcement of the winner. In the first few minutes I think I went into mild shock. It sounds awfully overdramatic, I know, but that's the only way to describe it. I feel embarrassed to admit that something so trivial could induce such a profound reaction, but that's the way it was. I felt numb, in a void. There was a soundproofed Perspex shield around me, which meant I couldn't communicate with anyone, nor they with me. According to Jackie, I turned into a cyborg.

'We lost you for about ten minutes. You retreated into yourself. No one could get to you, you didn't react, you just went blank, like you'd gone into a tunnel.'

Jackie tells me she was a lot more sanguine in the immediate aftermath. She was more elated than depressed, she says, thanks to the fact that she'd just given of her best in front of more than four million viewers.

I can remember other details now. There we were, in one corner of the studio, standing around, looking desolate, while about twenty yards away Jessica Garlick was singing her song again to round off the show. Once she'd finished, just to rub it in, a lorry-load of ticker-tape confetti stuff came down from the heavens and filled the stage. Then she got mobbed.

Where she was, there was energy, noise, euphoria, movement.

Where we were, there was stillness and silence, punctuated by the odd shell-shocked comment. '. . . fourth? . . . fourth! . . . we've come last . . .'

We were like a soccer team that's just lost a penalty shoot-out in a Cup Final. You know the scene: lots of players sitting around dazed on the pitch, while the management try to console them. Except that our losing margin wasn't just the one penalty, but 60,000.

Dominic Smith, the producer of the show, told me in the bar afterwards that we were just 100 votes behind Jamie from Level Best. So we got roughly 8000 votes then. So much for my plan of 1000 people voting for us 60 times. When it came down to it, an awful lot of people just couldn't be arsed to vote. And who can blame them? Why should they? The root of the problem can be ascertained from a chat I had with a secretary in the *Tonight* office in Manchester, where I found myself the day after the show. (I was there to finish the report on traffic jams on the M6: back to life, back to reality.) She asked me how I felt. 'Shit,' I said. 'Did you vote for me?'

'Oh, no. We don't do things like that. I was watching, you know, but I was too busy doing the ironing.'

Anyway. Back to Dominic Smith, in the bar. He said he knew Jessica was going to win it within a minute of the lines opening. She got 10,000 votes in the first 60 seconds.

Steve Anderson, Head of Quite a Lot at ITV, was there in the bar too, with a bottle of champagne, which was dispatched rapidly. Steve Levine was muttering darkly about how, in his opinion, the result was preordained and that we never stood a hope. He reckoned 'they' wanted Jessica to win and engineered it accordingly. He kept quoting examples to back up his grassy knoll-style theory, i.e. the fact that the confetti was already in place on Jessica's side of the studio. That, he said, proved that 'they' knew that she was going to win beforehand. Nonsense, I replied. Why would 'they' want her to win, rather than us? There are always cries of 'fix' after a contest like this, and they are virtually all without any foundation whatsoever. At least they are in this particular case. Having said that, a senior BBC person I spoke to recently told me an interesting story. A few years ago, he said, a performer who was considered 'unsuitable' looked like she was going to win the *Song for Europe* contest. (I can't tell you why she was deemed 'unsuitable', as that would identify her.) In the end she came second. But, the senior BBC person told me, had she come first, they would still have made her come second. 'This is entertainment, after all,' he told me with a wink.

It slowly dawned on me, there in the bar, that we never actually stood a hope of winning the thing outright. Rather like the bloke trying to fly who runs off a cliff and ends up in the sea, we shouldn't now be asking ourselves 'where did we go wrong?' but 'hang on a minute, it was never going to work anyway'. Dominic Smith said the *Song for Europe* contest was never going to be won by a pub band, fronted by a singing mother of two from Stoke Newington, and he's right, of course. I can see that now. But why didn't I see it then?

But far, far more important, as Steve Anderson, Head of Quite a Lot at ITV, pointed out in the bar, over glasses of champagne numbers three, four and five, an awful lot of people have made a huge emotional investment in Jessica Garlick: ten million members of the public – that's ten million potential voters – were watching her, and sympathizing with her, every week, for ten weeks. We can't compete with that. We have been crushed under the wheels of the *Pop Idol* juggernaut.

But . . . we could have competed with that. By playing the Jessica camp at their own game. Mind you, it would have meant thinking the unthinkable. I could have done what Jessica's team did, when their song reached the last eight. They simply ditched the person singing it and, cutely and cynically, harnessed the power of the *Pop Idol* phenomenon by bringing in Jessica.

But that would have meant sacking Jackie and Matt and Pete, our pretty Scottish drummer, and getting in someone like Hayley Evetts, another failed *Pop Idol* but one who went a lot further than Jessica did in the show. Had we got Hayley in, I would now be applying for visas to Estonia. But I didn't have the ruthless killer instinct when it mattered. Mind you, as Matt says: 'That wouldn't have been the Surf 'n' Turf way.'

But at least this whole episode has answered, partly at least, the question posed by the title of this book. In order to have a number-one hit single, or at least the slightest chance of one, you need to enter the *Eurovision Song Contest*, get down to the last eight, and then sack your mates and replace them with whoever happens to be one of the flavours of the month. Then again, maybe my mistake was one of omission: what with all the tension in the run-up to the big day, I forgot to ring my mate Uri Geller to ask him to send out his positive thought vibes.

After we'd had enough in the bar, me, Matt and Jackie got into the lift with some of the other performers (i.e. Tricia Penrose's dancers and a couple of the lads in Jamie's backing band). Despite our crushing defeat, spirits in the Surf 'n' Turf camp were artificially high, thanks to the large quantities of champagne ingested. I was just proposing a 'sing-off' in the lift between the various factions, and a re-vote, when the lift suddenly came to a halt. Which was fine, except the doors didn't open. And it was hot. Very hot. Here we were, having just come last in the *Song for Europe* contest . . . and stuck in a lift at the BBC.

At first, there was amusement and weak jokes. As in 'shame about the view' and 'if I'd wanted a sauna I'd have gone to the gym'. As the minutes trickled by, so did the sweat. Small butterflies of panic started to flutter. Maybe, I whispered to Matt, this is karmic payback for all those times we used to play that game, i.e. who-would-you-least-want-to-be-stuck-in-a-lift-with-Esther-Rantzen-or-Anne-Robinson? How wonderful if either (or both) had been in there with us right now, he said.

Ten minutes later, no one had come and nothing had moved.

I began to sense claustrophobia. But every time I felt it creeping up on me, I managed to banish it, aware it wasn't a good thing. A few seconds later, it would return, slightly more intense than the last time.

What a way to go, I thought. In a lift, at the BBC. Cause of death: lack of oxygen and shattered *Eurovision* dreams.

After about fifteen minutes the jokes and the patter had stopped, apart from the odd stifled expletive punctuating the non-stop distant trilling of the emergency alarm bell we'd activated. Then we heard a voice. It was like *The Poseidon Adventure*, the famous '70s disaster movie where the passengers on a fast-sinking cruise ship finally realize they are seconds away from potential rescue.

The voice was nearby: it was male and, it told us, was on the ground floor. Clearly, if we could get the doors open we would be in with a chance of escape. But how were we going to do that? No one had a crowbar on them, strangely enough. Then one of Jamie's backing singers snapped. He prised his fingers between the minuscule gap in the lift doors and forced them open. And, thank the Lord, they stayed that way. Suddenly, less than two feet below us, was the owner of that voice: a uniformed BBC bloke.

'Where are we?' I asked.

'The ground floor. Sorry, sir. You'll have to stay put until the Head of Security gets here.'

'How long is that going to be?'

'I don't know. We haven't made contact with him yet.'

'But that's ridiculous! All we have to do is step out of this lift and we're free.'

'I'm sorry. I can't allow you to do that,' said the uniformed BBC bloke. 'Head of Security has to make an assessment first.'

'What if the lift plummets to the basement before he gets here and we all die?'

'Well, you can take a risk if you want, sir, but it's a risk at your own expense.'

'Fine.' I laughed, stepped out and triggered the exodus.

Minutes later, me, Matt and Jackie were in our dressing room. It was time for the goodbyes. There I was in my 'sombre black and white attire' clutching my one souvenir of the whole experience: a drum skin (i.e. a cover that goes over the big bass drum at the front of the kit) with our logo on it. Steve Levine reckoned it was essential that we had one specially made up, so I went to someone recommended by him and paid £110 for a piece of white, circular plastic with bits of black gaffer tape stuck on it, to form the words 'Surf n Turf' (he couldn't even get the apostrophes right). I felt like one of those sad tourists who comes back from Brighton with a T-shirt bearing the legend 'I went to the seaside and all I got was this lousy T-shirt' except in this case it should have read 'I entered the *Eurovision Song Contest* and all I ended up with was this lousy drum skin'. I wandered off into the night and left the two of them waiting for a taxi.

It now transpires the cab never came. Poor old Jackie, who had arrived that morning in a posh, plush BBC courtesy car, ended up going home on the tube. Frozen and alone. As did Matt. But while they were waiting they saw a familiar, slightly orange figure weaving his way towards them: Milk Tray Martin, the writer of 'Come Back', the winning song. Martin had clearly had too many glasses of whatever it was he was quaffing. Sweet bloke that he is, he made a genuine (but unsuccessful) attempt to be sympathetic.

'I'm really shorry, y'kno . . . I really wish we could've all won, but . . . I just wish we could all be going to Eshtonia together, y'kno . . .'

Matt congratulated him, told him not to worry, and to have a great time. And off he staggered.

When I got home that night I got a timely reminder of exactly what we had been up against. On the news there was a piece about Will Young, the winner of *Pop Idol*, entering the charts at number one with the fastest selling debut single in history. He'd shifted over a million copies in just one week. Like I said: just like the cold, wet birdman who fell into the sea, we never stood a chance.

TUESDAY, 12 MARCH

Things have been ominously quiet down my brother's end. I've spoken to him only once since the contest. He said he was OK, but his tone was flat and he sounded very down. He kept saying that it was 'back to oblivion' for him. I told him that doesn't have to be the case. One or two doors are now open, albeit temporarily. Look at Jackie, I told him. She has already done stuff, as a result of the contest, which she wouldn't have been able to do beforehand. Last week she did a couple of singing sessions for Steve Levine, which might lead to something. And even if they don't, she enjoyed them. He (my brother, that is) should ring some of the phone numbers he was so assiduously collecting throughout the day (of fellow song-writers and local Svengali types) and see if he can get something together. His response? A grunt.

TUESDAY, 19 MARCH

I have done it. I have put my hand back in the fire. I have con-fronted my demons. After two and a half weeks, I have finally managed to make myself watch the video of us performing on the *Song for Europe* programme. It wasn't the most enjoyable forty-five minutes of my life. We were spirited, but not sparkling. And at this stage of the game, spirited ain't good enough. I also couldn't help noticing shots of an overweight, uncool forty-year-old, sway-ing – only slightly out of time with the music – from side to side, with a perma grin on his face and a red hanky in his top pocket.

When it came to the bit where Claire Sweeney announced the winner, I felt nervous, curiously. In what must be the most extreme case of hope over expectation ever, I found myself urging her to say it was us who had won. Not surprisingly, she didn't. I also found myself agreeing with the producer of the show, Dominic Smith, that a pub band like us – or at least a pub band who look like us – were never going to win. If only we had got an all-singing, all-dancing *Pop Idol* evictee to do our song instead. But as my uncle Alf likes to say: 'If ifs and ands were pots and pans, you'd have a very nice kitchen.'

The bit where dear old Sir Trevor wished us luck was entertaining, in an incongruous kind of way. The nation's favourite newscaster is the last bloke you'd expect to pop up in the middle of the *Song for Europe* contest 2002, but pop up he did. I'm not sure how many votes he won (or lost) us, but the sight of him in the *News at Ten* studio saying, in that inimitable, singsong way of his, 'Let's hope . . . that Surf 'n' Turf . . . go all the way . . . and represent Britain . . . in the *Eurovision Song Contest 2002* . . .' was a Top TV Moment and certainly a bit of a jaw dropper.

So where does that leave me now? Well, I'm slightly closer to having a number one than I was at the start of this book, in that I at least have a good pop song recorded, and ready to release. But I need to find a record company who's prepared to put it out. And I also have the Dale Winton project, which could be shunted from back to front burner. It is time to renew old acquaintances. Hence the following e-mails to Muff Winwood (as in the record industry legend who is now Senior Vice-President at Sony) and Colin Barlow (as in the big cheese at Polydor):

From: jmaitland@ukgateway.net
To: Muff Winwood
Sent: 19 March 2002
Subject: You know it makes sense

Dear Muff
Hello, Jonathan Maitland here, from Surf 'n' Turf.
As you may well know, since we met my band has scaled the peaks of the pop

music mountain. Yes, indeed. We were actually one of the last two songs left in this year's *Song for Europe* contest. Ironically – given your reaction to our tape – it was partly down to you that we got there as you were one of the judges that whittled the initial 600 songs down to 20.

A lot of people (not just close relatives) thought our song was far and away the best and should have won. In fact, a lot of people are asking me when it is going to be released as a single. I think you know where I'm heading.

Would Sony fancy putting it out? I can get a fair bit of PR to coincide with the release and we have a stonking video to go with it, which, although it cost approximately ten million dollars less than George Michael's new one, is actually much better.

Whaddya think?

Cheers, Jonathan

PS We now do 'Gimme Some Loving' as part of our set but it is causing ructions. Matt, our guitarist, thinks the chords to the opening riff are EEEEE E octave. I think they are EEEEE B. Given that you wrote it, you are surely the best person to resolve this one.

Cheers again, Jonathan

From: jmaitland@ukgateway.net
To: Sorcha Macdonald
Sent: 19 March 2002
Subject: Hello Sorcha do me a favour and pass this on to Colin while putting in a good word for us at the same time by the way are you related to Sir Trevor?

Dear Colin

Hi, Jonathan Maitland here: since we met my band have successfully completed phase one of our plan to dominate pop music the world over by successfully managing to be one of the last two songs left in this year's *Song for Europe* contest.

Everyone agrees ours was the best tune and the only reason we didn't get through was because a) the hulking great oil tanker that is *Pop Idol* obliterated the small wooden rowing boat that is Surf 'n' Turf and b) we looked a bit crap anyway. But neither of the above reasons will matter, of course, when people hear our song on the radio. I think you may well have a hit on your hands.

Do you fancy striking a huge blow for proper music played by professionals and putting our track out as a single? What have you got to lose? This could be the start of a U2-type journey!

Cheers, Jonathan

PS We also have a great video to go with it which cost just £247 (including sandwiches) but you would never know it by looking at it.

From: jmaitland@ukgateway.net
To: Clive Black
Sent: 19 March 2002
Subject: We need to ring Dale Winton on his mobile. I bet he's Orange.

Clivey Baby!

No doubt you have heard about our near miss. Only 60,000 votes in it. I am bloodied but not bowed.

Minutes after the contest, a woman – Anne I think her name was – came up and started going on about Dale, and how she was involved with him, and how she was hoping that Surf 'n' Turf were going to do something with him, and wouldn't it be a good idea if we did, etc., etc. Due to post-traumatic shock disorder I wasn't able to have a proper conversation with her. But now that my brain is back I can't help thinking it might be worth remounting, as it were, the horse marked 'Dale'. After all: everything is in place. Especially Ian Levine, who rang me the other day, frothing at the mouth, raring to go.

Whaddya say?

Cheers, Jonathan

WEDNESDAY, 20 MARCH

From: Clive Black
To: jmaitland@ukgateway.net
Sent: 20 March 2002
Subject: Remounting Dale

I can only guess at the massive buzz it must be to come 4th in the *Song for Europe*. Have you thought about doing a solo record? Songs for Swindling Plumbers?
It feels like time to break bread again.
Love, Clive

From: jmaitland@ukgateway.net
To: Clive Black
Sent: 20 March 2002
Subject: Songs for Swindling Plumbers? You cannot be serious. I have a day job to think about.

Clivey Baby!
Yes, we must break bread again. And not just because I have had Ian Levine on the phone. Again. He says that Dale, no less, has been in touch. Dale has now decided that he doesn't want to do that Dusty Springfield cover version after all. Ian is miffed as he has already done the backing track (and, as he keeps telling me, he hasn't been paid a penny for it) and he will now have to start all over again. I asked him if I could come to the studio to watch when Dale finally decides to record the vocal to his chosen song but he said, 'No way. Dale will be too embarrassed.'
Still, at least we are moving in a direction that appears to be forward, I think.
See you soon!
Rock on
Jonathan

FRIDAY, 22 MARCH

From: Muff Winwood
To: jmaitland@ukgateway.net
Sent: 22 March 2002
Subject: What Have I Done To Deserve This?

All right, then. Send me a copy of your song on CD and I will take a listen.
'Gimme Some Loving' is EEEEE . . . B.
Muff

THURSDAY, 28 MARCH

From: Sorcha Macdonald (no relation)
To: jmaitland@ukgateway.net
Sent: 28 March 2002
Subject: Sorry he hasn't been in touch sooner but Colin is now MD of the
company and very busy!

Hi, Jonathan
Congrats on your fantastic achievement in Eurovision (final 10!).
Unfortunately, we will not be pursuing our interest in the project. I wish you much
success with it!
Regards
Colin Barlow

From: jmaitland@ukgateway.net
To: Sorcha Macdonald
Sent: March 28 2002
Subject: If you can treat those twin impostors of triumph and success, etc., etc.

Hi, Colin
I won't quote the entire Kipling poem. Suffice to say that while I am disappointed
you won't be putting out our song as a single, I will get over it.
Having said that, I dreamed last night that I bumped into Lenny Kravitz. He was

being very respectful about Surf 'n' Turf and going on and on about what a good
song 'I Give In' was.

I think this is a sign. Then again, you probably don't.

Good luck in your new job.

Jonathan

FRIDAY, 29 MARCH

From: Muff Winwood
To: jmaitland@ukgateway.net
Sent: 29 March 2002
Subject: You must be joking

I got the CD. It's dreadful. I can't possibly release it. I have an impeccable
reputation to maintain.

Muff

From: jmaitland@ukgateway.net
To: Muff Winwood
Sent: 29 March 2002
Subject: You have made a big mistake

Do you remember that bloke who turned down the Beatles, saying 'Guitar groups
are out'? Alan Williams, I think his name was. You may have just made a howler of
similar proportions. Don't say I didn't warn you.

Jonathan

PS Can I apologize, in advance, for what we are about to do to 'Gimme Some
Loving' at our wedding gig this weekend? If your reputation doesn't feel quite as
impeccable on Sunday morning you'll know why.

SUNDAY, 31 MARCH

Actually, our version of 'Gimme Some Loving' wasn't that bad. It
was helped mightily by the addition of Julian, a tall, Jewish architect

from North London, and an old busking chum of Matt's, on percussion and backing vocals. The job of percussionist with Surf 'n' Turf comes with some baggage, mind you. It has previously been carried out by Martin Bashir, no less, at one of our gigs at Numero Uno, my local Italian bistro. Martin, the famed inquisitor of Princess Diana and a fellow reporter on *Tonight*, is actually quite handy. Pleasingly, his appearance also enabled me to announce to the diners present, once he had finished doing some impressive stuff on 'Black Magic Woman' by Santana, 'Ladies and gentlemen . . . on bongos . . . Martin Bashir!', much in the style of that Bonzo Dog Doo Dah Band song where Vivian Stanshall says, '. . . and now . . . on vibes . . . Adolf Hitler . . .'.

Talking of the Führer, we could have used him at our wedding gig last night – on vibes, backing vocals, anything. At least the audience might have noticed us. It was one of those nights. We spent it up one end of a dimly lit pub function room, while the guests spent it up the other end. You'd have thought we were in quarantine. The low point, for me, was when I attempted the bass introduction to the wonderful Fontella Bass song 'Rescue Me'. Despite having practised it on my own many hundreds of times, successfully, in the past week, I cocked it up royally. Just when it mattered. My excuse – that I had learned it while I was sitting down, and now that I was standing up it threw me – cut no ice with my fellow band members. Mind you, I still enjoyed the evening. Especially after John, Jackie's husband, produced what looked like a whistle and told me not to blow, but suck. Turned out that the whistle was in fact a pipe, of sorts, and full of interesting tobacco.

Talking of which, I am currently trying to do a report for the *Tonight* programme which involves trying to persuade MPs to go over to Amsterdam and smoke joints on camera. The reason for this is that there are lots of people threatening to open up cannabis cafés in Britain. One MP has already said yes, several are thinking about it, and one has thrown all her toys out of her pram and rung me up to say how disgusted she is that I have even suggested such a thing in the first place. I tried reasoning with Ann Widdecombe and argued that sometimes you have to expose yourself to something you find abhorrent in the name of research: for instance, members of the Obscene Publications Squad must find themselves leafing through magazines that appal them on a regular basis. She wasn't impressed. 'Are you suggesting I should go out and commit murder then, just to see what it's like?' she harrumphed. 'I don't think you can really equate the act of murder with smoking cannabis,' I ventured, 'but if I've offended you I'm sorry.' I don't think we'll be seeing Ann on the other end of a Camberwell Carrot in the near future.

Anyway. On to more important matters – i.e. releasing our single and winning my bet. I have a plan. Here goes . . .

Clearly, no one is going to put our single out in the UK. (See e-mails from Colin Barlow and Muff Winwood, above.) This is because it would cost at least £50,000. And anyway singles nearly always lose money. However, if we were young, good looking, committed to a career in the music biz, had six great albums in us, and the sky was full of airborne porkers, then someone somewhere might be prepared to take a chance on us.

But there is an alternative. I could put the single out myself. I could use my own money to have it manufactured and distributed in the UK. But even if I did everything as cheaply as possible, I'd still end up spending at least £35,000. And even then, if I failed to persuade the Most Powerful Man in Pop – i.e. the bloke who decides what singles Woolworths are going to stock that particular week – of the merits of my single, I would be left with a huge overdraft and a bedroom full of CDs. And anyway I've already written one book which involved me shovelling wheelbarrows of my own cash into the shredder, and I'm not prepared to go through all that stress and trauma again. Having said that, if I don't have faith in my own 'product', as we like to call it in the music industry, then who else can be expected to?

I am going to have to think seriously about mortgaging my house again. But first, I need to speak to someone very important.

MONDAY, 1 APRIL

There is no point in me putting my house on the line again, for the
sake of a two-and-a-half-minute song, unless the big radio stations
are prepared to play it. And they don't come any bigger than Radio
1. It may not be the all-conquering, dominant force it once was,
and it may have been overtaken in the ratings by Radio 2, but if
you want to get your single in the charts, Radio 1 is still the best
place to start. This is because its listeners, unlike Radio 2's, buy singles. And this is why I have just asked for, and got, an interview
with a bloke called Alex Jones-Donnelly, who is in charge of the
Radio 1 playlist. I am seeing him tomorrow.

TUESDAY, 2 APRIL

Popped over to Radio 1 HQ at Yalding House, near Oxford
Circus, after work today to see Alex Jones-Donnelly, armed with a
copy of 'I Give In'. Alex, who is thirty-four, was not what I was
expecting. He is nondescript and pudgy, with the beginnings of
what could turn out to be a quite impressive beer gut. Friendly,
though. Extremely powerful too. Alex, along with the producers of
Saturday morning children's TV programmes, the bloke who buys
the singles for Woolworths and a handful of record company bigwigs, could justifiably lay claim to the title of One Of The Most
Important Persons In Pop, If Not The Most Important. When Alex
says 'Yes', it has the same effect as when the Man from Del Monte
used to say it. This is because he has ultimate authority over what
songs Radio 1 plays every day. It's not solely down to him, mind
you: every week, around twenty-five achingly trendy, in touch, hip
young things employed by Radio 1 meet to discuss what should go
on the playlist. They will choose anything up to ten new songs each
time. They don't vote, however. In the same way that the Tory
Party used to choose its leader, it's done by consensus. Except that,
unlike the Tory Party of old, one bloke, i.e. Alex, has the power of
veto over any selection. He can also, if he feels so inclined, insist
that a record goes on the list even if the other twenty-four people
present think it's cack.

So what qualifies him to do the job?

It turns out Alex has been in the record business since he was six-teen. He has, among other things, run music clubs, been a singles buyer for Our Price in Manchester, worked for the organization that collects performers' royalties, and been the music librarian at Kiss FM. He has also, crucially, perfected the art of saying things like: 'The big difference between us and Radio 2, Jonathan, is that they have a musical identity, but they don't have a music policy. We have a music policy.' This is the sort of thing that gets BBC bigwigs nodding sagely in agreement even though they have no idea what it actually means. To keep his hand in, even though he is married and has a kid, he still goes out three nights a week to find out 'what's going on out there'. Clearly, Alex has never come across Surf 'n' Turf on his thrice-weekly jaunts as he showed not the slightest flicker of recognition as I pressed a copy of our CD into his hands. 'Why don't you put this on your playlist?'

'Why should I?'

'Because it's good.'

'That's just your opinion.'

'Obviously. But then your entire playlist is a matter of opinion, isn't it?'

Reading the above exchange, it may look like we were at each other's throats: we weren't. It was all good-natured stuff. As it was indeed when after just thirty-five seconds of the track, Alex turned it down and gave me his not entirely unexpected verdict. 'That isn't going to get on our playlist. It's just bog standard. It's got no edge, no direction.'

'How do I give it edge and direction then?'

'Remix it and put some beats on it.'

H'm. I could do that. But it's not really the kind of song that lends itself to that kind of treatment. It has a tune. And a melody. Great big thudding beats would ruin it. I have a better idea.

WEDNESDAY, 3 APRIL
My idea can be summed up in just one word.

Ireland.

I am going to release the song in Ireland. As in the Republic of Ireland. Here are four reasons why it makes wonderful sense:

1) I would need to sell only 1500 to 2000 copies to get to the top of the Irish charts, as opposed to the 30,000 to 130,000-odd (depending on what time of year it was released) that I'd need to shift in the UK.

2) I would need to spend only a couple of grand or so on getting the thing into the shops. And with a bit of luck I might make that money back. Or even – who knows? – turn a profit.

3) My betting slip with William Hill says that I have put £100 on myself at 50–1 simply to 'Have a number one'. The bet expires on 31 December 2002. Happily, it doesn't specify any particular chart. If I got to number one in Ireland, William Hill would then owe me £5,000, although I expect they wouldn't pay up without a fight.

4) For some reason this escapade, like my last one, has gone down very well in Ireland: I have given countless radio and press interviews to Irish hacks over the last eighteen months. Surely that will be enough to shift roughly 2000 copies of our song, and take it to number one? Off we go!

Tomorrow I am going to see a bloke at a record company called Vital, based in Ladbroke Grove. They have a satellite operation in Ireland. It was Vital, funnily enough, who got Gordon Haskell to (almost) number one last Christmas. Here's hoping they can go one better, with Surf 'n' Turf, over there.

THURSDAY, 4 APRIL

The bloke at Vital said he would tell his man in Ireland about me and said it would be a good idea if I went over there to meet him. So I am. I have arranged to meet a bloke called Jay Ahearn, who runs Vital Records in Dublin, this weekend.

FRIDAY, 5 APRIL

Remember Bill 'Congratulations' Martin, canny silver-haired Scot and author of the aforementioned tune, which plays every time his mobile rings? He said he would take me out to lunch after *Eurovision*, win or lose, to tell me where I'd gone wrong. I rang him this morning to arrange a meeting, but he sounded as keen to see me as Ann Widdecombe was to get the first flight over to Amsterdam. He told me to ring him back on his mobile, which I did twice, leaving messages both times. I haven't heard from him since. Oh, dear. I have outlived any potential usefulness he may have had for me. Not to worry. When this kind of thing happens to my brother Pete, he takes it very personally and has even been known to ring up the offending person, pretending to be someone else. Once, a large North London landlady terminated one of his Saturday night gigs after just ten minutes and refused to pay him. He rang up afterwards asking for his money but she refused, colourfully. He tried a few more times, but she wouldn't take his calls. He then rang pretending to be a Mr Smythe from the local council, saying he'd had a complaint from the Musicians' Union about her failing to pay one of their members and that if she didn't cough up quickly she would lose her live music licence. Remarkably, this tactic bore some fruit. The North London landlady sent him a cheque for twenty-five quid, which was half of what he'd agreed to do the gig for, but better than nothing. I don't think I'll be taking this approach with Bill Martin.

SUNDAY, 7 APRIL

I met Jay, who runs Vital Records in Ireland, yesterday. We got together in a pub in Dublin which, like all pubs in Dublin, was absolutely humming even though it was four o'clock in the afternoon. Jay was enthusiastic about helping to get the single out over there, even though Surf 'n' Turf don't really fit in with the prevailing Vital Records house style: the other bands he handles include the White Stripes and the Strokes, who are young, hip and approximately one million times more cutting edge than us. He said he'd call me in a few days to sort out logistics.

WEDNESDAY, 10 APRIL
Oh, dear. Jay rang from Dublin today and said he couldn't help me after all. Seems he has been quite vocal in the past about the Irish charts, alleging that one or two hits may have been hyped into the top ten. Add to that, he said, the fact that I am a so-called 'investigative TV journalist'* and important people will think the whole thing is a scam and run a mile. He wasn't being paranoid, he told me; he had asked a few influential people in the business over there and they had all said the same thing. Everyone will think I am planning an exposé of corruption in the Irish music industry and want to have nothing to do with it. The irony is, I'm planning nothing of the sort. I could if I wanted to, I suppose: attempt to hype the single to number one by buying 2000 copies myself. But it would take a lot of time, money and effort, and if I failed I would end up looking like a complete arse. And I would also stand to lose the £5000 for winning my bet with William Hill. Jay knows I have nothing up my sleeve (except my arm) but says the combination of me and him would scare too many people off. He has, however, told me to get in touch with someone else who might be able to help me. She is called Su ('without an "e"') and she runs another record company in Dublin, called Pinnacle.

FRIDAY, 12 APRIL
Spoke to Su (without an 'e') from Pinnacle Records in Dublin. She made me promise I wasn't plotting a scam, and once I'd done that she said she would think about helping me, and let me know her decision next week.

Mind you, this isn't the first time that people have accused me of being up to something when I'm not. When I was interviewed on

---

*I wouldn't use this description myself as it is tends to be used by people who take themselves far too seriously.

the *Song for Europe* programme on BBC1 by Christopher Price (bald, camp and witty), he asked me if I was worried, given that I was a journalist, that some people might think I was being a bit cynical and planning something. No, I replied, trying to elicit sympathy and votes, but getting neither. I'm doing this because I love music and being in a band.

I'm also doing it because I want to see how easy it is to have a hit.

The answer, as you may have guessed by now, is that it's not very easy at all.

SUNDAY, 14 APRIL

Went round to Steve Levine's house for dinner last night, cooked by his lovely wife Karen. Nearly choked on my dessert, though, when Steve said that someone sounding uncannily like my brother had rung that afternoon, claiming to be a big cheese from Sony Records. The caller asked him all sorts of strange questions, before ringing off abruptly when Steve started getting suspicious. Steve said he had quite a good idea of what my brother's voice sounded like as he (i.e. my brother) had left a couple of messages on his ansaphone that week, which he (i.e. Steve) hadn't yet responded to. Fortunately, Steve found the whole thing highly amusing and went on to get me to tell a few anecdotes about my brother, which he loved.

WEDNESDAY, 17 APRIL

Bingo. Su (without an 'e') from Pinnacle Records in Dublin has called to say that they will help me release the single in Ireland. She also said that a bloke called Kevin, who is apparently the best plugger in the business over there, has agreed to help. His services will cost, mind you – a few hundred quid – but if I'm serious about getting to number one I'm going to need someone like him, who can get the song played by all the right people in all the right places.

I'm not the first person to have done things this way: David Gray, the hugely successful solo artist (who to my mind sounds a bit like a singing sheep), found, like me, that getting a record deal was about as easy as pole-vaulting for beginners. So he, like me, decided to release his stuff in Ireland himself. And look at him now. His album got to number one in the UK charts and at the time of writing has spent ninety-nine weeks in the top forty. He may be a singing sheep, but he is a very rich one. That could be me!

MONDAY, 22 APRIL

22.29: They have just announced on the news that Christopher Price, the bald, camp, witty bloke who presents *Liquid News* and hosted the *Song for Europe* show, has been found dead at his London flat. He was thirty-four. The police are investigating, but no one else is thought to be involved. Jesus Christ.

MONDAY, 29 APRIL

I can't stop thinking about Christopher Price. The papers are speculating that it may have been suicide. But he had a lot to live for. He was popular, successful and rich. He was in the middle of a two-year contract worth £250,000 with the BBC, and everyone was predicting big things for him. He was also genuinely talented. Few people can do entertainment programmes without coming across as vacuous arse lickers, but he managed it. His mates at the BBC have, quite understandably, told the press that it was a tragic accident as they don't want him remembered as someone who took his own life. They say he was on painkillers for an ear infection, that he took some barbiturates to make himself feel better, and that the mixture killed him. He choked on his own vomit.

But then again there have been several reports that he was suffering from depression, and yesterday there was an interview with him in the *Mail on Sunday*. He'd done it three weeks before his death. In it he spoke about having had therapy. He was, the article said, adopted and living on his own after a failed love affair with a French bloke. He also talked about the subject of suicide, and then immediately afterwards said: 'Now why on earth did I say that?'

But on the other hand there was no suicide note. And as one of his mates said: 'If Christopher had wanted to kill himself, he would have done it with a flourish.' I guess we'll never know for sure whether his death was by accident or design but wherever he is now, I hope he's happy.

WEDNESDAY, 1 MAY

Have been attending to all the piddly, irritating things you have to do when you are releasing a single in Ireland on your own. Like:

1) Sorting out the artwork for the front cover. This is being done by Lucy, a graphic artist and, conveniently, my neighbour. She is doing it for £175 as long as I give her website, www.lucyash.com, a plug. She has designed a rather fine logo, as in:

As you may have spotted, there is an apostrophe issue. The BBC, on my instructions, used two. As in Surf 'n' Turf. Grammatically speaking, this is correct, of course: one apostrophe to replace the missing 'a' of 'and', another to replace the missing 'd'. As in 'rock 'n' roll'. Lucy, however, in suitably wild who-gives-a-damn-about-grammar rock 'n' roll style, has jettisoned one apostrophe. I am happy to leave it this way as I feel the second apostrophe may, rather like the extra 'e' that stalled Dionne Warwick's career, have contributed in a cosmic-type way to our *Eurovision* voting massacre.

I was tempted to put something on the front cover to attract our target audience, i.e. young kids. How about, I suggested to Lucy, putting 'This song is particularly appealing to young children' across the bottom?

'Er . . . you might want to go for a slightly more subtle approach,' she said.

One thing which has not been added to the cover, front or back, is a picture of the band. If I did that, our target audience would feel like Superman after a Kryptonite sandwich. If you don't believe me, look at the picture on the back of this book. (Admittedly, it doesn't include Pete, our pretty Scottish drummer, or Matt, but even if it did, no amount of smoke, mirrors, soft-focus cameras or discreet lighting would create the necessary silk purse.)

2) Joining the Performing Right Society (PRS). These are the bods who collect royalty payments once your single has been released commercially. Assuming there are any to collect, that is. It all depends how many times the song gets played on the radio. I have just checked with the Irish branch of the organization, who tell me I will earn only a couple of quid each time it gets aired. That means it will have to be played more than 50 times in order to recoup the cost of joining the PRS in the first place (£100) and will have to be spun more than 500,000 times if it is to generate a million pounds. Unlikely, but possible.

There was a section on the membership form which asked: 'How would you describe the music you play?' I put down 'Proper Music Played by Professionals'.

3) Working out what other tracks should go on the CD. OK, I know it's a single but you always need at least two tracks, don't you? To that end I have decided to include the charming but slightly thin and crappy-sounding original version of the song, as recorded in Neil the Hippie's basement studio-cum-outside toilet in Streatham. I've called it the '£23.33p mix', as that's what it cost me to record it.

4) Deciding what witticisms to put on the inner sleeve of the CD. Some bands put acknowledgements, as in 'Thanks to Martha for love, peace, understanding and her lovely moist fruit cake'. Others use the opportunity to rant a bit, as in 'Please help save the Amazonian rainforest by sending money to this address'. But in the end I went for 'If you want to

book Surf 'n Turf for your wedding, birthday party, bar mitzvah or even funeral, contact jmaitland@ukgateway.net'.

WEDNESDAY, 8 MAY

Graham Sharpe, the bloke from William Hill who accepted my bet, took me out to lunch today. We went to a posh fish restaurant called Rudland and Stubbs in the City. We spent practically the whole meal discussing how easy/hard it is to get one over on the bookies. I suppose you could argue that's exactly what I'm trying to do, by releasing the single in Ireland. But as I've already pointed out, my betting slip says simply: 'Odds on having a number one: 50–1.' And the one thing I've learned as a so-called consumer journalist is 'caveat emptor', i.e. 'let the buyer beware'. And the buyer in this case is most definitely William Hill. For obvious reasons, I chose not to tell Graham about my plans to put the song out in Ireland. But he did tell me an interesting story which gave me a strong clue as to how William Hill would react if indeed the song did get to number one over there.

About fifteen years ago, he told me, a bloke called Moo Young told William Hill he wanted to bet on himself winning Wimbledon. Graham had to be careful: Moo Young could have been a brilliant, but hitherto unheard of, tennis rookie. After doing some research, however, Graham found that Mr Moo Young didn't even play the game for a living and was forty-five years old. So he offered him 50,000–1. Mr Moo Young immediately slapped £20 on himself, which meant that, in the unlikely event of him winning Wimbledon, he would end up one million pounds richer. For a laugh, and because he knew it would create good publicity, Graham then organized a tennis match between Mr Moo Young and one of the top British players of the day, Nick Brown, at the Queen's Club. Poor old Moo Young got a pasting, of course, and everyone had a good laugh. But the smile was wiped off Graham's face the next day when Moo Young announced to the papers that he still had every chance of winning Wimbledon that year, because the tournament he was referring to in his bet was not what you or

I know as Wimbledon but his local tournament, which just happened to be held at a club down the road from him, called . . .
Wimbledon.

Graham told me that there was a good deal of nervousness at
William Hill – particularly on his part – as Moo Young progressed
smoothly through the Wimbledon Tennis Club annual tournament.
When he got to the quarter-finals, William Hill's HQ was alive
with the sound of brows being mopped. But then he got knocked
out, and Graham started sleeping soundly again. What would they
have done if he had won?

'We would have disputed it, certainly,' said Graham. 'We would
have taken the case to the Green Seal Committee – you know, they
decide these things, as bets aren't enforceable in a court of law –
and we would have argued that we weren't liable, due to deliberate
deception.'

H'm. Would I be guilty of deliberate deception if I got to number
one in Ireland? I'd love to find out.

WEDNESDAY, 15 MAY
Have just sent all the artwork for the single, and the two tracks, over
to a bloke called Aidan, who runs a company called Masterlabs in
Dublin. I sent it registered post, in a brown envelope. I hope it gets
there. Masterlabs are the people printing the CDs for me.

MONDAY, 20 MAY
Jessica Garlick has gone straight into the charts at number thirteen
with 'Come Back'. It looks like she is heading for the top ten. If she
does well in the *Eurovision Song Contest* this Saturday she could
even go to number one. But as that Irish bloke used to say in that
beer advert: 'Like the Murphy's, I'm not bitter.' Good luck to her.
And even better luck to Milk Tray Martin, the bloke who wrote it.

THURSDAY, 23 MAY
Jessica Garlick is haunting me. Every time I turn on the radio or the
TV, I hear her. Sometimes she's singing, sometimes she's telling me

to make sure I tune in this Saturday, when she will be 'representing the UK in the biggest music event in the world.' This morning I read she had been flown out to a battleship called HMS Chatham off the coast of Estonia to sing to the British troops on board. Old wounds are being reopened. That could have been us. All those old 'if's are revisiting my brain. As in, if only we had done things differently. But then, as my Uncle Alf used to say when I would complain after a cricket match that I had, yet again, been caught in the gully for a pathetically low score but if only I'd hit the ball harder, it wouldn't have happened, 'If you had tits and no c**k, you'd be a woman.'

FRIDAY, 24 MAY
Saw Del Amitri at the Shepherd's Bush Empire tonight. Iain, the band's hard-to-understand Scottish guitarist who lives in the flat above Matt, laid on free tickets and backstage passes. Del Amitri have three songs:

1) The Slow One
2) The Medium One
3) The Fast One.

Fortunately I love all three, so I had a great time. Later on, at the après gig lig, Iain's girlfriend Madeleine was bemoaning the fact that the band weren't bigger stars. She was comparing them to Ronan Keating, who has apparently been working with Del Amitri's singer, Justin, recently. How come Ronan is huge and Del Amitri aren't, when the latter are every bit as talented as the former? she asked. Aha, I was able to reply, utilizing the facts gleaned from my meeting last year with Colin Barlow, the then head of Polydor. Ronan is the Kevin Keegan of pop. He might not be the most naturally talented bloke in the world but he is dead keen, knows how to play the game, will gladly go to the opening of a record store in Norway and sign albums for the punters every day of the week, and what's more he will love doing it.

But who cares anyway? Everyone at the gig tonight thought Del Amitri were completely fantastic. There were, Madeleine and I agreed, several 'Moments', rather like that Surf 'n' Turf wedding gig last year, when both band and audience became one and went to a slightly higher place. Madeleine, a book binder, didn't balk at the comparison between the two bands but instead went on to tell me, as many hundreds of others have done in the last two months, that she voted for us not once, but several times, in the *Song For Europe* contest. I am beginning to think my only major achievement in all this has been to raise copious amounts of revenue for BT and the BBC. Rocking Bob, Matt's guitar-playing independent financial adviser who lives in Watford, told me that when he got his phone bill the other day, he noticed that a staggering £85 worth of calls had been made to just one number. The prime suspect, his little girl Nicole, pleaded innocent so he rang up BT to complain. But he had to stop, mid-harangue, when the BT person said the number in question was a BBC voting line. A quick check of the relevant dates and times revealed that the culprit was in fact Rocking Bob himself. He had managed to phone in and vote for us an heroic sixty-five times in the space of ten minutes on March 3rd.

SUNDAY, 26 MAY

Watched the *Eurovision Song Contest* last night. Jessica Garlick came third. She got 111 points. She was never really in with a chance of winning though. It was a two-horse race between the Maltese and Latvian entries. The latter, an unremarkable Ricky Martin style ditty sung by a sexy blonde in a tight pink satin dress, eventually won, scoring 176 points. This is the second year in a row that the contest has been won by a former Soviet republic. This is not a coincidence. Because there are so many of them, and because they all vote for each other, they have a much higher chance of winning than countries from other regions of Europe.

The highlight was the Slovenian entry. It was sung by three transsexuals dressed up as air stewardesses and performed in the manner of an in-flight safety video. Mind you, our song was better than any of them.

MONDAY, 27 MAY

Turns out that 11 million people watched the *Eurovision Song Contest* on Saturday night. In this day and age of multi-channel TV, the internet, Sony Playstation, et al, this is phenomenal. The figures are well up on last year's. There appears to have been a surge of interest this time round. Is it arrogant to suggest that Surf 'n' Turf may, in some small way, have had something to do with that? It appears not. I spoke to a BBC big cheese today who said, yet again, that thanks to us, they'd got more publicity for the contest this year than they'd had in ages. Jessica Garlick, meanwhile, has dropped down four places in the charts to number 17. But given the TV ratings for the contest, she may experience a healthy surge in sales over the next few days. It will be interesting to see where she is in next week's chart.

TUESDAY, 28 MAY

Today I interviewed the prime exponent of Proper Music Played By Professionals. Sir Cliff Richard. Oh yes. I am doing a piece for *Tonight* about the Golden Jubilee (again) and Cliff is one of the stars taking part in a massive pop concert next Monday in the grounds of Buckingham Palace.

I did the interview at Cliff's office, in a posh suburb of Surrey called Claygate. It was just round the corner from an excellent deli which sold jars of caramelised onion chutney. I bought two. You wouldn't know it was Cliff's office from the outside though: the only clue that the most successful solo artist in pop music history (64 top ten hits, a number one in five different decades) was based there was a sign, no bigger than my hand, with the letters 'C.R.O.' on it. This stands for Cliff Richard Organization, a charitable venture set up by Cliff, to help tennis in this country. The most surprising thing about Cliff – apart from the obvious, i.e. that he looks nothing like a sixty-one-year-old man – was that he was really quite angry. Angry that his records weren't being played on the radio any more. ('OK, I get played on Radio 2 but only a bit. I'm on the C List there.') Angry that his last song had only got to number twelve in the charts. Angry that the press slagged him off so much when he played Heathcliff in a West End musical. So angry in fact that whatever question I asked him, even if it had nothing at all to do with pop music, he would end up ranting about one, or all, of the above. When, for example, I asked him what changes he'd noticed in people's attitudes towards the monarchy in the last twenty-five years, off he went . . .

'Well, we're more opinionated but sometimes our opinions are formed by people, and this is where the press comes in, people who have the power to form opinions because they give us all the information and all I know is that I don't trust that information any more because I have read so much crap about me . . . because when you see what's written in the paper, whether it be about pop singers, or plays in the West End, or musicals, or the monarchy, why can't the people who write that stuff realize the fantastic power they have? I don't trust them any more.' After a few more tirades along these lines, I tried to mollify Cliff as he was starting to get a little bit heated (he was jabbing his finger in the air a lot by this stage) and I didn't think it would look too good on camera.

'Come on, Cliff,' I said. 'They don't really write that many bad things about you, do they?'

'Yes, they do.'

'No, they don't!'

'Yes, they do. And they are not concerned about who gets hurt. I mean, I could understand it if I had done something criminal . . .'

'But the press you get is generally pretty good, isn't it?'

'Pretty good is not good enough. You know in fact actually 25 per cent has been good 50 per cent intermediate and some really terrible stuff I mean for the five years when I was planning to play Heathcliff they were the most vicious vile people to me ever and I kept saying to them I've done nothing to you why can't you support me? I'm sorry it's unforgivable.'

He may have a surprisingly thin skin then, but Cliff's unquench-
able drive, enthusiasm and undimmed ambition is something to be
admired. I mean, you'd have thought, with more than a hundred
chart hits under his belt and a reputed 93 million pounds in the
bank, that he would be thinking of easing up a little on the old
career throttle, but not a bit of it. In fact, when I suggested – half
jokingly – that if he was so keen to hear his records played on the
radio, why didn't he set up his own radio station, and then they
could be played twenty-four hours a day, seven days a week, he
told me he was already considering it.

MONDAY, 3 JUNE
23.30: Have just watched the Golden Jubilee pop concert. Paul
McCartney took the whole thing over, as usual. Cliff wore a beaming smile throughout, and was decked out in an all-white outfit
(suit, shirt and tie) which made him look a bit like the dead one out
of Randall and Hopkirk (deceased). Which reminds me. When I
told Cliff about my Eurovision attempts, at the end of our interview,
he showed not the slightest bit of interest – which is fair enough –
but he did say that he would be prepared to represent the UK once
again in the contest, if asked. H'm. Maybe I should get my brother
to write another one especially for Cliff, for next year's competition.

Jessica Garlick, by the way, has dropped down to number 19 in
the charts. She is not going to get to number one. But we might.

FRIDAY, 7 JUNE
At last: we have beaten Argentina in the World Cup. I was shouting and screaming and singing so much during the game that I
have no voice left.

At last: the 3000 copies of our CD have finally been printed by
Masterlabs, the manufacturing plant in Ireland and delivered to Su
(without an 'e') Thomas at Pinnacle Records in Dublin. She will be
responsible for distributing them. The release date has been set for
Friday July 5th. On Monday I am going to ring Kevin the ace
plugger and talk tactics. Number one here we come!

MONDAY, 10 JUNE

Kevin the Irish plugger says he thinks he can get me loads of airplay on Irish radio but first he wants me to send him the story in a nut-shell. So I have.

From: jmaitland@ukgateway.net
To: Kevin Fennell
Sent : 10 June 2002

Dear Kevin.
Here we go! Hopefully this will get their noses twitching. Our timing looks good: the song should hit number one in same week that England play Ireland in the World Cup final.
Cheers,
Jonathan

Investigative TV reporter and author Jonathan Maitland (*House of Horrors, Watchdog, Tonight with Trevor McDonald*) is set to put one over the bookies. Maitland, 41, who plays in 'a crap wedding band' (his words) called 'Surf 'n' Turf' bet £100 with William Hill at odds of 50 –1 that he would get to number one by the end of 2002. To that end, Maitland's band is releasing a song, 'I Give In', which he confidently expects to top the Irish charts when it is released on Friday, July 5th. The song, which he describes as 'appallingly catchy, like smallpox', recently beat 600 other tunes to make it to the last two in the UK *Song For Europe* Contest. 'We could have won, but when voters saw us on TV they gave us the thumbs down as we looked like a shambolic pub band. Fair enough: we are.'

'The band's music,' says Maitland, 'appeals to "mature audiences"'. So mature that at a recent Surf 'n' Turf gig at an old people's home in Kent, two members of the audience actually passed away during the performance. 'I like to think we gave them a good send off,' says Maitland. 'At the venues we play, that kind of thing is an occupational hazard.'

Maitland, who used to work with TV dominatrix Anne Robinson ('She's a massive fan of the band'), stands to make £5000 if he wins his bet. He chose to release the song in Ireland when he realized 3000 sales in a week could get you the top slot. In the UK, 100,000 might not even do it for you. But what about objections from the bookies? 'I don't see a problem,' he says. 'My betting slip says "odds on having a number one : 50-1" but it doesn't specify which chart .'

Maitland's efforts are for his book, *How to Have a Number One Hit Single (and what to do if you don't)*, which is out in October. His last effort, *How to Make Your Million From the Internet (and what to do if you don't)* topped the bestseller charts but saw him lose a fortune after he mortgaged his house for £50,000 in an attempt to make a million from the dot com boom.

This project has lost him money too, but considerably less than his last venture. He has financed the single himself at a cost of £3000 as well as shelling out £247 on a promo, shot in the style of a wedding video, naturally.

'It cost about a million dollars less than George Michael's video for "Freeeek",' says Maitland. 'But funnily enough, it's better.'

OK, so what I've written may not be 100% shot through with truthfulness (i.e. the bits about Anne Robinson being a big fan, the old people's home gig, and getting down to the last two in the *Song For Europe* contest), but in pop music, like war, truth is always the first casualty.

TUESDAY, 11 JUNE

Got an e-mail from Kevin the Irish plugger. He has sent out my story, as above, to every single pop radio station in Ireland. All 23 of them. Whether they will play the song, and whether or not the punters will actually buy it, remains to be seen.

WEDNESDAY, 12 JUNE

Saw England draw 0 – 0 with Nigeria this morning. We are through to the last 16 of the World Cup and playing Denmark next. I have watched each of our three qualifying matches at different houses, but the only victory – against Argentina – came when I went to my mate Thommo's house, in Wimbledon. I shall be watching the Denmark game there.

THURSDAY, 13 JUNE

Today I interviewed one of Ireland's most famous sons. Not Kevin the plugger, Sir Bob Geldof. It was for a *Tonight* programme about fathers' rights. Bob thinks men are getting a raw deal when it comes to custody cases involving their own children. Yesterday, if I could have invited any ten people in the world to a fantasy dinner party at my house, Bob would have been the first on the guest list. Having met him, today I'm not so sure. He's a tremendously charismatic, articulate man, but if he did come round to dinner, it really wouldn't be worth inviting anyone else of interest as they wouldn't get a word in edgeways. He hasn't kissed the Blarney Stone, he's snogged it vigorously, several times. I didn't interview him: I couldn't. It was a 75-minute monologue. On one rare occasion, when I managed to slip in a question, he told me to shut up and let him finish. He even carried on ranting after we'd switched the cameras off. You can't help but admire someone who is spilling over with so much genuine passion, even if talking to them (or rather, being to talked to by them) is a bit like being repeatedly hit over the head with a thesaurus. Once the flow of words had eased slightly, I managed to establish that we had something in common: a shared love of one of the greatest bands of all time, Essex R'n'B hardmen,

Doctor Feelgood. Bob said that his band, the Boomtown Rats, were simply a speeded-up version of them. When I told him about the *Eurovision Song Contest*, he looked at me like I was a nutter.

FRIDAY, 14 JUNE

The Irish are starting to sniff. Kevin the plugger has set up a radio interview for me this Sunday afternoon. It clashes with cricket, but never mind.

SATURDAY, 15 JUNE

Went to my mate Thommo's in Wimbledon to see England play Denmark in the World Cup. I sat in exactly the same spot and wore exactly the same clothes as I did when I watched us beat Argentina 1–0. Sure enough, we won 3–0. I know where I'll be and what I'll be wearing when we play Brazil this Friday.

SUNDAY, 16 JUNE

Did interview with Ken O'Sullivan from radio LM FM this afternoon. He was sounding remarkably chipper, given that Ireland had just crashed out of the World Cup after missing four penalties. LM FM is based in County Louth, about thirty miles south of Dublin, and plays non-stop '80s music. It was an interview of two halves. The first was about Surf 'n' Turf, the second wasn't. This was because after a couple of minutes Ken heard a big cheer go up in the background and asked what was happening. I explained that I was talking to him in my cricket whites while standing on the boundary watching our number 11, who is just 11-years-old, go into bat. Consequently we spent the rest of the interview talking cricket. Unfortunately, just as the interview came to a close, so did the 11-year-old's innings. We lost by 29 runs. But at least Ken played our song.

MONDAY, 17 JUNE

My report on fathers' rights went out tonight. It very nearly didn't though. Two hours before it was due on air, we were still working on it and worrying about making the deadline when Bob Geldof got put through to the editing suite. He launched into a lengthy diatribe. Everything had to be put on hold while he vented his spleen. The more he went on, the more panicky the glances at watches became. Bob had seen a clip of the interview I did with him on GMTV this morning (they sometimes preview our show) and he was worried that the programme tonight was going to be more about him than about the issue. Fortunately, after 25 minutes, our editor managed to placate him. If I ever get in trouble, I want Bob on my side.

WEDNESDAY, 19 JUNE
Let us not forget Plan B, i.e. Surf 'n' Turf's proposed duet with camp orange TV game show host Dale Winton. That project is – technically at least – not dead yet. (A bit like Norman Wisdom.) Today I rang Ian Levine, the eccentric former Take That producer who lives in that strange Elvis-style house in Ealing. I asked if he'd heard from Dale and whether there was any chance of us getting a single out together by the end of this year. Turns out Dale had been in touch. He now wants to do a cover version of a song called 'Gimme Little Sign', which got to Number 8 for someone called Brenton Wood in December 1967. (You'd recognize it if you heard it.) However, despite all the e-mails and all the chats I've had with various people about the project, Dale doesn't seem to be overly aware of Surf 'n' Turf. He seems to think, quite reasonably, that this is a solo venture. Ian Levine however, for some reason, is massively keen to do something with us. Which is quite something given his current success: he is heavily involved with the boy band sensation of the moment, Blue. Last month he arranged a new version of the old Miracles song 'Get Ready', which they performed at the recent Golden Jubilee concert at Buckingham Palace. But as far as we and Dale Winton are concerned, it feels very much like it isn't going to happen. This is just as well because to be honest I don't think I could live with the shame of being in Dale Winton's backing band. I know that *Eurovision* was the nadir of naffness,

but at least we were in control of what we were doing. With Dale, I don't think we would be. I couldn't go through with it. Not even for a book. I think it's better that I keep my eye on the ball which, at the moment, is bobbing enticingly in Ireland's penalty area. Come Friday July 5th, when our single gets released, I hope to lash it home.

THURSDAY, 20 JUNE

Ireland is going Surf 'n' Turf crazy! Six radio stations – yes, six! – want interviews with me on Monday, and Kevin the plugger claims he has got me a slot on Irish breakfast telly on Friday July 5th, the day our single gets released. Perfect. This is excellent. Mind you, on Monday, the day of the six radio interviews, I will be on the Greek Island of Rhodes, doing a report about the appalling behaviour (drinking, shagging, fighting) of British Tourists there. I hope the mobile works.

FRIDAY, 21 JUNE

Watched England play Brazil in exactly the same clothes and surroundings – i.e. Thommo's place in Wimbledon – as the victorious matches against Denmark and Argentina. But we lost. So much for superstition. Deeply distressing. But I know how our boys feel. Because I felt something very similar on Sunday March 3rd, at the BBC. I too had allowed myself to believe that the Big Prize was within my grasp, only to see it brutally snatched away. Like David Seaman, England's goalie, who was lobbed from 40 yards out, I didn't see it coming.

MONDAY, 24 JUNE

The day of six Irish radio interviews. Managed, skilfully, to slot them in between interviews of my own with a Greek policeman, a Club 18–30 rep and a young British bloke who claimed he'd recently slept with three different women in one night. Every one of the radio stations played our song afterwards. This publicity is fantastic but I am now wondering whether it will really help us. I'll know in a couple of weeks, I suppose, when the song is released and the sales figures start coming in. I'm worried all this PR may backfire : if we'd marketed the song more subtly, then maybe more radio stations would now be putting it on their playlists, and airing it regularly. As it is, I suspect they see it as a novelty, and will play it just the once, as an adornment to their interview with me. Oh well. Too late now.

FRIDAY, 28 JUNE

Back from Greece. Even if we don't make it to number one, I really hope we break the top 30. Then we will have achieved something. We will have secured our place in Irish pop music history. (Not a very big one, admittedly.) We will also be in the *Guinness Book of Irish Hit Singles*. If there is one, that is. And we will be able to put 'Got to number 23 in Irish charts' on the bottom of our business cards. (Alongside, of course, 'Down to last two in *Song For Europe Contest* 2002'.) I'm not after a whole chapter in the Great Book Of Popular Music History: the tiniest asterisk will do just fine.

FRIDAY, 5 JULY

0655: Our single is being released today! Hence am in Dublin for mini publicity tour. Met Kevin the plugger in the reception of the musty-smelling Temple Bar Hotel. He had a taxi waiting to take us to the studios of TV3, on the outskirts of the city, where I am due to appear on Irish breakfast telly. Good for Kevin. He said he reckoned he could get me some big time TV exposure and he has delivered. We bonded quickly, after realising that the hotel's large female receptionist had been rude and unhelpful to us both in the last twelve hours.

0745: Have just met Su (without an 'e') Thomas from Pinnacle Records in the corridor of the TV3 studios, while waiting to go on. Su is ultimately in charge of making sure the record gets to the right shops and is displayed prominently. She wore trendy black horn-rimmed style glasses, the type favoured by Islington trendies (she actually comes from Potters Bar, which is twenty miles north of

Islington), green combat trousers and several small rings through her nose. She was very friendly and enthusiastic and, before I knew it, we were embroiled in a conversation with a bloke from *Hot Press*, Dublin's premier music magazine, about the many virtues of Phil Lynott, the deceased Irish front man of Thin Lizzy.

0834: Have just done my slot. The show was just like GMTV. There was a couch, a lot of bright pastel colours flying around, and two presenters, one of each sex.

This is clearly a formula that works: remarkably, the show has quadrupled its audience in the last year. They chatted to me for eleven minutes. This is good. Normally, items last no longer than five. They also played our video. The only blip came when I asked the co-hosts what they thought of the song. They spluttered a bit, before – rather unconvincingly – claiming that they liked it.

11.15: Have just finished a 45-minute slot on RTE radio, which is the Irish Radio 2. The show, which was presented by a bloke called Dave Fanning, is one of the most popular in the country. Dave wasn't, by his own admission, on top of his game: he kept telling his listeners how crap he felt and how he had been out all night. Not that I'm complaining. He played the song twice, and got people to ring in to discuss its merits (or otherwise). Sample call:

Dave Fanning : 'On the line now we have Linda. What did you think of the song, Linda? Did you like it ?'

Linda : 'No. I can't stand it meself.'

JM: 'Linda! Hi! Jonathan here. How long have you been hearing-impaired?'

Linda : 'Dat's very funny. But me kids loved it! They're in the car with me now. They've been jiggling around in the back, loike.'

JM: 'If I were you, Linda, I'd buy them ten copies each just to make sure.'

Linda: 'Lemme tell you what . . . I'll buy it anyway, not coz I like it, but coz ya got balls. Know what I mean?'

The last few minutes of the interview took the form of a pop quiz. Dave and I competed against each other, answering questions set by callers. The deciding question, from a bloke called

Sean, was 'who wrote the song "Can't Get You Out Of My Head" sung by Kylie Minogue?' While Dave floundered – still clearly suffering from the excesses of last night – I was able to triumphantly announce to the listening masses that it was in fact Cathy Dennis, from Norwich, and Rob Davis, the ex-guitarist from Mud, who, five years ago, could be found doing a duo gig in a wine bar in Carshalton, with my brother Pete.

1234: Have just finished very agreeable brunch with Su (without an 'e') and Kevin the plugger. They want me to do a story for *Tonight* about a tanker full of nuclear waste which is heading for Ireland. I said I would see what I can do. We also discussed what I should do with the leftover copies of 'I Give In', if, God forbid, it fails to sell in the quantities we are hoping for. Trying to flog them to drunk punters after future Surf 'n' Turf wedding and birthday gigs seems the best option. Kevin told me about his days on the road with Boyzone. Inevitably, Ronan Keating came up. Ronan, said Kevin, immediately stood out a mile from the rest of the band, even though he was only 18 when he first met him. 'He was, like, 18 going on 40,' said Kevin. 'It was uncanny, he knew exactly what he was doing and where he was going.' It was Ronan, for instance, who persuaded the other lads in the band not to kiss adoring female fans straight on the lips, but to proffer their cheek instead. This, argued Ronan, was more classy. Once again, we got into a debate about whether or not Ronan was too clean-cut for his own good. You might recall that Colin Barlow, the record industry big cheese who is one of Ronan's mentors, told me a few months ago that he was worried Ronan lacks the 'edge' that Robbie Williams appears to have. Turns out there was a story doing the rounds recently in Dublin, involving Ronan and fellow Irish pop artist Bryan Kennedy which, if it were true, would have transformed Ronan's image overnight. Ronan denied it strongly though. Maybe he shouldn't have.

1315: Have just been to HMV in Grafton Street, in the middle of Dublin, the biggest record store in Ireland. As I walked in, there on my left was a huge stand laden with about 200 copies of the new single by Six, the latest protégés of Ireland's Local Svengali *par excellence*, Louis Walsh. Louis' most famous charge, by the way, is Ronan Keating. It's a pity he hasn't taken us on, too. But why should he? He's after artists with long-term career prospects, not one-off novelty artists. Anyway. Enough self-flagellation. Went downstairs in search of our single. Suddenly, there, piled high next to an unattended till, I saw 40 copies of 'I Give In' by Surf 'n' Turf. This is it! It's happening! We are on sale! Bought 5.

1323: Have just bought a pair of dark glasses from Boots in Grafton Street.

1327: Have just gone back into HMV, wearing dark glasses, and bought another 3 copies of our single.

1359: Just returned to HMV with the aim of snaffling 5 more. Encouragingly, the pile of 32 CDs I left next to the unattended till at 1327 is now down to a mere 7. That means 25 copies have upped and gone in the last half hour. This could mean a) that they have been snapped up by eager Irish punters or b) that they have been slung in the 99p bargain bin, somewhere out of sight, at the back of the shop. Anyway, bought 5 more which means I have now created 11 official sales. Every single one will have been recorded and will count towards the Irish chart, which comes out this Friday. We will be needing all the help we can get come chart day: Surf 'n' Turf's new release will be battling it out with the latest offerings from, amongst others, Elvis Presley, Six (see above) and Kylie Minogue.

1421: Similar inspections of the two other big record shops on Grafton Street have just revealed a distressing lack of Surf 'n' Turf product anywhere. At first, in a fit of ludicrous over-optimism, I made myself believe that this was because the single had sold out within minutes of appearing on the shelves. Then, after discreet enquiries, I realized that neither shop was stocking the song in the first place.

1443: Am fighting the urge to go back to HMV to polish off the remaining 2 copies.

1444: Decide not to, as am due at next interview in five minutes.

1543: Have just finished interview with Talk FM, a radio station so new they don't even know if anyone is listening yet. During the chat, they asked me what you need to have a hit single and so I went into my 'a hit single is like a stool, it needs three legs to get off the ground' shtick but then I realized that I was wrong and that a hit single is, in fact, more like a chair, in that it needs four legs. Airplay, press coverage and a good song are not enough. Crucially, you also need a shiny, happy act to sell the thing. Preferably a group of adolescent boys, or girls, or a mixture of the two. That, of course, is something we conspicuously lack. All of a sudden, I don't fancy our chances.

1800: Am on plane home having done a quick interview at the airport with Ken O'Sullivan, the DJ from LM FM who interviewed me during that cricket game a couple of weeks ago. He recorded it and will broadcast it in three weeks' time, as he is off on holiday tomorrow. This is a bit unfortunate as we need all the publicity we can get right now, not then. For some reason we ended up talking about golf for half the interview but then, the last time we spoke, we spent several minutes discussing cricket.

MONDAY 8 JULY

Did another interview tonight, on a late night talk show on a station called Red FM, based in Cork. The host, an American called Charlie, played the song three times and told everyone listening to go out and buy it immediately.

PART SEVEN

★★★★★

ANOTHER NAIL IN MY HEART

TUESDAY 9 JULY

1846: Just rang Kevin the plugger in Dublin to see how the sales are going. He says he has no idea but will be in a much better position to comment tomorrow morning as that's when the mid-week sales figures are issued to people in the industry. I have a feeling that, despite all the publicity, we have not sold much more than 11 copies.

WEDNESDAY 10 JULY

1326: I was wrong. We have sold 26 copies. *26 copies*. We have crashed into the Irish Hot 100 mid-week chart at number 98. I have a strong suspicion that we may be crashing out of it very soon. I am going to lie down for a while.

1435: Have just rung Jackie and asked her how on earth we are going to shift the remaining 2,974 copies of 'I Give In'. I told her my brother Pete's suggestion – that we should set up a stall in Covent Garden, play the song through a ghetto blaster, and get her to mime to it, while we flog copies of it from the back of a van – but the response was not favourable. She did point out, however, that CDs make excellent coasters. And frisbees. I have sent out an e-mail to those closely connected with the project – i.e. Matt,

Steve Levine and Rocking Bob – asking for their suggestions re the 'unsold stock' as it must now be called.

1644: Looking on the bright side, 15 people appear to have actually bought our single of their own free will. That means they must like it. And us. If each one of them booked us for their wedding/birthday bash/fleadh or whatever, at £1000 a time, we would be £15,000 better off. That, as they say in the City, is a valuable potential revenue stream.

THURSDAY 11 JULY

Had a chat with Kevin the plugger today. He is desperately disappointed. Touchingly, he tried to make me feel better by saying that he has represented artists in the past whose singles have sold even less than ours. But tellingly, when I asked him what they were called, he said he couldn't remember. Kevin says the problem is that we have been getting sporadic airplay but not making it onto those all-important playlists. Most stations in Ireland are run like Radio One: they have 'A', 'B' and 'C' lists. An 'A' listing guarantees around 30 plays a week, 'B' means 15 or so, and 'C' about half a dozen. We appear to have scraped onto the 'Z' list, hence our appearance in the – ahem — lower foothills of the charts. Kevin says we have two problems. One is that our sound 'just isn't what the kids are listening to right now . . . everywhere you go, Jonathan, even in Singapore, it's all dat Drum and Bass stuff, you know?' The other, as I have long suspected, is that we are not exactly the perfect pop package: i.e. we need to be young, pretty and choreographed but we are, in fact, old(ish) and look rather like a bag of spanners.

On the positive side, however, I have had a useful e-mail from Thommo, my mate who lives in Wimbledon, about the problem of the 'unsold stock'. Thommo is the bloke at whose pad I watched all those World Cup games but he was also, impressively, 'West Croydon Young Businessman Of The Year 1985.' Thommo, who made a fortune by selling out at the height of the dotcom boom (unlike me), has come up with five ways of shifting the remaining

2,974 CDs. The idea that intrigues me the most is his suggestion that I should do a deal with a restaurant chain that has Surf 'n' Turf on its menu – i.e. Harvester, or Beefeater – and get them to give away a free copy of our single every time someone orders that particular dish.

(Just in case you didn't know, Surf 'n' Turf is steak, with prawns and/or lobster. There is usually a jacket potato involved too.) Well, there's no harm in trying, is there?

Mind you, there is always the chance that in the next 24 hours 2,974 Irish people will descend on the HMV shop in Grafton Street demanding that they each be sold a copy of 'I Give In', thereby improving our chart position by 97 places. I doubt it though.

FRIDAY 12 JULY

Some people did descend on their local record shops, but not in the numbers I was hoping for. We have sold 3 more copies in the last 24 hours. We have ended our first - and, I think it is safe to assume, last - week on the Irish charts at number 111, having shifted a total of 29 singles. I would have loved to print this week's chart right here, with us listed in it, so you could at least see our name up there in lights, so to speak: but unfortunately they only publish a top 50. Oh dear. What a journey. I started this book dreaming of pop stardom. I'm ending it trying to do a deal with Harvester.

PART EIGHT

★★★★★

DON'T DREAM IT'S OVER

MONDAY 15 JULY

The music industry, like any other, is based on a very simple economic theory.

If you make money, for yourself and your record label, you're a success.

If you don't, you're not. By that yardstick, this whole project has been a quite spectacular failure, as the following table shows:

MONEY SPENT BY JM TRYING TO GET SURF 'N' TURF TO NO.1	INCOME RECEIVED BY JM ALONG THE WAY
Neil the Hippie's studio fee: £70	
Song for Europe Entry fees: £240	
Fees to musicians when we re-recorded the song properly at Steve Levine's: £300	Performance royalty for appearing on BBC *Song For Europe* programme: £390

Cost of mixing master CD: £230	
Cost of ridiculous Surf 'n' Turf drumskin (which I've since lost): £110	Performance royalty for appearing on the Gloria Hunniford Show: £150
Hospitality/ sweeteners eg. bottles of Champagne: £200	Performance royalty for John Daly Show on BBC Northern Ireland: £750
Cost of shooting pop video i.e. wedding suit hire, editing, make-up, sandwiches etc: £247	Performance royalties from song being played on Radio 2: £75
Artwork for CD: £175	
Cost of manufacturing 3000 CDs: £1560	
Cost of distributing 3000 CDs (and getting 2,971 of them back): £1300	Estimated royalties to come from CD being played on Irish radio: £50
Kevin the plugger's fee: £400	
2 visits to Ireland, one to discuss release, one to publicize it: £550	Sales of 29 Surf 'n' Turf CDs in Ireland (mind you, I bought 11 of them myself): £58
Cost of joining Musicians' Union and Performing Rights Society: £180	
TOTAL £5562	TOTAL £1473

On a purely Mr Micawber-ish basis then, as you can see, my gross expenditure has exceeded my net income by more than £4,000. So the net result should, in theory, be unhappiness. I am, however, clinging to two possibilities. One is that the very charming-sounding Joanne Blake, who is the Marketing Director of Harvester Restaurants, will take up my offer of buying 1500 of our CDs at the bargain price of £3000, which she will then give away free to customers who have the good sense to order a plate of Surf 'n' Turf. The other is that you, having read this book, will, quite understandably, be seized by the overwhelming urge to hear what all the fuss is about. Hence this:

OWN YOUR VERY OWN LIMITED EDITION SURF 'N' TURF CD!

- AUTOGRAPHED BY THE BAND!
- DOWN TO LAST 2 IN BBC SONG FOR EUROPE CONTEST!
- GOT TO NUMBER 98 IN IRISH CHARTS!
- AS SEEN ON TV!

Yes, I would like to receive . . . . copies of 'I Give In' by Surf 'n' Turf.
In fact, I can't wait. I enclose a cheque for . . . . (see prices below)
My name and address is: . . . .
. . . .
. . . .
. . . .
. . . .

Costs (inc. P & P)
1 copy :   £4.99
2 copies: £8.00
3 copies: £10.00
1000 copies: £2000.00 (and we'll play your wedding/ birthday party for nothing)

PLEASE CUT OUT THIS FORM AND SEND IT TO:
JONATHAN MAITLAND,
SURF 'N' TURF SPECIAL OFFER,
PO BOX 98
c/o 21 BENNERLEY ROAD
LONDON SW11 6DR

I'm not kidding: send me your cheque(s) and I'll make sure you get the goods within 14 days. Any problems, e-mail me at jmaitland@ukgateway.net

FRIDAY 19 JULY

From: Blake, Joanne
To: jmaitland@ukgateway.net
Sent: Friday, July 19 2002 8:13 AM

Hi Jonathan

Thanks very much for the CD – I quite enjoyed it!

I've talked your offer over with my MD and Communications Director and I'm sorry to say the outcome isn't favourable.

We're currently undergoing a lot of strategic work to re-position the brand.

Whilst Surf 'n' Turf is a semi popular dish, it's not what the brand is famous for – or certainly where we'd like to be. Fresh, salad cart, spit roast and flame grilling is what we're all about.

As we're currently on this re-positioning journey (and only just at the beginning) we're not yet in a position to communicate through any media – as I said to you on the phone, we're trying to move away from the 'Hello, Sir, have you been to a Harvester before ?' legacy.

But good luck anyway and thanks for the call!

All the best

Joanne

What a marvellous e-mail. I just love that marketing jargon! Especially 'Re-positioning journey' and 'Fresh, salad cart, spit roast and flame grilling is what we're all about.' These are phrases to treasure. What she's trying to say, I think, but is too polite to say it up front, is this:

Dear Jonathan,
You lot are too naff. Even for us. And that's saying something.
Yours, Joanne

Oh well. There's always Beefeater.

And there is also William Hill, or, to be more precise, Graham Sharpe, hence this:

From: jmaitland@ukgateway.net
To : Pressoffice@WilliamHill.co.uk
Sent : Friday July 19 14:21
Subject: Just keeping you posted

Dear Graham
In the interests of tying up the loose ends of this project, I thought I should let you know that you can now sleep easy as Surf 'n' Turf have failed, albeit narrowly, to get to number one. We peaked at number 98 in the Irish charts, selling 29 copies, 11 of which I appear to have bought myself. So, as someone once said, or rather sung, I give in.
By the way I now have quite a few copies of the single going spare. Interested?
Cheers
Jonathan

From: Sharpe, Graham
To: jmaitland@ukgateway.net
Sent : Friday July 19 16:34
Subject: Phew that was close

Jonathan
I can now reveal that it was William Hill who bought the other 18 copies of your CD: after a top level board meeting it was felt that we should send a trouble shooter over to Ireland with instructions to buy up as many copies of the song as possible, in order to take them out of circulation and to protect the public.
Looking forward to details of your next bet!
Cheers
Graham

PART NINE

★★★★★

I CAN'T LET GO

So, where are we now? Well, I'm back concentrating fully on the day job. Which currently involves exposing dodgy estate agents. And planning my next book. I think it might be called *How To Make Your Million From Television (And What To Do If You Don't)*. I mean, you've got to stick to what you know, haven't you?

I have also learned a few things on the way about the do's and don't's of trying to have a hit single, so here goes:

DO:

1) Get yourself an enormously powerful Local Svengali type to manage you, like Louis Walsh or Simon Cowell. They might make loads of money out of you, but who cares? 10% of something is better than 100% of nothing, as Jonathan King once said. (In fact, that was the title of a 10cc song that the band wrote in his honour.)

2) Make sure that your demo sounds as good as it can possibly be. In fact, some people now say there's no such thing as a demo: your track should be pretty much the finished article. If it isn't, people like legendary A&R man Muff Winwood will simply throw it out of the window or use it as an ashtray.

3) Make sure that your act is as young and pretty as possible. If

you are neither of these things, get someone in who is. It's not unheard of for older, uglier acts to make it: there was once a band called The Motors who were briefly big in the 70s, for instance, who all had faces like a smacked arse. But once their album appeared in the shops, with their picture on it, they were roundly rejected by the record-buying public and never heard of again.

4) Make sure the song is either a) a drippy ballad, b) a cover version of a well-known song or c) has loads of beats on it.

5) Pretend that the song was recorded in your bedroom and cost £3 to make, even if it didn't.

6) Make up lots of ludicrous stories about how the band met, i.e. at a fight in a Mongolian launderette. This will guarantee lots of useful PR. Other useful promotional tools include: getting the band arrested, swearing on live TV, and getting the song banned. (See: Pistols, Sex.)

DON'T:

1) Enter the *Eurovision Song Contest*, if you want to retain the slightest scrap of credibility.

2) Bother learning an instrument or how to sing. Looking good and being able to dance is far more important.

3) Expect overnight success: it took Gordon Haskell 35 years, for goodness sake.

4) Worry about nicking the best bits from your favourite songs. Everybody does it. It's not the ingredients that make the cake taste nice, it's how you mix them together.

5) Take it too seriously, whether you make it or not. Pop music is cheap, ephemeral, and really doesn't matter. But be realistic. For every artist or writer who makes it, there are approximately 1000 who don't. If you're part of the 1000 though, it doesn't mean you can't have a good time: music is its own reward. (Cue strings)

Surf 'n' Turf, meanwhile, are back on the wedding/birthday circuit.

Only the other week we played an absolute corker in a marquee in someone's back garden in Beckenham. For some reason, we are huge in Beckenham. After that particular gig, three 39-year-olds who all lived within 400 yards of the gig booked us for their 40th celebrations. I can't help feeling that it is that environment – i.e. Beckenham — and not the higher reaches of the charts, which is our natural environment. My brother Pete, meanwhile, continues to play his pub and working man's club gigs and has written a new song – 'My Dream' – which, I am afraid, has *Eurovision* stamped all over it. It sounds like a cross between Paul McCartney's 'We All Stand Together' and, curiously, 'Whatever', by Oasis.

You may not have heard the last of him. Or indeed us.

I think it was an old Chinese sage who once said, 'it is better to travel than to arrive'.

He was right: we may not have quite made it to where we were hoping to get to, but it was a fun journey. Music is the best!

POCKET
BOOKS

OFFICIALLY OZZY

The Osbourne Family

The authorised companion to 'The Osbournes', a pop culture phenomenon of the first magnitude whose appeal is massive.

Officially Ozzy is the authorised tie-in book to the highly popular MTV show that follows Ozzy Osbourne and his family. Whilst a reality-based series, 'The Osbournes' is really a sitcom about curfews, pets and pooper-scoopers, unwanted guests, lost credit cards, remote controls and folk-singing neighbours. Already commissioned for a further two series, one to be filmed in the UK, 'The Osbournes' is a global hit, breaking all viewing figures both in Europe and the States.

PRICE £12.99

ISBN 0 7434 6619 5

POCKET
BOOKS

THE OSBOURNE'S PET BOOK

The Osbourne Family

The perfect gift for the millions of fans of *The Osbournes* TV show and their pets!

The book will feature the furry members of the Osbourne family including Minnie, Maggie, Lola, Crazy Baby, Pipi, Martini, and Puss. They have all played a large part in the success of the hit show with Sharon Osbourne bringing them home and Ozzy getting aggravated with their antics. The book includes personal stories of the Osbournes and their beloved pets, with over fifty never-before-seen photos of the adorable dogs and cats from the Osbourne family collection.

PRICE £5.99

ISBN 0 7434 7006 0

POCKET
BOOKS

WHITE LINE FEVER
Lemmy Kilmister

White Line Fever is the warts-and-all autobiography of the
front man of one of the loudest rock bands in the world.

Inspired by Little Richard and Buddy Holly, Lemmy
formed what would become the ultimate metal group in
1975: Motorhead. The group went on to embrace a rock 'n'
roll lifestyle fuelled by drink, drugs and women. After a
brief spell in the early '90s when the band fell from grace,
Motorhead came back with a vengeance, gathering
more fans and achieving further critical acclaim for
their latest album.

Lemmy is a survivor and a rock legend. Few could claim to
have taken more drugs, drunk more bourbon or entertained
more women than Motorhead's lead singer. In this
autobiography, Lemmy relates tales of unbridled excess in
his unpretentious, hugely entertaining style and ruminates
on what has kept Motorhead going after 27 years.

PRICE £16.99
ISBN 0 6848 5868 1

**POCKET
BOOKS**

THE GOOD LIFE
Tony Bennett

His career has spanned over four decades, he has won countless
awards including eight Grammys, and created a lasting musical
legacy with such classics as his signature song 'I Left My
Heart in San Francisco'. Today, Tony Bennett has become the
hottest – and coolest – pop-culture icon of the MTV generation,
while remaining beloved by their parents and grandparents.

Written with wit and charm, *The Good Life* is a wonderfully
revealing self-portrait that lets us get to know Tony Bennett as he
really is: a man of integrity, an enduring artist and a true class act.

'The epitome of classy cool'

Sunday Telegraph

'A record of a class act who has remained throughout a
remarkably sympathetic human being'

The Times

PRICE £6.99
ISBN 0 6710 2958 4

Scribner

Such Sweet Thunder
Benny Green on Jazz

Edited by Dominic Green
Forward by Elvis Costello

An encyclopaedic journey through the Jazz Century, from the world's leading authority on Jazz and the Popular Song.

Benny Green (1927-98) was a saxophonist and prolific writer whose work spanned every aspect of the musical arts. *Such Sweet Thunder* gathers this lifetime of Jazz into one volume: essays, concert reviews and obituaries join previously unpublished material and Grammy-nominated sleevenotes in a unique collection compiled by his son and fellow-musician, Dominic Green. It is a truly definitive guide to Jazz and the Popular Song.

'A magnificent collection' *Independent on Sunday*

PRICE £8.99
ISBN 0 7432 0727 0

SIMON &
SCHUSTER

This book and other **Simon & Schuster UK Ltd** titles are available from your
bookshop or can be ordered direct from the publisher.

0 7434 6619 5	**Officially Ozzy**	**The Osbourne Family**	£12.99
0 7434 7006 0	**The Osbourne's Pet Book**	**The Osbourne Family**	£5.99
0 6848 5868 1	**White Line Fever**	**Lemmy Kilmister**	£16.99
0 6710 2958 4	**The Good Life**	**Tony Bennett**	£6.99
0 7432 0727 0	**Such Sweet Thunder**	**Dominic Green**	£8.99
0 6715 1645 0	**In Black & White**	**Twiggy**	£6.99

Please send cheque or postal order for the value of the book, free postage and
packing within the UK; OVERSEAS including Republic of Ireland £1 per book.

OR: Please debit this amount from my VISA/ACCESS/MASTERCARD:

CARD NO:. . . . .

EXPIRY DATE: . . . .

AMOUNT: £. . . . .

NAME: . . . .

ADDRESS:. . . . .

. . . .

SIGNATURE: . . . .

Send orders to SIMON & SCHUSTER CASH SALES
PO Box 29, Douglas Isle of Man, IM99 1BQ
Tel: 01624 836000, Fax: 01624 670923
www.bookpost.co.uk
Please allow 14 days for delivery. Prices and availability subject to
change without notice